OXFORD THEOLOGICAL MONOGRAPHS

Oxford Theological Monographs

THE LEONINE SACRAMENTARY
By D. M. HOPE. 1970

CLEMENT OF ALEXANDRIA'S TREATMENT OF
THE PROBLEM OF EVIL
By W. S. G. FLOYD. 1971

CLEMENT OF ALEXANDRIA: A STUDY IN
CHRISTIAN PLATONISM AND GNOSTICISM
By S. LILLA. 1971

THE ENGLISH SEPARATIST TRADITION
By B. R. WHITE. 1971

ANCIENT RHETORIC AND THE
ART OF TERTULLIAN
By R. D. SIDER. 1971

THE PRINCIPLE OF RESERVE IN THE WRITINGS
OF JOHN HENRY NEWMAN
By R. C. SELBY. 1975

GELASIAN SACRAMENTARIES OF THE 8TH
CENTURY
By M. B. MORETON. 1975

THREE MONOPHYSITE CHRISTOLOGIES

Severus of Antioch,
Philoxenus of Mabbug,
and Jacob of Sarug

BY

ROBERTA C. CHESNUT

OXFORD UNIVERSITY PRESS
1976

Oxford University Press, Ely House, London W.1

OXFORD LONDON GLASGOW NEW YORK
TORONTO MELBOURNE WELLINGTON CAPE TOWN
IBADAN NAIROBI DAR ES SALAAM LUSAKA ADDIS ABABA
KUALA LUMPUR SINGAPORE JAKARTA HONG KONG TOKYO
DELHI BOMBAY CALCUTTA MADRAS KARACHI

ISBN 0 19 826712 6

Printed in Great Britain by
William Clowes & Sons, Limited, London, Beccles and Colchester

PREFACE

IN any study of monophysite theology, we must begin with an expression of gratitude to two scholars above all: to A. de Halleux, and to J. Lebon, the first for his pioneering work on Philoxenus, and the second for his work on Severus. It would be no exaggeration to say that this present book could hardly have been written at all before they had done the work they did, especially in the matter of editing texts.

In its original form, this work was written as a doctoral dissertation for the University of Oxford. Here I should like to give my thanks to my supervisor, the Revd. L. H. Brockington, who not only encouraged me throughout, but also furnished me with suggestions that were full of common sense and practicality. I also owe a particular kind of debt to two others. I could never repay Father Derwas Chitty for the stories he told me of the ancient monks and their monasteries; when he talked, the twentieth century would disappear and I would find myself in the world of late fifth-century monastic life, among the monks whom Severus, Philoxenus, and Jacob must have known. It was he who gave me confidence, when I was first beginning this project, that the effort would be worth while. I owe a similar debt to Father Gervase Mathew, who kindly read my manuscript in progress and gave me the benefit of his knowledge of patristic theology. As Father Chitty encouraged me at the beginning, Father Mathew urged me on when my courage was faltering later on.

As most of this work was completed in the United States, and I found myself for a considerable length of time cut off from libraries where the necessary texts were available, I must especially thank Dechard Turner, the librarian at Perkins School of Theology, Southern Methodist University, for his extraordinary generosity in the long-term loan of many of the texts I needed.

Finally, I wish to thank my husband Glenn, whose sensitive insights into the period, arising out of his own research in Greek patristics, have been invaluable. It is rare, I suspect, to be married to one's most valuable colleague!   R. C. C.

CONTENTS

INTRODUCTION

THIS book is a study of the relationship between Christ and our knowledge of God, in the theological systems of three Syrian monophysite theologians who lived and worked in the exciting—and excited—period around the end of the fifth century and the beginning of the sixth, the great age of monophysite creativity and vitality. Each of the writers, Severus of Antioch, Philoxenus of Mabbug, and Jacob of Sarug, had a great reputation in his own age, Severus as a brilliant theologian and churchman, Philoxenus as a theologian and zealous supporter and promoter of both the monophysite cause and the Syriac language, and Jacob, the 'Flute of the Holy Spirit', as an inspired homilist.

The christological systems of the three theologians chosen for study are particularly suitable for three reasons. First, there is a tremendous volume of their works extant: page upon page of letters, public and private, hymns, sermons, treatises, confessions of faith, polemical works. One is not working from fragments, nor is one dependent upon the statements of theological opponents, who may or may not have understood their positions and described them accurately. Further, because of the quantity of surviving material, one is able to see the balance and range of interests of each of these writers. For example, a study of Philoxenus' letters allows the reader to see him not simply as a warrior, but as a director of souls. Again, it is both fascinating and useful to see Severus in his role of preacher to the Antiochene flock, a congregation apparently addicted not only to the theatre but to the use of magic amulets.

Second, even though there has been a relatively small amount of work done on these three, apart from the impressive theological and textual studies of J. Lebon and A. de Halleux on Severus and Philoxenus, and the important textual work of A. Vööbus on Jacob, a large number of major texts by all three of these men have been edited and published. This means that Severus, Philoxenus, and Jacob are all readily available to the scholar. Unfortunately, although the texts of Severus and

Philoxenus have been translated for the most part into modern western languages or Latin, the five published volumes of homilies and the letters of Jacob remain almost entirely untranslated from the Syriac, with the exception of one very important group of letters. For this reason, Jacob is not accessible to the scholar unfamiliar with Syriac in the way that the other two are. Nevertheless, the general accessibility of the modern editions of these three makes them peculiarly attractive for study.

Third, these men in themselves display the rich variety and creativity of the monophysite theologians of the period. Theologically speaking, Severus is all Greek (and in fact he wrote in Greek, though his works survive for the most part only in Syriac), Philoxenus moves freely both in the Syrian and the Greek theological worlds, while Jacob chooses to express his ideas almost purely in Syrian forms. Severus understands himself to be the rightful heir of Cyril of Alexandria, and his own thought is a brilliant development of the vocabulary of Cyril. Philoxenus, as a self-conscious Syrian, finds his master in the most respected and beloved of the Syrians, Ephraem Syrus, and he writes exclusively in Syriac. But Philoxenus does not regard himself as a defender of the position of the simple pious Syrian: he sees himself as the man who must for the first time introduce real theological technical language into the Syrian tradition; he must develop Syriac as a language in which theological inquiry can be conducted, as it can in Greek. Philoxenus is fully capable of using the language he inherits from the Cyrillians, and indeed, he uses it continually, but the total thrust of his thought is quite different from that of a man like Severus, and his christology is not at all a mere modification of Severus': it is a genuine alternative. Jacob, whose temperament was irenic, and whose Christian conscience was outraged by the division in the church caused by the christological controversy, never, to my knowledge, willingly and without coercion, used the catch phrases and jargon of the monophysites. That he both understood it and was able to use it is obvious from his correspondence with the abbot of Mar Bassus; that he found it offensive to be forced to take a monophysite loyalty oath is equally obvious. Jacob's way of looking at the person of Christ, though clearly monophysite, is even farther from Severus'

vision of Christ than Philoxenus'. Jacob sees Christ and his
work in mythological images, just as the gnostics in his region
had earlier used such images to describe the plight of the human
race and the means of acquiring salvation. Jacob is the most
'biblical' of the three. He is not constructing a theological
system of the sort that Severus so beautifully builds; nevertheless
Jacob, just as fully as Severus, presents a consistent, structured
christology, which, like that of Philoxenus, is a genuine alternative to Severus'. From the writings of Severus, Philoxenus, and
Jacob, then, the reader is able to see something of the variety
of the monophysites of this region.

There is an additional reason for studying these men and the
monophysitism of this period: It has often been the case that the
serious study of Chalcedon has ended with 451, while what
came after it was regarded as a mere tidying up of loose ends.
But the period following the Council cannot be understood in
this fashion without giving a truncated and unbalanced picture
of Chalcedon itself. No one attempting to make sense of the
Arian controversy would stop at 325. In the same way, Chalcedon failed to end the conflict which had its historical beginning with Cyril and Nestorius, and in fact, temporally
speaking, the Council of 451 does not stand at the end of the
christological controversies of the early church, but in the
middle. A study of the monophysites of the late fifth and early
sixth centuries, then, is important not only for an accurate
understanding of the reasons for the continuing division in the
church, but also for the vitally important light it throws back-
ward on those theological events which had split the church
some three-quarters of a century earlier.

Of course one cannot see the entire theological picture without also taking into account the historical, non-theological
factors contributing to the controversy centring on Chalcedon,
and a good survey of the history of this has been provided in
English recently by Professor Frend in the third and final
volume of his social history of the early church, *The Rise of the
Monophysite Movement*. In this work the student of the period is
again reminded of the role that the various rivalries between
the great sees played in this crucial period, as well as the roles
of nationalistic feeling and popular piety. Fortunately, having
been freed by Professor Frend from the necessity to review

issues of this sort, I am able to focus upon the purely theological questions in themselves.

I have, in fact, chosen not to present the 'fighting side' of the
monophysites at all. I have tried to understand their various
positions as more than responses to their opponents; I have
tried to present the epistemologies and christologies of these
three men as they were rooted in basic Christian faith. To a
certain extent, this approach might appear artificial, for both
Severus and Philoxenus seemed to relish battle for its own sake.
But there is far more to the thought of both men than the
polemical element. They are working out of firm theological
foundations, which give meaning to their positions, but do not
always enter directly into the material used for combat.
Philoxenus' doctrine of faith is a case in point: unless one understands his thought here, one cannot understand his conception
of the union of humanity and divinity in Christ, and yet he
himself does not really use this doctrine of faith in his arsenal
when he combats the dyophysites. The question to be asked in
the following work, then, will not be, 'how and why did the
monophysites oppose the Chalcedonians?', but 'what did the
various monophysites, whose works are examined here, believe concerning the identity of Christ, the manner of the union
of Godhead and humanity within the Incarnation, and the
means whereby we know God through Christ?'.

Before we go on to look at the thought of these three men, a
short summary of the life of each may be useful.

According to Zacharius Rhetor,[1] Severus of Antioch was
born in Sozopolis in Pisidia about 465. He seems to have come
from a distinguished family with a Christian background. As a
student he went to Alexandria with two older brothers to study
grammar and rhetoric; then he went on to Beirut to study law.
During his years at Beirut he was baptized, and at the end of
his legal studies he became a monk at a monophysite monastery
at Maiuma. Here he was associated with Peter the Iberian.
About 508 Severus went to Constantinople with a group of
Palestinian monks to see the emperor Anastasius for support
for the monophysite monks in Palestine. Here he remained for
a number of years. In 512 Severus was made Patriarch of
Antioch after the removal of Flavian II, following the Synod of

---

[1] P.O. ii.10 ff.

Sidon. After Severus served six years as monophysite Patriarch of Antioch, Justin became the emperor, and in 518, both Severus and Philoxenus were removed from their sees, Severus going into hiding in Egypt. In 531 or 532, in the reign of Justinian, but with the support of the empress Theodora, Severus was recalled to Constantinople; in 536 he was again condemned and returned to exile in Egypt. The date of his death is uncertain, but it seems to have been between 538 and 542. Severus is generally called the best of the monophysite theologians, and he is credited with being the real unifier of the party, which at the time of his exile was probably too fragmented to survive without his leadership. Though he wrote in Greek, his writings survive almost exclusively in Syriac.

Philoxenus, or Akhsenaya, as he is also called in ancient sources, was born most probably between 440 and 455 into a family belonging to an Aramaic community in Persia. He apparently had a brother, Addai, who may have been a teacher at the school of the Persians at Edessa, and he had a sister. He himself was educated at the school of Edessa, which at that time was divided into two factions, one supporting the tradition of Theodore and the other the tradition of Cyril. While Philoxenus sided with the Cyrillians, he also tells us that he read the works of his opponents. At this time Jacob of Sarug may have been a fellow student at Edessa. Leaving Edessa, Philoxenus moved west to Antioch. During this period Calandio, then Patriarch of Antioch, expelled him for his monophysite teachings and his support of the Henoticon. In 485, when Peter the Fuller became Patriarch, he made Philoxenus bishop of Mabbug, or Hierapolis, at that time the centre of a thriving pagan cult dedicated to the Syrian fertility goddess Atargatis. During all this time, Philoxenus was firmly monophysite. De Halleux suggests[1] that in 489, when the Persian school of Edessa was closed for doctrinal reasons, Philoxenus may have had a hand in its closing. In 489 Flavian II became Patriarch of Antioch: up until this time he had been anti-Chalcedonian; from the time of his election, however, he declared himself in favour of Chalcedon. Philoxenus therefore immediately began to work with unabated zeal to have him removed; the culminating point of his crusade was the Synod

[1] A. de Halleux, *Philoxène de Mabbog: sa vie, ses écrits, sa théologie*, p. 49.

of Sidon in 511. In 512 Flavian was removed and Severus became Patriarch in his place. Some time between 513 and 515 the Synod of Tyre took place—de Halleux[1] finds it probable that it was actually held at Antioch—presided over by Philoxenus and Severus jointly: this council decreed that the Henoticon was in contradiction with the decrees of Chalcedon, and Chalcedon was anathematized. In 519, when Justin became emperor and Severus went into hiding in Egypt, Philoxenus was captured and taken into exile first to Gangra in Paphlagonia and then to Philippopolis in Thrace, where he died of suffocation, probably in 523. Philoxenus had been an ardent supporter not only of the monophysite cause, but also of Syrian language and culture. He wrote, of course, exclusively in Syriac.

Jacob of Sarug was born in a little village on the Euphrates in 451 or 452. His father was a priest. Jacob was educated at Edessa, and may very well have been a fellow student of Philoxenus there. For many years he served as episcopal visitor for the rural diocese of Sarug. (The capital of the district was Batnan, also called Bathnae, in Osrhoëne.) In 519, the same year that Philoxenus and Severus were removed from their sees, Jacob was made bishop of Batnan; he was around sixty-eight years old at this time. He served in this office two and a half years, until he died in 521. Unlike Severus and Philoxenus, Jacob appears to have had a peaceable temperament, only entering into theological controversy with great reluctance. His monophysitism was not widely known in the early period, and even in modern times his monophysitism has been questioned.[2] His episcopal appointment, as we have just noted,

---

[1] Ibid., pp. 81 ff.

[2] Two twentieth-century scholars have argued that Jacob was a Chalcedonian. P. Peeters in his article, 'Jacques de Saroug appartient-il à la secte monophysite?' (*Analecta Bollandiana* LXVI (1948), 134–98) explains all the monophysite material in Jacob's writing as later additions. P. Krüger, in 'War Jakob von Serugh Katholik oder Monophysit?' (*Ostkirchliche Studien* 2 (1953), 199–208), also argues Jacob's orthodoxy. In a later article, however, Krüger came round to the position that Jacob was a monophysite, but that his homilies had been brought in line with Chalcedonianism, to be made suitable for liturgical use ('Das Problem der Rechtglaübigkeit Jakobs von Serugh und seine Lösung', *Ostkirchliche Studien* 5 (1956), 158–76; 225–42). My own position is that Jacob was clearly a monophysite. T. Jansma has convincingly demonstrated that Jacob was a moderate monophysite; see particularly 'The Credo of Jacob of Serugh: A Return to Nicea and

came at the very time when the more zealous monophysites went out of favour. He was the author of some hundreds of metrical Syriac homilies, for which he was given the title 'Flute of the Holy Spirit'.

Constantinople', *Nederlands Archief voor Kerkgeschiedenis* 1961, 18–36; and 'Encore le credo de Jacques de Saroug', *L'Orient syrien* 10 (1965), 75–88; 193–236; 331–70; 475–510.

PART I

SEVERUS OF ANTIOCH

Hypostasis and Prosopon

THE foundation of Severus' system is the concept of the hypostatic union of the divinity and the humanity in Christ. The key to the understanding of the union according to Severus lies in his use of the word 'hypostasis',[1] for when he used such key monophysite phrases as 'the natural union' or 'the one nature of God the Word incarnate',[2] he used 'nature' as a synonym of 'hypostasis'.[3] In this section, then, we shall look at what Severus had in mind when he spoke of one hypostasis or nature in Christ.

Unlike the term 'nature', which, depending on the context and the preference of the writer, could refer either to the specific or the generic,[4] the term 'hypostasis' always refers to the individual.[5]

There are two kinds of hypostases, the 'self-subsistent' and

---

[1] Though nearly all the surviving texts of Severus are Syriac translations of the Greek, Severus' translators were generally careful to translate the standard Greek technical vocabulary with an equivalently technical vocabulary in Syriac. In general however, in the following pages the (transliterated) Syriac will be given; though we know that *qnômâ* always (probably) translates the Greek ὑπόστασις ('hypostasis') and that *kyānâ*, translates φύσις ('nature') and *'ûsîâ* is the Syriac of οὐσία ('ousia'), we cannot always know the exact Greek word that the Syriac translates. In all cases I have tried to use the generally accepted English equivalents of the Greek technical vocabulary, without trying to guess at the exact Greek word lying behind the Syriac. For comments on the translation of the technical vocabulary, see J. Lebon, *Chalkedon*, I. 454, n. 5.

[2] For the distribution of the formulas in their various forms among the monophysites, see J. Lebon, *Le Monophysisme sévérien*, chart between pp. 308 and 309.

[3] P.O. xii.200, Letter VII. A typical statement: 'Accordingly it is the same thing to say that God the Word was united to flesh possessing an intellectual soul in nature (*bakhyānâ*), and in hypostasis (*baqnômâ*), and in ousia (*b'ûsîâ*).' See also Letters XV, pp. 210–11, XVI, p. 211, etc.; also Letter II, pp. 186 ff. where Severus explicitly rejects any notion that the union was a union of 'generalities' (*gensê*), i.e. of 'humanity' (*'nāsûthâ*) in the general sense with the whole of the Godhead. See also *Contr. Grammat.* 2, 21 (CSCO, vol. 111), 179 ff.; 2, 28 (CSCO, vol. 111), 218 ff.

[4] Letters V, p. 195; VI, pp. 196–97; LXV (P.O. xiv.28–9).

[5] Letter V (P.O. xii.195); *Contr. Grammat.* 2, 28 (CSCO, vol. 111), 218 ff.

the 'non-self-subsistent'.[1] Christ is one self-subsistent composite[2] hypostasis, the product of a union of a simple self-subsistent hypostasis with a non-self-subsistent hypostasis. We can most easily explain the two if we make use of Severus' favourite example, that of the union of soul and body to make up one individual man,[3] let us say, Peter. Peter's living body is a non-self-subsistent hypostasis. It only exists in combination with Peter's soul.[4] It never stands on its own apart from him; it does not come into existence before being united to his soul. It belongs to Peter who experiences life on earth through it. It serves him in all ways as an instrument. What makes it a non-self-subsistent hypostasis[5] is the fact that Peter's living body never did and never will have a separate existence outside its union with Peter's soul.

If we assume that Peter's soul *could* exist by itself at any stage without his body, then Peter's soul is a self-subsistent hypostasis, for a self-subsistent hypostasis is one that exists in its own right. A simple self-subsistent hypostasis is one that exists in its own right and is not composite: the Father and the Holy Spirit both are simple self-subsistent hypostases.[6] Peter, as are all men, and Christ, however, are *composite* self-subsistent hypostases: this means that they owe their existence to a union

---

[1] A self-subsistent hypostasis is a 'hypostasis existing in individual subsistence' (*qnômâ dhabhdîlāyûth qûyāmâ mqayem*); a non-self-subsistent hypostasis is a 'hypostasis that does not exist in individual subsistence' (*qnômâ law badhîlāyûth qûyāmâ mqayem*). See e.g. Letters II, pp. 189, 190; XV, p. 210; *Contr. Grammat.* 2, 4 (CSCO, vol. 111), 74 ff.

[2] Root, *rkb.* 'Composite', *brûkhābhâ.* See e.g. Letters XV, p. 210; XXV, pp. 229–230, etc.

[3] Some typical passages: Letters XXV, pp. 230 ff.; LXV, p. 18; Homilies LXVII (P.O. viii.359); LVIII (P.O. viii.219, 222–3); *Contr. Grammat.* 2, 4 (CSCO, vol. 111), pp. 76–7.

[4] Letter II, p. 190: soul and body are non-self-subsistent hypostases. Letter XXV, p. 230. Severus would not appear to accept the Platonic-Origenistic notion of the pre-existence of the soul with its concomitant idea of a fall into the body. He explicitly rejects the thought that the body is a punishment for sin. See Draguet, pp. 127 ff., and the following section, 'Christ the Word and the New Creation'. Severus accuses those who hold to the doctrine of indwelling of believing that the baby was formed in the womb of Mary, then the Word came and dwelt in it. A typical statement: 'It is false that the infant pre-existed in the womb of the Virgin, and the Divine Word appropriated it to himself by an adhesion inspired by love . . . in virtue of a design decided on by will.' Hom. LVIII (P.O. viii.221–2); Letters II, p. 190; LXV (P.O. xiv.17–18).

[5] Letter II, p. 190; *Contr. Grammat.* 2, 4 (CSCO, vol. 111), 77.

[6] *Contr. Grammat.* 2, 4 (CSCO, vol. 111), 76.

of two hypostases, either two non-self-subsistent hypostases, or a self-subsistent and a non-self-subsistent one. In the case of Peter, this means soul and body; in the case of Christ, the divinity and the humanity.[1]

The term 'prosopon' is equivalent to self-subsistent hypostasis: it implies 'existing in individual existence'.[2] A prosopon is counted as a concrete reality, and most important, it bears a name[3]—'Peter' or 'Paul' or 'Christ'. A *non*-self-subsistent hypostasis is not a prosopon and is not named in this way: this is why Severus never calls the humanity in the Incarnation 'the Man', or anything like it. Thus Severus speaks of the 'one nature, one hypostasis, and one prosopon of God the Word Incarnate'.[4]

Hypostasis refers to the individual, rather than to the generic. In the case of human beings, individuality comes from historicity—Peter is distinguished as an individual from Paul by the fact of their different past histories, although both share the same generic humanity.

The set of properties of Peter is one; the fact that he is from the little village of Beth-Saida, the son of John, the brother of Andrew, and a fisherman of skill, and after these things, an apostle, and because of the orthodoxy and firmness of his faith had been newly named 'Rock' by Christ. But another is the set of properties of Paul, the fact that he is from Cilicia, that he used to be a Pharisee, that he was taught and learned the law of the fathers at the feet of Gamaliel, and that after having persecuted, he preached the Gospel . . . *and all these other things that are written concerning him in a history*. In the same way hypostasis does not deny genus or ousia or abolish it, but it sets apart and limits in particular icons the one who subsists. For

---

[1] Severus uses these two terms almost exclusively for the two elements in Christ, rather than, e.g., such terms as 'the Word' and 'the flesh', when he pairs them in this way. He never calls the human element 'the Man' or 'Jesus'.

[2] See e.g. Letter XV: 'The peculiarity of the natural union is that the hypostases are in composition and are perfect without diminution, but refuse to continue an individual existence so as to be numbered as two, and to have its own prosopon impressed upon each of them . . .' See also Letter XVI, p. 211; *Contr. Grammat.* 2, 4 (CSCO, vol. 111), 78; Lebon, *Chalkedon*, pp. 473–4.

[3] See e.g. Letter LXV (P.O. xiv.28–9).

[4] It is not strictly correct, therefore, to say that hypostasis, nature (in its individual sense), and prosopon are synonyms. This is only true if we specify that the hypostasis is self-subsistent, and that nature in this context is also equivalent to self-subsistent hypostasis. But see Lebon, *Chalkedon*, pp. 461; 464–5.

in ousia and in genus Peter is a man as is Paul; but in propriety he is distinguished from Paul.[1]

(Could Theodore of Mopsuestia be working with a further development of this idea when he says that animals do not have hypostases?[2] That is, perhaps rational beings are the only creatures that have hypostases because they are the only creatures that have real historicity, as opposed to mere existence as part of Nature.)

There is only one operation arising out of a self-subsistent hypostasis: one does not speak of Peter's *body* eating, strictly speaking, if we mean by it that Peter's body somehow ate apart from Peter himself. Just as the self-subsistent hypostasis, Peter, is characterized by his one history, which immutably belongs to him, out of Peter arises only one operation or activity. This means that whatever Peter does, whether he eats, dreams, thinks, plans, or builds, while we may distinguish between the proper sphere of activity of body and soul, we do not say 'Peter's body did it' or 'Peter's soul did it', but 'Peter did it'.[3] In the same way, in Christ, we do not speak of two operations: we do not say that 'the man wept', 'God raised Lazarus from the dead', but 'the Incarnate Word did it'.[4]

Hypostatic and Prosopic Unions

Severus contrasts hypostatic union,[5] or, as he also calls it, natural union, with prosopic union.

---

[1] Hom. CXXV (P.O. xxix.236). I have translated *bthaš'ithâ* 'in a history', but it could also be 'in the narrative'. See also Letter LXV (PO xiv.29).

[2] Hom. V. 15, 16, *Les Homélies catéchétiques de Théodore de Mopsueste*, ed. and trans. R. Tonneau and R. Devreesse, Studi e Testi 145, pp. 121–3.

[3] Cf. 'First Letter to Sergius' (CSCO, vol. 119), 82–3.

[4] Letter I, pp. 180–2; Hymn 35-1-VIII, 'The Hymns of Severus and others in the Syriac Version of Paul of Edessa as Revised by James of Edessa', ed. and trans. E. W. Brooks (P.O., vi). *Critique du Tome* (CSCO, vol. 244), pp. 153 ff. Homilies XLVIII (P.O. xxxv.316–18); CXX (P.O. xxix.86).

[5] Severus prefers the phrase 'hypostatic union' in place of 'natural union', just as he prefers to speak of the two hypostases which are preserved within the union, rather than of the two natures, in spite of the fact that in the context of discussion of the union, 'nature' and 'hypostasis' are properly synonyms. Generally speaking, Severus used 'nature' as a synonym of self-subsistent hypostasis, rather than of non-self-subsistent hypostasis. He believed, of course, that the Nestorians and the Chalcedonians always used 'nature' as equivalent to 'self-subsistent hypostasis' when they were talking about the union. (He did not generally distinguish between the Nestorian and the Chalcedonian positions.)

A prosopic union is one in which two prosopa, two self-subsistent hypostases, are joined in some way: the union of Peter and Paul, who are united by a union based on the authority of apostleship, is a prosopic union; the Nestorian, and to Severus, the Chalcedonian concept of the union of Christ as a union of the Man and the Word would also be a prosopic union:[1]

When hypostases subsist by individual subsistence, as for instance, those of Peter and Paul, whom the authority of apostleship united, then there will be a union of prosopa and a brotherly association, not a natural union of one hypostasis made up out of two which is free from confusion.

These are some of the things characterizing a prosopic union: even after the union, there are two countable entities[2] remaining which can exist apart[3] from each other, say Peter and Paul. Each has his own name—Peter, Paul, the Man, Jesus, the Word. Each arises out of his own historical situation[4] and affects the world through his own independent operation or pattern of behaviour.[5] The vital being, the lives of the members of the union do not, then, depend on the union for their very existence in the world, at the natural level (the spiritual level is another matter). Most important of all, the members of a prosopic union are not in an iconic relationship to each other: one does not present a picture of the other on a different level of reality from the other. Some of the typical phrases Severus uses to describe the prosopic union are 'partnership', 'union of brotherhood', 'conjunction in honour', 'union by assumption', or 'presence'.[6]

[1] Letter II (P.O. xii.189–90). See also e.g. Hom. LVIII (P.O. viii.221–2); Letter XVI, p. 211.

[2] It is a characteristic of self-subsistent hypostases (but not non-self-subsistent hypostases) that they are subject to numeration. (See Severus' treatment of how number enters the Trinity: Letter XXII, pp. 215–16). Letter XV, p. 210; Hom. LVIII (P.O. viii.221–2).

[3] Letter X, p. 201 etc.

[4] Hom. CXXXV (P.O. xxix.236).

[5] See e.g. Hom. CXX (P.O. xxix.82–6). The two distinct operations of the two natures of Christ within the union are to Severus one of the more obnoxious features of the Tome of Leo. See Letter I, pp. 180–2; 'First Letter to Sergius' (CSCO, Vol. 119), 80–8; see also Sergius' problem with the Tome, 'First Letter to Severus', pp. 70 ff.

[6] Letters II, pp. 189–90; X, p. 201; XVI, pp. 211; XXV, p. 244; Hom. LVIII (P.O. viii.221–2).

Severus points out that the expression 'indwelling' is not
alien to Biblical language. Paul uses the expression 'to dwell'
to refer to the way that our soul is present to our body; thus,
according to Severus, the expression 'indwelling', when applied
to the union of humanity and divinity in Christ in the New
Testament, must refer to a hypostatic union. What is forbidden
is to interpret 'indwelling' to mean that God was in Christ as
he was in the prophets.[1]

The actual union of the divinity and humanity in Christ,
says Severus, was not a prosopic union, but a 'natural' or
'hypostatic' union, not of prosopa, but of hypostases, non-self-
subsistent with self-subsistent.[2]

... the peculiarity of the natural union is that the hypostases are
in composition (*brûkhābhâ*) and are perfect without diminution,
but refuse to continue an individual existence so as to be numbered
as two, and to have its own prosopon impressed upon each of them,
which a conjunction in honour cannot possibly do.

From the section on hypostasis we recall that the prime example of this type of union is that of body and soul to make up
one man. These things, then, characterize a 'natural' or
'hypostatic' union: First, the two elements 'differ in kind'[3]
from one another, and are not of our ousia, like body and soul,
humanity and divinity. After the union, although the two
hypostases remain, they have no individual, *separate* existence
of their own,[4] just as soul and body do not exist apart. After the
union, there is only one countable entity:[5] if we are looking at
Peter and somebody says, 'how many do you see?', we always
say 'one'. The two components in the union bear only one
name between them—Peter, Paul, Christ, or the Incarnate
Word.[6] There is only one history referred to the end product
of the union. There is only one centre of activity, one source of
operation out of which arise all the actions of the one prosopon.[7]

---

[1] See e.g. Letter LXV, pp. 21–2.   [2] Letter XV, p. 210.

[3] Letter X, p. 203. See also Letter XXV, p. 233.

[4] Letter XV, p. 210 etc.

[5] Homilies CXX (P.O. xxix.86); LVIII (P.O. viii.222–3); Letters I, pp. 178–9;
XVIII, p. 212. 'He who is united is fixedly one, and does not again become
two . . .' See also Lebon, *Chalkedon*, pp. 467–76; he defines *henosis* as 'unification or
reduction to unity'.

[6] 'First Letter to Sergius' (CSCO, vol. 119), p. 78.

[7] Letter I, pp. 180–2 etc.

Further, the two hypostases stand in an iconic relationship to each other: one reflects the other on a different level of reality: the body is an image of the soul on the sensible level,[1] and in the same way, the humanity is an image of the divinity on the created level in such a way that, looking at the one, we see the other. Thus the Incarnate Word is one nature, one hypostasis, and one prosopon.

Difference and Division

To talk about the way in which the two hypostases remain within the hypostatic or natural union, Severus made use of these nouns: 'difference' or 'distinction' (*šuḥlāphâ*), which is always used positively,[2] and 'separation' (*pûlāghâ*), which is always used negatively.[3] In addition he used the verbs 'to distinguish' (*prš*), which, depending on the context, is either negative or positive,[4] and 'to separate' (*plg*),[5] 'to cleave' (*psq*),[6] and 'to put far from each other' (*raḥeq men ḥdhādhê*),[7] which are always used negatively.

The word 'difference'[8] was used to talk about the way in which the sets of properties (called sometimes 'proprieties')[9] of the two hypostases within a hypostatic union continue to exist within the union, while nevertheless avoiding being divided

---

[1] Homilies LXXXI (P.O. xx.356); LXVIII (P.O. viii.379, 384–5); see also Hom. CXXI (P.O. xxix.98–101).

[2] There are so many examples of these terms in the Letters that we shall refer to only a few. For Lebon's guess at the Greek lying behind them, see *Chalkedon*, pp. 537–8. Letters I, pp. 177, 178, 181–2, etc.; VI, pp. 198–9; X, pp. 201, 202; 'First Letter to Sergius' (CSCO, vol. 119), 77–8.

[3] Letters I, p. 178; X, pp. 201–2; 'First Letter to Sergius', pp. 77–8.

[4] Letters I, p. 180, 182; II, p. 190; III, p. 194. For the noun derivative, Letter XXXIV, p. 273.

[5] Severus uses this word most often. Letters I, pp. 180, 185, 186, etc.; III, p. 194; Hom. CXX (P.O. xxix.86).

[6] Letters I, p. 177, 180; VI, p. 199, etc.

[7] Letter I, p. 177 etc.

[8] In an Origenistic-Evagrian system, what distinguishes souls from each other and from God is the result of sin: in such a system the concept of difference cannot be elevated to a place of importance as it has in Severus' system, where the difference between God and man, the individual members of the Trinity, and the hypostases of individual men is certainly a stable and important and positive element in existence. See Evagrius Ponticus: When God will be all in all, individual souls will disappear 'and this unification will be made by the disappearance of names and numbers, introduced by movement'. Frankenberg, 616–17, quoted in I. Hausherr, *Études de spiritualité orientale*, p. 38.

[9] See supplementary note, p. 55 below.

and apportioned out as though each propriety belonged to a self-subsistent hypostasis, or prosopon. What Severus meant to say is again made clear by his ubiquitous example, that of the union of soul and body. While neither the soul nor the body of Peter exists in this earthly life without the other, the soul and body each has its own propriety (or set of properties)[1] which exclusively characterizes it. Thus, Peter's body has brown eyes, Peter's intellect has the power of thought. These 'natural characteristics',[2] as Severus calls them, are real and not removed or annulled or confused within the union:[3] soul continues to be soul, and body, body; the divinity continues to be divinity, and the humanity in the union, humanity.[4] Propriety follows hypostasis in such a way that to *divide* the proprieties, setting them apart from each other, implies that we are also thinking in terms of two self-subsistent hypostases, two identities, and two operations:[5] It is as though we were thinking of Peter again in terms of two identities. But in the case of Christ,[6]

Where, then, we confess the one out of two, Lord and Son and Christ, and one incarnate nature of the Word himself, we understand the *difference* as it were in the natural characteristics of the natures from which Christ is. But, if we speak of two natures after the union,

[1] See e.g. *Contr. Grammat.* 1, 9 (CSCO, vol. 111), 47; Letter LXV (P.O. xiv.18); see also 'Second Letter to Sergius', p. 105; Letter XXV (P.O. xii.233).

[2] *mšawdi'ûthâ khyānāythâ*, Letters I, pp. 177, 182; X, p. 201. Letter XI explains that we are, in the context of the union, talking about 'the different principle underlying the existence of Godhood and manhood [in Christ]: for the one is without beginning and uncreated . . . while the other is created . . . This difference we in no wise assert to have been removed by the union', p. 204. See also supplementary note, p. 55, on the proprieties in Christ.

[3] Letters I, p. 177; X, p. 201; 'First Letter to Sergius', p. 86. The 'property of the natures of which Immanuel consists, which is shown in the natural characteristics, continues constant and fixed', Letter I, p. 182. Furthermore, because the two sets of natural characteristics or properties both belong to the incarnate Word, each propriety acts to reveal the other: 'By means of the properties of the flesh the Word is known and the properties of the manhood will be the properties of the Godhead of the Word. And again, the properties of the Word and the properties of the flesh will be confessed, and he will be the same, for he is seen by means of both, i.e. the tangible and the intangible'. 'First Letter to Sergius', p. 79. See also Homilies LXXXIII (P.O. xx.410); LIX (P.O. viii.236).

[4] Letters I, pp. 176–7; XXV, p. 238, etc. See also 'First Letter to Sergius', p. 90. See Cyril, Ep. 45 (P.G. 77.228–37), Lebon, *Chalkedon*, p. 514.

[5] See Severus' remarks on Leo's Tome, Letter I, pp. 182–4; 'First Letter to Sergius', pp. 79–80.

[6] Letter X, p. 201.

which necessarily exist in singleness and separately, as if divided into a duality, but united by a conjunction of brotherhood [i.e. a prosopic union] . . . the notion of *difference* reaches to the extent of *division*, and does not stop at natural characteristics.

The notion of the preservation of difference within the union allows Severus to say clearly and without contradiction or paradox how it is that, while the incarnate Word suffered death upon the cross, one does *not* say that the divinity itself suffered passion and death. One does not say that Peter's soul is suffering a burn on his finger, because it is the body that is actually burnt, not the mind. What we properly say is, 'Peter's finger is being burnt', referring the burn to the composite hypostasis, 'Peter'. In the same way, it is not a 'natural characteristic' of Godhead to suffer natural death; natural death belongs only to the created realms, and in the case of a man, it means the separation of soul from body. Nevertheless, just as we rightfully refer the burn to Peter, we rightfully refer the death to Christ, the incarnate Word.[1] Thus, we see what Severus is driving at when he emphasizes the centrality of the notion of the preservation of 'difference', and the rejection of 'separation'.

Mixture and Confusion

The concepts of 'difference' or 'distinction' and 'separation' are absolutely fundamental to Severus' christology. None the less, the monophysites were regularly accused of mixing and

---

[1] Physical death to Severus is what it was to most Greek theologians, the separation of body and soul (see e.g. Letter LXV, p. 242). Jesus suffered death in this sense, and we may rightfully ascribe this death to the Word because his body and soul were his own, as body and soul belong to every man. Nevertheless, the divine nature itself did not suffer death, being impassible and immortal; it is outside the realm of the possible that the divine hypostasis of the Word should suffer or die. A typical remark: 'he was united to a suffering body, and as it is his body, so also it is called his suffering; nevertheless as God he remained without suffering, for God is not touched by suffering', Letter LXV, p. 42; cf. 'Second Letter to Sergius', pp. 90–1; Hom. LIX (P.O. viii.237, 238); *Critique du Tome* (CSCO, vol. 244), 153. In the *Critique*, pp. 147–9, Severus rejects the analogy of the burning bush to describe the passion of Christ: it is not true to say that 'the passible flesh at the same time suffered and did not suffer' as the bush was burned and was not consumed. The monophysite addition to the Trisagion could give offence to neither Chalcedonian nor Nestorian if one were to accept Severus' doctrine of the suffering of Christ.

confusing the natures of Christ in some way or form, and it is obvious from reading Severus' letters, sermons, and treatises directed toward fellow monophysites[1] that there indeed were among them many who must have confused or mixed the human and divine natures in some way. So far we have been examining the *way* in which the hypostases were kept distinct; in this section we shall see why Severus could not have confused or mixed them.

The basic mistake, says Severus, of those who mix or confuse the two natures or hypostases in Christ is that they are thinking in materialistic terms, as though the two natures in Christ are material substances which could be mixed together.[2] Though Severus does not say so, it is not surprising that such a notion of the union would be prevalent in some circles: the Greeks had debated the way in which substances united with each other even before Aristotle. The two most famous positions however, were those of Aristotle and the later Stoics. Aristotle distinguished two basic types of 'mixture'. One was a 'synthesis' (σύνθεσις)—one example of this would be a mixture of barley and wheat.[3] The other was a κρᾶσις or a μίξις—an example would be a solution of wine and water.[4] A σύνθεσις is an inert combination, a κρᾶσις one in which the elements interact with each other but can be analysed into the original elements; in the resulting product 'the distinctive properties of the ingredients remain potentially . . . but they are actually superseded by the properties of an intermediate substance'.[5] The way in which a large quantity of water combines with one drop of wine is a special type of κρᾶσις, for here there is not a mutual interaction, but for all practical purposes, the wine, the lesser component, is changed into the nature of the water, the greater component.[6] The Stoics further expanded and revised Aris-

---

[1] This is a consistent theme in all Severus' writings: those against the Chalcedonians (who accused the monophysites of holding to a doctrine of mixture, confusion, or change) and against his fellow monophysites. Those who transform the nature of the humanity into divinity Severus calls the 'Synousiasts'. See 'First Letter to Sergius', pp. 75–6; Lebon, *Chalkedon*, pp. 443–4. See also in particular Letters I and XXV.

[2] Letter I, pp. 179–80 etc.

[3] *De gen. et corr.* 327ᵇ 34 ff.

[4] *De gen. et corr.* 327ᵇ 34 ff.

[5] R. Norris, *Manhood and Christ*, p. 69; *De gen. et corr.* 328ᵃ 19 ff.; 327ᵇ 25 ff.

[6] *De gen. et corr.* 327ᵇ 34 ff.

totle's views on κρᾶσις. They distinguished between a σύγχυσις (one of the Chalcedonian adverbs was ἀσυγχύτως), in which the elements interact with each other but 'cannot be resolved again into its elements',[1] and a κρᾶσις δι'ὅλων, which was characterized by a 'mutual and total interpenetration of two material substances, in which each retained all of its characteristic properties unaltered, so that even in their intimate union, the two substances remain distinct'.[2] The Stoics, thinking of the soul as material, used the κρᾶσις δι'ὅλων to explain the union of soul and body. But the view that the soul is material was not simply that of a few Stoic philosophers. It was widespread in the ancient world at least up into the fourth century, and Augustine,[3] who in his Manichean days even thought God material, is probably an example of the belief of a large percentage of ancient men, Christians included. If one took the analogy of body and soul as the basic analogy to explain the union of manhood and divinity in Christ, and if one were to believe that the soul is mixed with body in some material fashion, then one would be apt to think of the union in Christ as a material one.[4]

Severus himself consistently argued that the analogy of a union of two material substances could not be used to explain the union in Christ because the union is one between elements from two different levels of reality, for it is one between 'things that differ in kind and are not of one ousia with one another, the suprasensual, I mean, and the perceptible'.[5] An intelligible will not 'mix' with a sensible: Severus says, in explaining

---

[1] Norris, p. 69; see Alexander Aphr. *De mixt.* 216. 22; 220. 29 ff.

[2] Norris, pp. 69–70.

[3] Augustine, *Confessions*, V.10; VII.1, 5 and 20.

[4] e.g. Severus quotes from a lost dialogue of Nestorius, preserved in part by Cyril, against whom it was written. In it a 'theopaschite' explains his doctrine of the union and is refuted by an 'orthodox': 'The theopaschite says: "What do you think of an egg-shell of water that has been poured into the sea?". The orthodox says: "What else except that the unstable addition of the water has disappeared in the great volume of the sea?".' (Severus, Letter XXV, pp. 235–6; Cyril, *Adv. Nest.* II.7.) The theopaschite goes on to explain that the same is true in the Incarnation: the humanity is transformed into the divinity. Though Severus and Cyril deny believing any such thing, there must have been those who *did* make use of the analogy of Aristotle's mixture of the one drop of wine in a large quantity of water in this way, as Gregory of Nyssa did in an earlier period. See J. N. D. Kelly, *Early Christian Doctrines*, p. 300.

[5] Letter X, p. 203.

Gregory of Nazianzus'[1] use of the word 'mingle' to talk about
the union:

Do not let the term 'mingle' disturb you: for he used it very clearly
and without danger with the intention of denoting the primary
union: for where there is a union of something incorporeal with
a body, no danger anywhere arises from mingling. For this is
manifestly a quality of fluid bodies, to be confounded together by
intertwining, and so to speak, comes out of their nature.[2]

Will

As we go on to the problem of the will or wills in Christ, we
shall find that, just as the other elements in Christ which come
from the two different levels of reality will not form a mixture
with each other but remain distinct to function in their own
level, the human will of Christ, belonging to the realm of human
moral decision, will not be merged with the divine will in
Christ, which lies entirely outside the realm of moral choice.
In this section then, we shall examine the whole notion of the
human will, its function, the relationship between the evil will
and necessity, and the doctrine of synergism. We then go on to
relate Severus' doctrine of the will in Christ to his doctrine of
the hypostatic union of the natures in Christ. We shall find that
Severus sees in Christ one will out of two, the human and the
divine, each existing within its own proper sphere of activity,
the one an iconic representation of the other.

The human will in its healthy state, to Severus, is first of all
the inner drive in a person which inclines him to move toward
increasing participation in the uncreated goodness and bounty
of God. It is also that faculty by which men make individual
moral choices. It is always involved in good or evil: Severus
does not seem to think of it as the planning faculty or the
choosing faculty in other than moral terms. This is of utmost
importance to the question of the human will in Christ, for it
means that we are not talking so much about whether the
humanity could act apart from the Word in the Incarnation
(this is the question of the two *operations*), but whether the

---

[1] Gregory of Nyssa also used the term 'mixture' to talk about the union in Christ.
See *Contr. Eunom.* (P.G. 45.693); see also J. N. D. Kelly, *Early Christian Creeds*,
pp. 298 ff.
[2] Letter I, pp. 179, 180; *De gen. et corr.* 328ᵇ 1 ff.

humanity could make free moral judgements, including whether the humanity could really withhold its assent, let us say, to the crucifixion. In this section, then, we shall look at several related aspects of the human will which bear on the question of the will in Christ—the idea of the will as that by which a man participates in God as much as is possible, at the problem of where the corrupt will comes from (if Jesus is *homoousios* with us, did he inherit a corrupt will?), and how the will is actually said to be free.

In the following passage Severus sets out his doctrine of the purpose of the will and reason in an individual man. Here he is arguing against the suggestion that God should have created men not subject to the necessity of moral choice, and have made them good, without the possibility of turning away:

You say that it was fitting that we have been immutable with respect to evil and absolutely incapable of sin. You seem to want only to be a rock or a piece of wood instead of a man, and to honour the insensible creature before the one that possesses will and reason . . . As for rational natures, God has made them for this—to share in his bounty. And, because he is essential wisdom, righteousness, and light, we also by an intellectual movement and by the fact that we raise ourselves toward it have a share in his knowledge and in the light which is in us from this in order to arrive at being righteous and good, and to be enlightened in the knowledge of heavenly things according to what will be known by us. This is why wise men, not of us, enunciated this definition of philosophy: 'Philosophy is the imitation by a man of what is better, according to what is possible.'[1]

The will is God's chief gift to rational creatures, for by means of its exercise, a man appropriates to himself the gifts of God.

---

[1] Hom. CXXIII (P.O. xxix.180). Severus has carefully included the last clause 'according to what is possible' in the definition of philosophy: the idea that the created could ever lose its created characteristics completely and merge with the divine is entirely alien to his thought. The humanity of Jesus remains created even if it belongs to God as a man's body belongs to a man. In the same way a human *nous* or soul or body will *never* become part of the divine nature. Severus' position is in sharp contrast to such an Origenistic system as that held by Evagrius Ponticus: See I. Hausherr, 'De doctrina spirituali Christianorum Orientalium Quaestiones et scripta', in the collection of essays, *Études de spiritualité orientale*, pp. 23–55. Severus' whole system represents an attempt both to *acknowledge* the gulf between the created and the uncreated, the immaterial created realm and the sensible realm, and to bridge the gulf *as far as possible*.

Its natural tools, which are inborn, are conscience, memory, and natural law, the ability to know right from wrong.[1]

But most men's wills are sick: and this sickness is separation from God, which is called sin.[2] The basic driving force toward the good is not simply inborn, though one might call it part of human nature itself. While each man is born with the seeds of conscience and the ability to discern right and wrong when he comes of age, the will is also affected by society. In almost everyone, it is perverted by a failure of the parents, even Christian parents, to teach the child Christian values and goals instead of the values of 'the world'.[3] The result of this failure is that the child no longer has a natural preference for the good, and finds himself making moral decisions with difficulty.[4] As an adult, he further brings about the worsening of his own will through his own decisions, to such an extent that to the outsider who does not know the man, it might seem that his own evil actions are predetermined.[5] Severus uses two analogies for this deliberate self-perverting of the will—first, the same analogy of the eye and self-induced blindness that Gregory of Nyssa uses.[6] God has given us intelligence to be an intelligible eye

[1] Hom. LXIX (P.O. xxxv.342–4).

[2] See e.g. *Critique du Tome* (CSCO, vol. 244), 45; Homilies XLIX (P.O. xxxv.342); CXXIII (P.O. xxix.178–80); LXXXII (P.O. xx.393–5); CXIX (P.O. xxvi.401).

[3] Hom. LXII (P.O. viii.276–7). 'The world' in Severus' system, is a synonym for 'the wicked life, miserable, given to sin, and the sickness of free thought', Hom. LXXXII (P.O. xx.395).

[4] Ibid., pp. 393–5.

[5] Severus devotes some time to the problem of astrology: Homilies CXV (P.O. xxvi); CXIX (P.O. xxvi); and especially CXX (P.O. xxix). He rejects the notion that the moon and stars themselves affect the lives of men for evil, for they were created good by God. But he has some interesting hypotheses as to why astrology 'works': first there is a *demon* which places itself by the star in question and then deliberately misleads the astrologer, who has made himself a willing dupe. (In the genuine Platonic tradition, and to a certain extent, the Christian Platonic tradition, the stars are themselves both rational and semi-divine.) Second, Severus suggests that it is demons who produce the actual waxing and waning of the moon, maliciously shaving it off and building it up again. Third, demons, and not the impersonal lunar forces, are responsible on a personal basis for mental illness: this point puts Severus in direct conflict with the Greek medical theory of his period. Severus' demons are far more externalized than those, say, of Evagrius Ponticus or Maximus the Confessor; nevertheless, in their effect on men's *minds* (though not on their bodies) they may gain no entry without the assent of the individual will: 'If you are sick from avarice, at that very moment, the demon who kindles the fire has found a step to go forward . . . and throw himself on your soul', Hom. CXX (P.O. xxix.90).

[6] *De anima* (P.G. 46.120C–121A, 369D–372A).

through which we may participate in the divine intelligible light. But, as we may close our physical eyes and induce blindness in ourselves by our own will, we may close our intelligible eye and induce blindness: this blindness 'is separation from God; now separation from God is the privation of the light, and it is sin . . . which would not exist if I myself had not separated from the contemplation that is in nature. . .'.[1] Several times Severus calls sin a sickness of the will;[2] his meaning is illustrated by his other analogy, that of a sick man who has knowingly made himself ill.[3] Suppose a man is susceptible to terrible attacks of asthma. If he deliberately does something which provokes an attack, for example, he buys himself a pair of angora house cats, it is almost inevitable that he will become ill. His illness has come through his own fault, but once he has become ill, he cannot help it.

Here it is not necessary to blame necessity for this cruel sickness, but the one who has been the cause of it. For it is for this reason, that no one may say that the necessity of offences is bound up with our nature by allotted portion and by birth, that our Saviour did not say 'Woe to the human genus,' but 'Woe to the world! . . .'. The cause of offences is not the nature of man, but the world, i.e. the wicked life, miserable, given to sin, and the sickness of free thought . . .[4]

Human nature as such is not to blame for our inclination toward evil, and for the inevitable results of sin. Severus' doctrine of original sin does not include the notion of a corrupt will which comes to the child through his own birth.[5]

---

[1] Hom. CXXIII (P.O. xxix.178–80).

[2] See e.g. *Critique du Tome* (CSCO, vol. 244), 45; Hom. XLIX (P.O. xxxv.342) etc.

[3] Hom. LXXXII (P.O. xx.393–5). [4] Ibid.

[5] Julian of Halicarnassus insisted upon a doctrine of original sin in such a way that he felt Jesus would have had to have been conceived in some way outside the manner in which all other babies were conceived, for the sexual act itself was to him the means by which both sin and a corruptible body were passed along to each new member of the human race (see Draguet, *Julien*, pp. 118–27). Severus emphatically denied anything of the sort: he consistently argued that the body is neither the *source* of sin (Homilies CXXIII (P.O. xxix.180–4); LXXV, pp. 120–121; LXVIII (P.O. viii.298–9)), nor the *punishment* for sin (Hom. LXVIII (P.O. viii.375)) and that though virginity is better, marriage in this life has been blessed by God (Hom. CXIX (P.O. xxvi.414–18)). The union of the soul and Christ is compared to marriage 'because there is nothing among men more beloved and dear than the fleshly union in marriage, from which is equally born the love for

But let us look at how an operating will functions. We have already mentioned that the will is the faculty for making moral choices. These moral choices are not simply choices resulting in external activity. Whether the soul itself holds firmly to the good may be a matter of inner refusal to assent to evil in a situation where a man has no external choices to make, as in the case cited by Severus of the Jewish martyr who is physically forced to eat unclean meat.[1] The virtue of παρρησία or 'boldness' which the great Christian witnesses exercised arose out of the clear knowledge that, while kings and evil men could torture or kill them, their will was perfectly free: they could not be made to assent to the breaking of the divine law.[2]

God does not violate this liberty of the soul to give mental assent to its external circumstances or to reject them.[3] God works with the soul by setting up certain external circumstances, certain possibilities called 'the gifts of God' or 'the call' when they refer to specific work God desires of us. God annoints Saul king, but he does not make Saul kingly. When Saul turns away from God, God says 'I repent that I made him king, because he deserted me'. But

'I repent'. . . . is written to show that the calls and gifts of God are not forced and necessary and that they do not violate liberty. For it is not necessarily true that just because God made him king that he made him good: *this was the business of the will of Saul.*[4]

Severus, however, feels obliged to explain how it is that Paul says that the gifts and call of God are not subject to recall on

children. And if it were possible to find another image that would be greater [the Gospel] would necessarily supply it'. Hom. CXXI (P.O. xxix.96–8); see also Hom. XCII (P.O. xxv.36–41).

    [1] Hom. LXXV (P.O. xii.120–1).
    [2] Hom. LXXVIII (P.O. xx.283–4, 289). With respect to our own 'boldness' in the presence of God, it is Christ who 'confesses' for us who have no liberty near God, Hom. LXIII (P.O. viii.297).
    [3] See e.g. Hom. CXXIII (P.O. xxix.180–4). Expounding the parable of the Pharisee who thanked God that he was not like other men, Severus puts these words in Jesus' mouth: 'It is not you whom I have come to call, you who, by your own decisions declare yourselves just . . . but those who confess themselves sinners and run to my call . . . The call is not in anything necessary and forced, but it waits for the one [who answers it] by will . . . on the sole condition that you chase far away from you the presumption of righteousness which appears in you', Hom. XCII (P.O. xxv.32).
    [4] Hom. LXXX (P.O. xx.334–5).

God's part: While the individual may fall away from his possibilities and refuse to appropriate to himself what God would have him do, his basic moral possibilities remain fixed, and by repentance, he may reappropriate them to himself.[1]

The Human and Divine Will in Christ

Severus has much less to say about the will or wills than about the union of the two hypostases in Christ. Nevertheless his notion of the will in Christ is an integral part of his understanding of the hypostatic union: just as the two hypostases preserve their identities within the union, divinity and humanity remaining *distinct* but never *separate*, the two wills remain, distinct but not separate in Christ. In this section, then, we look at the specific passages on which this hypothesis is based, and try to establish what the actual human and divine wills in Christ are.

There are two major passages from which we may work out Severus' position: one from Homily LXXXIII (P.O. xx), pp. 415–17, and one from *Contr. Grammat.* 3, 33 (CSCO, vol. 101, pp. 182–3). In the first passage, citing Isaiah 7, he explains that because Jesus made moral decisions, this meant that he had a human will, for God, inasmuch as he is the Good itself,[2] does not make moral choices at all. However, because the humanity was intimately united to the divinity, Jesus did not have to *learn* to distinguish between good and evil; even as a baby he knew the difference. In the second passage Severus explains how it is that we do not rightfully speak of two wills in Christ, just as we do not speak rightfully of two wills in any man.

Jesus had a human will[3] in the sense that he made moral

---

[1] Ibid. 333–6.

[2] Gregory of Nyssa (*Contr. Eunom.* (P.G. 45.333CD)) also makes the distinction between willing the Good and being the Good: '. . . uncreated intelligible nature is far removed from such distinctions: it does not possess the good by acquisition, or participate only in the goodness of some good that lives above it: in its own essence it is good, and is conceived as such: it is a source of good, it is simple, uniform, incomposite . . .' Severus indicates in many places his agreement with this basic Platonic concept. See also *Critique du Tome* (CSCO, vol. 244), 96.

[3] Severus believed that Jesus had a human soul endowed with will and reason as well as a human body. Severus' peculiar position cannot really be described as falling within the category 'Word–flesh,' if one divides christologies into 'Word–flesh' and 'Word–man' types (see e.g. J. N. D. Kelly, *Early Christian Doctrines*, pp. 280 ff.). He usually speaks of Christ as possessing a rationally ensouled body (Letters LXV, pp. 18, 42; VII, p. 200; *Contr. Grammat.* 2, 21 (CSCO, vol. 111),

decisions. Explaining the text of Isaiah 7:15, 'before he knows how to choose evil, he will choose the good', Severus says,

[The] words, 'he scorned' and 'he did not obey' and this other, 'he chose' show us that the Word of God is united hypostatically not only to flesh, but still to a soul endowed with will and reason, for the purpose of making our souls bent toward sinfulness incline toward the choice of good and the aversion to evil.[1]

Yet in this same passage Severus qualifies this statement. He explains that

Each of us, in effect, examined at the age of infancy, has no knowledge of good or evil . . . But as by nature Immanuel was all God and the Good itself . . . he did not wait for the time of discernment . . . On the one hand he scorned evil and did not obey it, and on the other, he chose the good.

Because Jesus was God as well as man, though he *chose* good and rejected evil, he did not have to grow into the knowledge of good and evil.[2] Furthermore, while he was humanly tempted, he had foreknowledge of the temptations and of the thoughts of the devil.[3] In the same way, he did not have to learn the Law; like Adam in Paradise, he had internal knowledge of it written on his heart.[4] Jesus did not, then, go through a process of mental

---

179–80), Homilies LIX (P.O. viii.237); LXVIII (P.O. viii.221–2); CXV (P.O. xxvi.313–14)), but he gives a very unplatonic proof of the fact that Jesus was rational in a human manner: The Bible says of Jesus 'Then he began to be distressed and grieved, and to say, "My soul is sorrowful, even unto death". But it is plain to everyone that *distress and grief happen to a rational and intellectual soul*",' P.O. xiv, Letter LXV, p. 19. Gregory of Nyssa called the passions 'warts' on the soul. Here Severus is using the presence of certain passions as proof of the existence of a *rational* human soul. See Gregory's *De anima* (P.G. 46.55C). See also Hom. LIX (P.O. viii.239).

[1] The whole passage: Hom. LXXXIII (P.O. xx.415–17); see also *Critique du Tome* (CSCO, vol. 244), 179 ff.

[2] The whole side of Christ that was expressed in the working of miracles, knowledge of the future, healing illness, and defeating demons, even going long periods without food and drink, came later to belong to the stock-in-trade of the monastic holy men, and to form regular elements in the collections of the stories of the desert fathers. (Cf. Severus' list of extraordinary powers in Hom. XCVIII (P.O. xxv. 160.)) This is not to suggest that Jesus was conceived of as a super-holy man, though he was understood to be the model for the holy men. Nevertheless Jesus would not, during this period, have been regarded as divine or non-human, *simply* on the basis of his miraculous behaviour (with the exception of the resurrection).

[3] Hom. LXVI (P.O. viii.347).   [4] Hom. XLVI (P.O. xxxv.294).

growth,[1] and he was never without the knowledge of the motivations of the people around him, as ordinary men are.

Jesus had a human will, but it was not self-subsistent, so to speak, any more than his human hypostasis was. It did not function apart from the divine will to which it belonged.[2] If we ask whether Jesus' human will was the same as that of a prophet[3] like Jeremiah, whom God called even before birth, we must answer 'no'. All other human wills go through a process of growth, having as their end participation in the knowledge of God. God did not intend the humanity of Jesus to have as its end its own participation in God. Jesus, inasmuch as he was a man, had as his end and goal the inclining of the will of the rest of the human race toward God.[4] This was true for no other creature. As for participation in the knowledge of God, Jesus *is* the Wisdom of God Incarnate.[5] Second, the humanity of Jesus could not be free, as a prophet was, to assent to, or reject, God's calling. The humanity belonged to the Word, not as a prophet belongs to God, but as a man's own flesh belongs to him.[6]

But Jesus felt the things appropriate for a man to feel when faced with a terrible death—fear and reluctance.[7] At the same time, in the 'divine cheerfulness'[8] he knew that he would break the power of death in the resurrection. The fear, on the one

[1] Hom. CXIX (P.O. xxvi.381).

[2] The amount of freedom Jesus actually had and how we talk about it is a difficult problem. Severus several times mentions the *obedience* of Christ and his taking on of our disobedience as one of the saving factors in the Economy (see e.g. Hom. XLIX (P.O. xxxv.352–6); see especially Hom. LXXI (P.O. xii.56)). On the other hand, Severus says very strongly that no single instant in Jesus' life could be interchanged with any other: none is devoid of meaning, no matter how slight, even if it is unknown to us, and everything had to happen according to the pre-ordained divine timetable. Nevertheless, Jesus was not under *'anankî*, Greek 'necessity', Homilies XLVI (P.O. xxxv.298); CXIX (P.O. xxvi.381).

[3] Hom. CXV (P.O. xxvi.311–12).

[4] 'Every man is born for his own benefit, to participate in this light [of God] and the knowledge of God; but Christ, "the true light which enlightens every man who comes into the world" had no need [of this].' 'The Word of God is united hypostatically ... to a soul endowed with will and reason for the purpose of making our souls bent toward sinfulness incline toward the choice of the good ..', Hom. LXXXIII (P.O. xx.415–17). See also Hom. CXXIII (P.O. xxix.180–4).

[5] Hom. LXXXIII (P.O. xx.415–17); see especially Hom. LXX (P.O. xii.34–5), Letter LXV (P.O. xiv.16), etc.

[6] Hom. LVIII (P.O. viii.222–3) etc.

[7] Hom. LIX (P.O. viii.239); see also especially Letter LXV (P.O. xiv.19).

[8] *Contr. Grammat.* 3, 33 (CSCO, vol. 101), 183 (*ḥwîḥûthâ 'alâhâythâ*).

hand, and the courage, on the other, represent two wills of the humanity and the divinity only inasmuch as in a man the soul longs for spiritual nourishment and the body physical nourishment:[1] It was the same one, the Incarnate Word, who humanly rejected death and said,[2] '"Father, if it is possible, let this cup pass", and that which is flesh suffered; but divinely said, "the spirit is willing" and willingly he received the passion: we do not *divide* into [separate] wills or words or natures or images".' The same notion of accepting difference and rejecting separation applies to the wills as it does to hypostases and proprieties.

Severus is no Apollinarian. His Platonism, in the broad sense of the term, was such that he knew that the divine will is of an entirely different sort from created, human will: men *choose*, God *is*. In Christ there must have been a human will to make choices if there was to have been a human life.[3] But this human will was the iconic representation of the divine will, just as the body is the iconic representation of the soul.[4] One is a perfect image of the other on another level of reality. But while the two levels of reality correspond to each other, beings existing in the two levels exist only as it is possible for them in the mode of their own level (for example, the soul cannot be physical, the body immaterial). This means that the human will is an icon of the divine will, but is not a mirror image of it: it does not function in the same way that the divine will functions. This would be impossible. We find this same type of iconic relationship in Plato's *Timaeus*, where time, i.e. the moving stars and planets, is said to be a *moving* image, on a different level of reality, of changeless eternity. The system of Plotinus is built on the iconic correspondence between the One, the Many (Nous), and the Soul in the same way.

In a very real sense we can say that it is the Will of God[5] that is incarnate in Christ, the very liberty of God: this fact in itself must overshadow the question of the human will. To Severus

---

[1] *Contr. Grammat.* 3, 33 (CSCO, vol. 101), 182–3.

[2] Ibid., p. 184.

[3] Hom. LXXXIII (P.O. xx.416).

[4] See Hom. LXXXI (P.O. xx.355–7). See also Hom. LXVIII (P.O. viii.384–5). This idea was an old one. For Origen, the body is the natural expression of the soul. Bigg, *The Christian Platonists of Alexandria*, p. 226.

[5] Gregory of Nyssa sometimes referred to the Son as the Will of the Father, *Contr. Eunom.* P. G. 45.984A.

what matters is that God himself voluntarily[1] elected to take upon himself all the anxiety and suffering that goes with being a man or woman, fear of death included, and 'submitted himself to the laws of our nature', as he says in one way or another many times,[2] '[but] he is not susceptible to being dominated by a single one of [the factors affecting human life] . . . [But] by the very fact that he is incarnated he *accepted* to suffer all [human] things. . .'. It would be quite true to say that what all men possess by *nature*, within the Incarnation, the Word possessed by *will*. Sometimes Severus talks as though there was only one decision on the part of God to submit to the laws of nature; at other times, he talks as though there was a new decision to make every time, whether to grow hungry or sleepy or anxious. Either way, as far as Severus is concerned, by an act of *will* God *voluntarily* submitted himself to the laws of human nature or necessity and took upon himself a rational, willing human hypostasis. And this act of *God's* will is what is of significance to Severus, and not the human will.

The Operation of Christ

Arising directly out of the question of the will or wills in Christ is the question of the operation or operations in Christ: How does Severus conceive of them, and how many are there?

Severus uses the word 'operation' (ἐνέργεια, ma'bdhānûtha) in two major christological contexts: first, when he is talking about the one *source* of activity in Christ, and second, in the places where he is explaining how the humanity of Christ is said to be the operation of the divinity within the Incarnation.

When we talk about Peter making choices, we do not divide his choices up and say, 'Peter's body chose to fall asleep in Church'; 'Peter's mind decided to visit his neighbour who is ill'. We refer all his choices to Peter himself, and all arise out of

[1] *Contr. Grammat.* 3, 33 (CSCO, vol. 101), 183 ff. Hymn 108-1-VII (P.O. vi.146); *Critique du Tome* (CSCO, vol. 244), 125 ff.
[2] Hom. LVIII (P.O. viii.227); *Critique du Tome* (CSCO, vol. 244), 110. A typical statement: 'Even if the passions and death of our Saviour God were voluntary . . . they were, however, natural and proper to a truly passible and suffering flesh: the Incarnate Word permitted it to suffer according to the law of nature', *Critique du Tome* (CSCO, vol. 244), 133. Letter LXV (P.O. xiv.42); Hom. LXXXI (P.O. xx.355). The quotation is from Hom. CII (P.O. xxii.293-4).

Peter's one *will*. Nevertheless, the choices Peter makes can be roughly divided into those appropriate to the body and those appropriate to the soul—deciding to eat, deciding to pray, etc. In this sense, we recognize the *difference* between the two types of wishes, but we do not *separate*[1] them and say that there are two *wills* in Peter. In the same way, we do not say that there are two wills in Christ.

Now the one *operation* of Peter or Christ is the 'efficient motion' (*zawʿâ maʿbdhānâ*)[2] of Peter or Christ. The will chooses, but the operation is the source of energy—what sets the man in motion, so to speak, so that the choice of the will becomes a completed fact. Severus explains what he means by saying that the operation is the 'outreaching' or 'irruption' (*ḥîphâ*)[3] of the individual will. Peter wills to walk on water; Peter's will is translated into operation and he starts walking.

But just as there are two basic spheres of willing appropriate to the soul and body, there are two basic types of activities, one appropriate to the soul and the other appropriate to the body. Severus uses the example of a man who builds a house:[4] he draws up a plan, he decides on a location and what order to do things in; then he starts digging and shovelling, hammering and sawing, roofing and painting. He has performed mental and physical work, but all the work has sprung from the same source within the man:[5]

He who has acted is one man, who is composed of soul and body, and one operation, for there is one efficient motion, the outreaching (*ḥîphâ*) itself of what he wills. [But] of these different things done, this belongs to the intelligible realm, but that to the tangible and sensible.

The same is true of Christ: there are two types of activities,[6]

---

[1] Severus' correspondence with Sergius the Grammarian is probably the best source for his basic understanding of the meaning of the operation of Christ. 'First Letter to Sergius' (CSCO, vol. 119), 83 ff.; Letter I (P.O. xii), pp. 179–82, helps to fill out the picture.
[2] Ibid.   [3] 'First Letter to Sergius' (CSCO, vol. 119), p. 82.
[4] Ibid.   [5] Ibid.
[6] Ibid. 'Between the things performed and done by the one Christ, the difference is great. Some of them are acts befitting the divinity, while the others are human . . . Yet the one Word performed the latter and the former . . . Because the things performed are *different*, we shall [not] on this account rightly define two natures or forms as operating', Letter I (P.O. xii.181–2).

one that is appropriate to a man, and the one that is appropriate
to God. Jesus weeps and heals, dies and is resurrected; he also
suffers mental anguish and is filled with the 'divine cheerfulness'.[1]

Thus one also sees Immanuel [as one sees the builder] *for the one
who acts is one*—this is the Word of God Incarnate—*and the operation
is one efficient cause, but the things done are different* . . . Thus let no man
separate the Word from the flesh, and thus he cannot *divide* or
separate the operations.[2]

We are back again to the three technical terms, 'difference',
'divide', and 'separate'. Just as we do not divide or separate the
hypostases in Christ, though we recognize the difference, we
recognize the difference between the two types of activity in
Christ, but we do not divide and separate them, apportioning
them out to the humanity and divinity as though they spring
from two different operations and therefore from two self-
subsistent hypostases.

The Tome of Leo represents to Severus the epitome of all
he is fighting against, and he quotes the same passage in several
places to argue against it:[3] 'Each of the images performs what
belongs to it, the Word performing what belongs to the Word,
while the body completes those things that are of the body: one
of them shines in the miracles, but the other does the small
things.' To divide and separate the natures is to say that God
did all the things worthy of God and the Man did the rest.
And if we say this, then we have to say as the Nestorians did,
that the Man was crucified, while the Word whispered com-
forting advice in his ear. This is why Severus insists on the
hypostatic or natural union: one nature, one prosopon, one
will, and one operation. It is God himself who saved us, and
not a partnership of a man with a God who could not sully
himself by acting directly within the human sphere.

Severus has another way of explaining how it is that we do
not see two operations in Christ: Drawing implicitly upon the
distinction between a nature (or self-subsistent hypostasis) and
its operations, he explains that we might see the humanity and

---

[1] *Contr. Grammat.* 3, 33 (CSCO, vol. 101), 183.
[2] 'First Letter to Sergius' (CSCO, vol. 119), 83.
[3] Ibid., p. 84; see also Letter I (P.O. xii), pp. 182-4.

divinity in Christ in such terms that we could speak of the
humanity as the *operation* of the *nature* of the divinity.[1] We put
ourselves in the right area of thought if we remember that,
when we gain knowledge of God, what we know of him is never
his *nature*, but only his operations and properties,[2] for even the
angels do not know the divine nature.[3] The operation of a man
or of God, as we have just said, is the expression of the will, the
'outreaching' of the will, but it is something different from, and
to a certain extent separate from, the nature or hypostasis from
which it comes. Severus calls it both the 'efficient cause' and a
'middle term',[4] and explains how the operation is the link
between the one acting and the work performed.[5] It would not
be accurate to describe an operation in this sense as a tool,
though it is the means by which the work is done, because it
belongs to a man or God in a different way than a tool does.[6]
It is indeed the 'middle term' (*meṣʿāythâ*) between the invisible
and unknowable being of God or of a man (this unknowable
being in the case of a man is his mind)[7] and the visible, tangible,
concrete world in which the man and God act.

Severus uses the standard patristic analogy of the union
between fire and wood[8] to talk about the way in which the
humanity is the operation of the nature of the divinity in

---

[1] The Word 'performed all his own acts in [his body] and changed it, not into
his nature (far be it!), but into his glory and operation . . .', Letter I, p. 184;
see also pp. 180–2. Cf. Hom. LXVIII (P.O. xxxv.316–18). Eustathius gives a
quotation purportedly from the *Philalethe* (but not found in our extant texts) in
which the same point is made. See Lebon, *Chalkedon*, pp. 559–60.

[2] Hom. LXX (P.O. xii.9–10); see also Letter XXVIII (P.O. xii.259–60), etc.

[3] Hom. LIV (P.O. iv.61–2) etc.

[4] 'First Letter to Sergius' (CSCO, vol. 119), 82–3. Severus says of the Word,
that the 'whole hypostasis of the Only One [is present fully in the Incarnation],
although he is raised above all limitation, *he who imparts tens of thousands of operations to others*, and distributes graces by way of gifts as from a fountain', Letter
LXV (P.O. xiv.22).

[5] 'First Letter to Sergius', p. 82.

[6] 'First Letter to Sergius', p. 85; see also *Critique du Tome* (CSCO, vol. 244),
pp. 153–4.

[7] Hom. LXX (P.O. xii.15).

[8] Aristotle talks about the union of fire with wood, *De gen. et corr.* 327^b 10 ff.:
'Now we do not speak of the wood as combining with the fire, nor of its burning as
a combining either of its particles with one another or of itself with the fire: what
we say is that "the fire is coming-to-be, but the wood is passing-away".' The
important thing to note: wood and fire do not 'mix'. See also Bigg, *The Christian
Platonists of Alexandria*, p. 190, for Origen's use of the metaphor of the union of fire
and iron.

Christ.[1] He is explaining how the ember which purified the lips of Isaiah (Is. 6), is an appropriate symbol of Christ:

Because just as wood, interwoven with fire, burns with intensity and receives the flame in its depths, becomes, one thinks, entirely fire, and without ceasing to be wood, does not reject [this] from its own nature, but one thinks is inseparably one, named ember— the thing and the name being indivisible—doing what is proper to fire, namely, to shine and burn—in the same way, when the Word of God had been united to the flesh from the Holy Spirit and the Virgin Mary, possessing an intelligent soul, [to] which he had been united, not in a simple manner, but by the hypostatic union, in such a way that he himself should be comprised to be truly incarnated and made man, on the one hand he conserved the flesh . . . without having changed it into his own nature, nor being changed himself into its nature, and on the other, being united at the same time indivisibly, he is one, it seems, with the flesh, and he operates there and disposes everything that is proper to it, in such a way that it heals, it creates, it gives life, because in truth it has become the body itself of the creating and life-giving Word, a divine and intellectual ember.[2]

The important things in the analogy and his comments on it are: first, the wood 'becomes, one thinks, entirely fire' when united to the fire; second, the wood does not cease to be wood; third, the fire and the wood become inseparably one—an ember;[3] fourth, the ember *performs the operation* of the fire: it shines and burns. The Word, then, 'changed the [manhood] . . . into his glory and operation',[4] just as the wood 'becomes, one thinks, entirely fire'. But the Word 'conserved the flesh' as it was (Severus, of course, uses both 'flesh' and 'body' as synonyms for the humanity, usually including, as here, a statement near by that the flesh or body was rationally ensouled). Thus,

[1] Hom. XLVIII (P.O. xxxv.316–18); Hymn 35-1-VIII (P.O. vi.75–6); *Critique du Tome* (CSCO, vol. 244), 153–4. See also Hom. LXVIII (P.O. xxxv.330); Letter I, pp. 182–4; 180–1. Severus is presenting an alternative to the theory of two operations and at the same time rejecting the notion of change.

[2] Hom. XLVIII (P.O. xxxv.316–18).

[3] Severus' use of the metaphor of fire is significant: we know God only as an intellectual 'ember', not as pure fire. See e.g. Hom. XLVIII, p. 320: '. . . the one who spoke with Moses on the mountain was equally the one who according to the economy raised himself and appeared as an ember, not as the fire itself . . . to the end that he be accessible . . . to all men, and as far as we purify ourselves we can know him with the tongs of knowledge as . . . the seraphim . . .'

[4] Letter I, p. 184.

through the hypostatic union, manhood and divinity became inseparably one, as the wood and the fire are one in the ember. Finally, the Word 'operates there and disposes everything proper to it, in such a way that it heals, it creates, it gives life, because in truth it has become the body itself . . . of the Word, a divine and intellectual ember'.

In another characteristic passage from his 'First Letter to Sergius'[1] Severus explains fully how the Word expressed himself and performed his saving activities through the humanity. Severus begins by saying that Jesus did *not* use the humanity as a man would use a lifeless, irrational, and inert tool, but

it appears that he used the strength of his soul as God incarnate. . . . To the sea, he says, 'be still, be calm'. But to Peter, who cried out 'command me to come beside you on the water', he commanded, 'come'. And to the leper . . . he gives the law by God's authority and says, 'I say to you, do not be troubled'. It does not anywhere say that the Lord says this: 'In the name of the Lord I do such and such things . . .'.[2]

When Severus says that the Word used the strength of the soul of Jesus to perform the saving acts, we see very clearly again that he is thinking in terms of the iconic relationship between the two levels in Christ, recalling what was said in the section on the will of Christ: The Word uses the strength of the human soul as the 'efficient cause' of the activities of Christ because he is operating within the created level of reality, and must express himself in terms appropriate to it. God in his uncreated nature does not speak[3] to the sea and say 'be still!'. And, going back to the analogy of the ember, Severus says that what we know of God through Christ we know, not as the untouchable fire, but as the ember which, like the Seraphim, we may pick up with the tongs of knowledge.[4]

Epistemological Conclusions

There are, then, three basic epistemological distinctions of which Severus makes use to solve the christological problem

---

[1] (CSCO, vol. 119), p. 85; see also p. 87.   [2] 'First Letter to Sergius', p. 85.
[3] Just as God does not 'will' in human fashion. But see Letter XCV (P.O. xiv.178–80), where Severus attempts to explain what the Bible intends when it ascribes words to God. See Homilies CXXIII (P.O. xxix.142); LIX (P.O. viii.234–235).
[4] Hom. XLVIII (P.O. xxxv.320).

to his own satisfaction. The first is the division of reality into three genuinely distinct levels which stand in an iconic relationship to each other: the uncreated, immaterial God, the created realm of the intelligibles, and the realm of the visible, material creation. The second is the distinction between the very real duality in Christ, which is encountered only in thought, and the unity which transcends the duality and which is understood at the operational level. The third distinction is that between a subject or prosopon and its predicates or proprieties.

First, the division of reality into the three Platonic levels sets up the basis for Severus' ability to insist firmly that divinity must remain unconfusedly divinity in Christ, the body and soul of Christ also remaining firmly body and soul which belong not only to the realm of creation, but continue to remain human. The boundary line between the uncreated and the created is crossed by the Incarnate Word, but never blurred or removed.

Second, Severus' further distinction between the levels of thought about the union allow him to say that, while on the one hand, the duality[1] which we apprehend at the level of *theoria* or *epinoia* or subtle intellect is real (the body of Christ remains created, the soul remains a human soul), nevertheless, the unity in Christ is of greater significance than the duality, for it is in the unity of the humanity and divinity that the identity of Christ lies; it is through God the Word incarnate, who operates all things within the incarnation, that our salvation comes. Our recognition of this unity lies somehow in a level of thought higher than the recognition of the duality because it is the level of real insight; it is also a lower level of thought, because it is the level of the world of concrete objects, in which we deal with people as single identities, rather than as composite hypostases of body and soul. But let there be no mistake: the realm of thought is very real, too; it is the Cappadocian realm of *epinoia* in which creative thought takes place, the seat of the divine names, as well as of all real theology. It is

---

[1] Severus himself refuses to use the word 'duality' for fear of its being misunderstood. For him, duality must imply the destruction of unity. We shall use it, however, because of the peculiar danger of not seeing the legitimate twoness which really does exist in Christ according to Severus. Severus, at this point, genuinely appears to take his ideas from Cyril. See Lebon, *Chalkedon*, pp. 504–5.

unfair to call it the 'purely logical',[1] for the realm of *epinoia* is a real reflection of the world of the objects of thought as far as it is possible. Here we distinguish the natures in Christ; at this level we are forbidden to separate or divide the natures so as to set them apart from each other, or to speak of two prosopa[2]—we could not, at this point, separate them at any other level. The unity of Christ lies beyond it, in the realm of the objects of thought, yet we must make use of this realm of thought if we are to know and to name accurately what we meet with both in the world of spiritual experience and the concrete world.

Third, Severus' distinction between a subject or prosopon and its accompanying proprieties or sets of predicables allows him to state further that Christ is one in identity, one nature, to which belong two sets of properties, the humanity and the divinity. These proprieties belong to the nature and serve to identify it, acting as marks so that we may recognize the incarnate Word for what he is, but they do not make him what he is, since a nature is not a conglomerate of all its properties, but is something, an identity, to which predicables belong.

Christ as One of the Trinity

Severus' conception of Christ is closely tied to a particular kind of doctrine of the Trinity. To move further in our study of the relationship between Christ and knowledge, we must look at the relationship between Christ and the Father in Severus' system.

God the Father is the 'root' (*'eqārâ*) of the Trinity, the origin of the Son and the Holy Spirit, the one first cause (*melthâ dhrîshānûthâ lḥudhāythâ; ḥdhâ rîshîthâ*)[3] of the Godhead. He is a 'great intellect' (*tar'îthâ rabtâ*) and 'a mind above all things' (*hawnâ dhalhal men kol*).[4] God the Father is the 'living and hypostatic mind', incorruptible, invariable, and everlastingly the same.[5] He is the eternal begetter of the living and hypo-

---

[1] As Lebon calls it; see *Chalkedon*, p. 500: 'In reality this duality does not exist in the object; it is entirely a creation of the mind. . .'

[2] In *Contr. Grammat.* 2, 11 (CSCO, vol. 111), pp. 106 ff., Severus might appear to allow separation by the subtle intellect (*hawnâ qaṭînâ*), but he immediately takes back with one hand what he gives with the other. See also Letters XI (P.O. xii), pp. 203–6; II, p. 190; XXV, p. 231 (a long quotation from Cyril, Ep. 50, P. G. LXXVII, 257; but see Lebon, *Chalkedon*, p. 500, text and note 127).

[3] Letter LXV (P.O. xiv.14).　　　[4] Ibid., p. 9.　　　[5] Ibid., p. 11.

static Word, and from him eternally proceeds the living and hypostatic Spirit.[1] His own proper activity is his contemplation of himself, or rather of his eternal Wisdom, who is the Son.[2]

The Son is the Word of the living mind of the Father. As the Wisdom of God, he is the eternal object of the Father's contemplation. He is the perfect image of the mind of the Father.[3] But he is also the Father's Messenger.[4] Severus is very much within the broad tradition of the old Logos theology, which tended to regard the Father as the unknowable and unfathomable depths of God, while the Word (in one of his functions) was the Rational Structure of reality and the theoretically knowable element of God. This distinction between the directly unknowable Father and the partially knowable Son has an extremely important place within Severus' system, as it does in many Greek fathers, for the Son is both *revealer* of the knowledge of God and the *object* of the knowledge of God. But Severus thinks in christological terms. It is *Christ* who is the Door to our knowledge of God;[5] in Christ the Word is the invisible one made visible,[6] God who stooped to our level.[7] But the Word, even in the Incarnation, does not completely reveal God, because this is clearly impossible: the Word has descended only a little way from the secret storehouses of the knowledge of God[8] and has opened only one small part of the book of the knowledge of the Trinity which, before the Incarnation, was completely closed to us.[9]

Theoria

Christ as the incarnate Wisdom of God is therefore both the *means* to our knowledge of God, and the *object* of it. As the means to our knowledge, he is the 'Door', the initial entry, and then the guide through the three levels of *theoria* which culminate in the contemplation of the Trinity. As the object of our

[1] Ibid.   [2] Hom. LXX (P.O. xii.31–4).
[3] Letter LXV (P.O. xiv.9).   [4] Ibid.
[5] Homilies XCVIII (P.O. xxv.159–60); CXXIII (P.O. xxix.124, 126).
[6] Hom. LXXI (P.O. xii.62, 63).
[7] 'Christ, the Word of God, the true and unmixed light, was thrown from the height even as far as the depths . . . and has drawn us from there, and made us go up, who were submerged by sin and death' Hom. LXXI (P.O. xii.65–6). Cf. Homilies CXXIII (P.O. xxix.124–6); LXVII (P.O. viii.353); LXIII (P.O. viii. 289–90).
[8] Hom. CI (P.O. xxii.259).   [9] Ibid. 259–60.

knowledge, he plays a different role: At the same time he is perfect God and also a representation of God in terms of human activity. As object of our knowledge in this sense, he is our 'legislator' who has given us the 'evangelical law' and our model of perfect human life in the image of God.

Jesus, 'the Word of God, this One of the Trinity, this Door to knowledge', leads us up to God by first humbling himself so that he will be comprehensible to us at our low level of existence.[1] Then gradually raising our thoughts to higher levels of knowledge through *theoria*, he makes us 'dwell in the company of the Father'.[2] The ascent of the thought under the direction of Christ (perhaps through the three major levels of *theoria*—natural *theoria*, *theoria* of the intelligences, and *theoria* of the Trinity—)[3] Severus says is the Transfiguration; as Jesus made the three disciples go up the mountain and was revealed to them, so does he love to raise lesser Christians to the highest knowledge of God which is both profound and comprehensible.[4] Then, at the point where confusion might enter, the one who is led up is sent back down.[5]

This is the partial context of Severus' thought on the ascent of the mind to God during this life—the gradual ascent through the levels of *theoria*, the comprehensibility of knowledge which we enjoy at every level, the limitation of the knowledge attainable by each individual according to his own purification, preparation, and study.[6]

In this section we shall make a few comments on Severus' use of the word *theoria* and then look more closely at the levels of *theoria* through which one presumably travels to reach the highest knowledge of God attainable in this world: natural *theoria*, *theoria* of the angelic level, *theoria* of the Trinity.

[1] Hom. CXXIII (P.O. xxix.124–6). See also Homilies LVII (P.O. viii.353); XLVIII (P.O. xxxv.320).

[2] Hom. LIX (P.O. viii.231–2).

[3] These three levels were the standard three of the Origenistic-Cappadocian tradition. Severus does not usually list them together in this manner. See Hom. LXX (P.O. xii.9–10). See also Hom. CXXIII (P.O. xxix.124–32). This division nevertheless appears to lie implicitly behind his thought, and is useful for discussion. For the *theoria* of the Trinity, see Hom. LVX (P.O. viii.327).

[4] Homilies CXXIII (P.O. xxix.124–6); LXV (P.O. viii.327); see also Hom. LXX (P.O. xii.9, 10).

[5] Ibid.

[6] Homilies CI (P.O. xxii.259); CXXIII (P.O. xxix.126); see also Hom. LIII (P.O. iv.27) etc.

In line with the tradition of the Logos theology to which he belongs, Severus believes implicitly that *all* knowledge is knowledge of God, and that most knowledge, in so far as it is comprehensible, is knowledge of the Son, the Word, who lies behind all things as the comprehensible structure of reality.[1] For this reason Severus can call Jesus, who is the incarnate Wisdom of God, the Door to all knowledge of God and our guide through the levels of knowledge of God,[2] for as Wisdom Incarnate, Jesus also represents the comprehensible aspect of God.

Theoria is the term applied by Severus to the attentive studying of something for the purpose of finding its real underlying meaning or structure. It is a broad word which can refer to the bare analysis of something, or to insight at its profoundest level. It is probably best not to press for a general definition of *theoria* any more precise than this.[3] *Theoria* is the term Severus uses for what we do when we study Scripture;[4] it is the word he uses when he talks about our prayerful speculation on the Trinity;[5] and about the way we see God lying behind all created reality.[6] One wonders also if 'the subtle intellect' by which we see the duality in Christ is the same as *theoria*.

There are three major levels of *theoria* through which we may

---

[1] This is what the Christians meant when they called Jesus the Wisdom of God Incarnate, and connected this title with Proverbs 8:22 ff. It could also account for how one might say that God would teach Ephraim Greek.

[2] Hom. CXXIII (P.O. xxix.124–6).

[3] See Hans Jonas's summary statement, *The Gnostic Religion* (Beacon Press, 2nd edn.), p. 338: 'To look at what is there, at nature as it is in itself, at Being, the ancients called by the name of contemplation, *theoria*'.

[4] See e.g. Hom. LXXXI (P.O. xx.346–7): Scripture is easy to read in the literal sense, but by abundant and secret *theoria* one learns the hidden meaning. What is learned with great difficulty is harder to neglect than what comes easily. Severus does not, obviously, give gnostic reasons for the necessity of the hidden meaning of Scripture. See also Hom. XCVI (P.O. xxv.97); Letter LXIX (P.O. xiv.77–8).

[5] Hom. LXV (P.O. viii.327).

[6] See e.g. Homilies CXXIII (P.O. xxix.178); CXVI (P.O. xxvi.333–4).
Though Severus does not characteristically talk this way, he once describes a vision Stephen the martyr had. He begins by saying that, as a result of the heavens opening at Jesus' baptism, all those who believe in Jesus enter heaven freely by *theoria*: 'Thus Stephen, the first of the martyrs, as he was held in the middle of the assembly of the Jews and was ravished in his mind . . . "saw the glory of God", i.e. the opening of the heavens, [and] "Jesus standing at the right hand of God" . . . who taught him and instructed him to stand and not be humble or bow the knee in the fight for proper religion, for it is with respect to these things also that revelations and *theorias* are seen', Hom. CXVII (P.O. xxvi.352). Through *theoria* of this type Stephen receives explicit instruction in practical Christian behaviour.

travel to reach our highest knowledge of God. The first is natural *theoria*, the *theoria* of the visible, natural universe. We practise *theoria* of nature by using our spiritual eye, intelligence,[1] along with our physical eyes, to see, lying behind, or within, the physical world, the work of God himself. Severus, following the tradition of Scripture as well as the Platonic tradition, had at the base of his system the conviction that 'the heavens declare the glory of God, and the firmament displays his handiwork'. By natural *theoria*, which all men could be expected to exercise, without any special revelation, they could see the work of the Word, ordering and providing, nourishing and sustaining the universe.[2] All men could further be expected to know that it was God who made everything by means of his Word.[3] Natural *theoria*, then, is the basic knowledge of God available to all men: it is the 'outside' of God.[4]

Sin is the result of turning away from natural *theoria*, or one might even say that it *is* the turning away from natural *theoria*: through natural *theoria* we remain with God; if we refuse it, and see the natural world without seeing God at the same time lying behind it, we are separated from God, and this separation from God is sin.[5] To put it in more concrete terms, the sin of the

[1] Hom. CXXXIII (P.O. xxix.178–80). See also Hom. LXVIII (P.O. viii.385).

[2] Homilies LXX (P.O. xii.9–10); CXXIV (P.O. xxix.208); Letter XCIX (P.O. xiv.220 ff.), etc. See also Hom. CXVI (P.O. xxvi. 333–4).

[3] See e.g. Hom. CXXIV (P.O. xxix.208): A typical statement: 'God, who has made everything by means of the Word and by superior and ineffable Wisdom, by means of the grandeur and beauty of each of his works and the ordained and harmonious movement which they conserve with respect to each other makes known that he is the author of the universe, for while they are silent, the works themselves shout out the operation, the order, the sustaining of the one who created, the one who ordered, the one who sustains.'

[4] '. . . it is by the glory that surrounds him and by what is seen on him on the outside that God is known . . . and not by a consideration and an interior and hidden contemplation: he is known, for example, by the beauty and grandeur of the creatures, by the order and harmony seen in them . . .', Hom. CXXIII (P.O. xxix.126). Severus and Philoxenus appear to be of one mind in this respect: they are extremely mistrustful of 'mystical' experiences, and stress the essentially comprehensible element in the knowledge of God that we may have. This is quite different from saying, as Eunomius apparently said, that we can know God as well as he can know himself.

[5] In discussing the question of the origin of evil, Severus explains sin as the deviation of a free will: '[God] has . . . created the intelligence which is in us as an intellectual eye, in order that we have part in the divine and intelligible light and we make use of the contemplation of that which is seen and which by the beauty and harmony of the world we reflect by analogy on the one who has made and

Pharisees, self-righteousness, separates us from God in this way: it blocks the individual who is suffering from it from seeing how he needs to bridle his passions so that his intelligence may be full of *theoria*.[1] Thus, self-righteousness separates us from knowledge of God, and God himself, from Christ 'the light of Truth': 'The presumption of righteousness is a wall which bars all the roads that lead to salvation and stops God by seizing hold of the mind itself.'[2] Natural *theoria*, then, is linked to natural law and conscience: all men are born with an innate ability to see God in creation, to tell right from wrong, and to follow the right.[3]

But natural *theoria* itself leads the Christian up into the next realm, the realm of the intelligences. In Homily LXX[4] Severus describes the ascent:

I [shall] travel and cross over the natural *theoria* which is visible in this world which is seen, that which surrounds [me] like a wonderful tent, and thus I shall arrive at the house of God, the intelligences (*methhawnānē*), and the bodiless ones. In these especially God dwells as in a house (*badhmûth baytâ*) and from these is he known, while he is [in himself] incomprehensible and unapproachable.

The mind, then, crosses through natural *theoria* to the realm of the angels and bodiless spirits in which God dwells as in a house and from which he is known.

In other places Severus states that God dwells in the angels. In Homily CI[5] he explains that the 'place of God' in the vision of Ezekiel is 'the immaterial essences' who participate in the divine *theoria*. This is why the cherubim are called his throne and see, for by means of illumination he 'sits and rests upon them and at all times lives among them.' Thus they participate in the uncreated Light of the Trinity.[6]

---

ruled this order . . . But if by our will we separate our intelligence from this contemplation . . . we have closed our intellectual eye . . . and organized in it . . . blindness, which is separation from God. Now separation from God is privation of the light, and it is sin . . . which would not have existed if I myself had not separated from the contemplation which is in nature', Hom. CXXIII (P.O. xxix.178–180).

[1] Hom. XCII (P.O. xxv.35–6).
[2] Ibid. 33.   [3] See e.g. Hom. LXIX (P.O. xxxv.342–4).
[4] Hom. LXX (P.O. xii.9–10).   [5] Hom. CI (P.O. xxii.251–3).
[6] Homilies CXXIII (P.O. xxix.144–6); LXXII (P.O. xii.75–6); cf. Hom. CI (P.O. xxii. 251–2).

One of their functions is to bring us knowledge of God. They are able to do this because they participate in this uncreated and essential Light of the Trinity and are able to sustain the light and share it.[1] Light, of course, is the symbol of the illuminating power of God, so that when Severus says that the angels participate in it, he means that they share as directly as possible in true knowledge of God: because this means that they understand his desire for us,[2] they are able to perform the work of God and bring us his knowledge.

In both these tasks Severus' angels are related to the angels in the system of Dionysius, where they are arranged in hierarchies, each angel receiving his knowledge of God from the one directly above him, and each teaching the one directly below him, until the knowledge of God is passed down to men.[3] Severus' angels are arranged in hierarchies we know, for he tells us that some of the spiritual beings we shall know and name in this life, but others will only 'be named and known in the age to come according to the state of preparation and purification of each'.[4]

This brings us to Severus' use of the doctrine of the divine names. The doctrine of the divine names does not hold a central position in his theology; nevertheless, what there is of it is of importance where we try to sort out the problem of the angels as carriers of divine knowledge. The divine names are themselves not literal,[5] they are 'hints' and 'pointers' which serve the purpose of raising our minds and pointing them in the direction of the individual operations and properties of God[6]

---

[1] Homilies CXXIII (P.O. xxix.144–6); CI (P.O. xxii.251–2); LXXII (P.O. xii. 75–6).

[2] See e.g. Hom. LIV (P.O. iv.61–2).

[3] *Cael. Hier.* V; see also Evagrius Ponticus, Frankenberg, pp. 614–15, and the *Book of the Holy Hierotheus*, I. Hausherr, 'L'Influence du 'Livre du Saint Hierothée',' *Études de spiritualité orientale*, p. 39.

[4] Hom. LXXII (P.O. xii.73).

[5] Letters XXVIII (P.O. xii.259–60); XCIX (P.O. xiv.222–6), etc. Language cannot literally be applied to God. See also Hom. CXXIII (P.O. xxix.140–2); 'First Letter to Sergius' (CSCO, vol. 119), 94–5.

[6] e.g. Hom. LXX (P.O. xii.14). 'The divine book . . . makes use of the poverty of words which are in use among us, when it wishes to raise as far as possible [our mind] . . . as far as the height of the divine thoughts and when it humbles itself because of this to follow the habit of our ears, to the end of painting in us the icons of truth and making our intelligence advance . . . by the hinting of words, because it is not possible to show, other than by different words and well-chosen expressions, actions by themselves', Hom. LIX (P.O. viii.234–5).

(and not toward the unknowable *ousia* itself).[1] They are like metaphors, which serve to suggest far more than what they actually say: as we strike two rocks together to create a spark, we use the divine names to strike up the divine fire of the knowledge of God. But as we get only sparks from the rocks and not the fire itself, so also we get only sparks from the divine names.[2]

While the second level of *theoria* is that of the angels, the highest form of *theoria* attainable to a man in this life is *theoria* of the Trinity. This *theoria* is the same as the angels enjoy. Very few men, of course, reach this level.[3] Gregory of Nazianzus was one. Like the angels, he looked upon the Light of the Trinity with 'wide awake and unsleeping eyes'. Like the angels, because of his *theoria* of the Trinity, he was able to give us 'a theology [which was] exempt from all error and exact'— he both participated in the highest possible *theoria* and he passed on what he knew to those below him.[4] Again, however, as at all other levels, the encounter with the Light remains *comprehensible*,[5] and his theology was accurate because he did not 'strive for an abundance of grace' and seek more than he was capable of receiving. Even at this level, *theoria* must match preparation.[6] Severus quotes Gregory of Nazianzus with approval when he says that the tree of which Adam and Eve wrongfully ate was the tree of *theoria*; this tree would not have been forbidden to them forever, but only until they were prepared for it.[7]

These are the three interrelated levels of theoria characterized in Severus' system. We have already seen in the section on the human will in Christ that Severus conceives of the end of

---

[1] See Hom. LXX (P.O. xii.9–10).   [2] Hom. LXX (P.O. xii.14).

[3] Nevertheless, Severus says that men were originally created to be like embodied angels: each man 'lives on the earth as another angel, who is both visible and invisible . . .', Hom. LXVIII (P.O. viii.372–3). See also Hom. LXI (P.O. viii.257–258), where he says that the monks live like angels in that they shun material goods, avoid marriage, weep continually, offer constant praise to God, and read the Bible. See also Hom. CXVII (P.O. xxvi): John the Baptist lived in the desert of Jordan in imitation of the 'angelic and incorporeal' life of Elijah (p. 346).

[4] Hom. LXV (P.O. viii.327).

[5] Ibid. See also Homilies CXXIII (P.O. xxix.124–6); LXVII (P.O. viii.364–365), etc.

[6] This is why, even in the future life we shall not all know the names of the same angels, but some will know more, others less.

[7] Hom. CXIX (P.O. xxvi.409–11).

man for which he was created to be the enjoyment of, and participation in, the knowledge of God. He regards our advance in *theoria*, with its necessary study and purification, as only the beginning

[of] the future life, in which there exists a copious and abundant enjoyment of knowledge and which is such that it fills and satisfies ... the power of the desire of those who have part in it and which overflows because of its grandeur and spreads itself out like great waters which spread out, escaping the hand which tries to contain them.[1]

Our farthest advance in knowledge, then, comes after death, when we shall name and know the intelligences we cannot now know, and when our desire for knowledge will be satisfied. Nevertheless, even in the age to come, some will know more than others, depending on the state of purification and preparation of each.

Christ as Legislator and Model

But the Christian life is not simply contemplative. Hence our knowledge of God must be more than simply *theoria*, it must furnish us with a guide to the active Christian life as well. Christ is to us not only our leader in the ascent to God through thought—he is our Type, our Model, our Teacher in all human matters. He is both the new Adam who has, through his own birth, 'blessed our passage into existence', and the great Legislator who has, in baptism, written the Spiritual Law on our hearts. He has taught us all acceptable human ways, and has imposed a new meaning on the human objects of love and pity.

Severus interprets the passage from Proverbs, chapter 8, 'the Lord created me the beginning of his ways', in the following manner:

When the Word, the unique Wisdom and Power of the Father, was incarnate, it was for us that he was created, in that he was made man. But he has been created for the beginning of his ways, to the end that he make us go up, who were in error, toward the Father and the right way of the virtues ... [But] 'the way' is the direction and teaching of knowledge and virtue, by which 'the works,' i.e. ourselves, have been newly formed and adapted to the good. ...[2]

---

[1] Hom. XCVI (P.O. xxv.97); cf. Hom. LXIII (P.O. viii.292-3).
[2] Hom. LXX (P.O. xii.35).

The work of Christ, then, as it is conceived in this passage, is the establishment of the patterns of human knowledge and behaviour. Christ begins this work through the gift of baptism, and completes it through the offering of his life as a model for all men.

Severus sees the history of mankind as the history of the loss and regaining of the Law. Adam was originally created incomplete, in order that, of his own free will, he might be able to share in the good things of God.[1] To help him develop as he was supposed to, he was given the Law, which was written on the tables of his heart. This evangelical and spiritual law was to test his free will, to help him to preserve what he had and to come to those things that he did not yet have.[2] Needless to say, the Law was a very great gift. The Fall, however, cost mankind not only its immortality; through the Fall it also lost the evangelical and spiritual law which had been written on the tables of Adam's heart.[3] This meant that though the human race was left with 'natural law,'[4] i.e. a knowledge of the difference between good and evil, and a conscience, the ability to perform a genuinely virtuous act out of love of the good was lost.[5] But God took pity on mankind and sent the Mosaic law—a literal law written on tablets of stone and a spiritual law, which lay behind the obvious.[6] The history of God in the world from Moses to Christ is, then, the history of the gradual disclosure of the spiritual and evangelical law which was finally fully revealed in Christ.[7]

Christ's baptism in the Jordan as our representative, 'the

---

[1] Hom. XLIX (P.O. xxxv.342).

[2] Hom. XLIX (P.O. xxxv.342). See also Homilies XLVI (P.O. xxxv.294–5) and LVI (P.O. iv.75–6). Eve was given to Adam as a help-meet 'in the worship in Paradise and in the keeping of the Law', Letter LXV (P.O. xiv.46). Men and women were intended to have 'equal honour in the life of bliss in Paradise,' Letter XCII, p. 169. In Hom. CXIX (P.O. xxvi.410), Severus cites Gregory of Nazianzus, saying that God gave the Law to Adam as matter to his free will.

[3] Cf. Hom. LVI (P.O. iv.75–6).

[4] Hom. LXIX (P.O. xxxv.342–4).

[5] See e.g. Hom. XLIX (P.O. xxxv.342–4). In Severus' Hymn 340-I-III on the verse 'because none that liveth shall be justified before thee' he says, 'all the righteousness that comes from man is before thee, my Lord, as a rag of her that sitteth at her menstruation; but thou as being merciful justifiest all those that have loved thy commandments. . .'.

[6] Hom. LII (P.O. iv.12–14).

[7] See e.g. Hom. LXXIX (P.O. xx.299 ff.).

first born of our race' as members of the Church, is the beginning of our new life under the evangelical Law, which through baptism is written on our hearts. The story of Moses who received the law on the tablets of stone is, then, the story of our own baptism and[1]

shows by a symbol that when God created man at the beginning, and when he was finally created anew by the baptism of the infant, he wrote on the tables of his heart, which were pure, that he was created and renewed following his proper laws: first, the natural law, and at the end, the evangelical and spiritual law.

The recreation and restoration of a human being begins with the rewriting of the law in his heart, both *natural* law, which is the ability to discern right from wrong, and the *evangelical* law, the well-spring of virtuous activity which arises from a real understanding of the goodness of God at such a level that it produces a response arising out of the depths of the heart: following the evangelical law, a man will naturally not only distinguish between good and evil, he will have a natural inclination toward the good, and an understanding of the basic premises of the law.[2]

But the work of Christ the Law-giver goes far beyond the gift of the law at baptism. His baptism in the Jordan is symbolically the marriage between Christ and the Church: but the period of time following his baptism, the time he spent with his disciples, was the symbolic time of marriage which follows the ceremony, when the groom goes about with the bride and teaches her her new way of life and offers himself as a model for

---

[1] Hom. LVI (P.O. iv.75–6).

[2] In Hom. LII (P.O. iv.11–14), as in other places, Severus calls the evangelical law the 'spiritual' law. See Homilies LXII (P.O. viii.277); LVI (P.O. iv.75–6); also LXI (P.O. viii.257), where Severus says that after having 'gone up the mountain of philosophy' in a visit to the monks, he has seen 'not God descend in fire, but men inflamed by the divine fire of great and elevated desires going up to heaven. They did not receive the law on tablets of rock, but they possess written on the tablets of their hearts the laws of the Spirit; not only do they meditate in them day and night and have them in their mouth, but they accomplish them in reality, and they are a law for those who see them. . .'. Occasionally Severus contrasts the Law as given to men with the requirements of Nature, Hom. LII (P.O. iv.12–14). Nature regulates the behaviour of animals, the Law, of men; there is, however, a high level of human behaviour, that of the voluntary: the life of virginity belongs to this level, which goes beyond the Law, Hom. CXIX (P.O. xxvi.376–7). Occasionally the Law is also contrasted to the Gospel, of which it is the incomplete forerunner: Hom. CXVI (P.O. xxvi.328–9). See also Hom. XCII (P.O. xxv.30–3).

her imitation.[1] Christ is seen to be our 'legislator'[2] not only through the gift of the Law on Sinai, but also through the gift of the law at baptism. He is our legislator by the setting of a perfect human example and precedent, as the one who 'pre-establishes our ways'[3] by rewriting, so to speak, the laws of human behaviour. Christ is our 'model of philosophy',[4] our 'type',[5] whose every action to the most infinitesimal instant of time, has a didactic meaning for us.[6] All the details of his life serve this purpose: the angels at the crucifixion, for example, were there to teach us that when we are in need of help, God will sustain us, though of course, Jesus was not in any need of sustaining himself.[7] As the wisdom of God incarnate, even the exercise of the virtues served no other purpose than a didactic one.[8] In all things, the Word, being made man, 'appropriated our imperfection and gave us a doctrinal model of perfection'.[9] Thus has Christ 'made shine on us the rays of the knowledge of God; he has also practised equity and righteousness on the earth, when he extended his laws over all the earth with an absolutely superior righteousness'.[10]

Holy Men

Just as the life of Christ serves as the primary model for our imitation, and hence our participation in the Good Things of

Nevertheless, Severus feels the necessity of affirming that the 'God of the Law and of the Gospel' is the same, Hom. XCVI (P.O. xxv.107). To live by the evangelical law is to dispose one's whole life in accordance with the interior meaning of the law—e.g. '. . . the true fast is a life pure from every evil act, and that we should break bread for those who are hungry', Letter XVII (P.O. xii.212).

[1] Hom. XCII (P.O. xxv.40–1).

[2] 'Christ the Legislator', Hom. LXXIV (P.O. xii.104); 'your spiritual legislator', Hom. LIV (P.O. iv.58); 'the God of love and the Lawgiver, Christ', Letter XXV (P.O. xii.247). See also Hom. LXIII (P.O. viii.292).

[3] Hom. LXX (P.O. xii.34–5).

[4] See also Hom. CXXIV (P.O. xxix.212), where by his teaching Jesus made the apostles 'statues of perfection' and 'models of philosophy' for the whole world. Severus often spoke of the philosophic life: Basil and Gregory were 'washed with the waters of philosophy and the monastic life', Hom. CXVI (P.O. xxvi.328). Elijah lived 'philosophically', Hom. CXVII (P.O. xxvi.346).

[5] Hom. LXXI (P.O. xii.56).

[6] Hom. XLVI (P.O. xxxv.298). See also Hom. CXIX (P.O. xxvi.381).

[7] Hom. LXIV (P.O. viii.318–19).   [8] Hom. CXVI (P.O. xxvi.331).

[9] Hom. LIX (P.O. viii.242). See also the article by I. Hausherr, 'L'Imitation de Jésus-Christ dans la spiritualité byzantine' in Études de spiritualité orientale, p. 224.

[10] Hom. LXIII (P.O. viii.292).

God, the lives of the great teachers, apostles, monks, martyrs, and patriarchs serve as secondary models, and are themselves a major source of our knowledge of God.[1]

God has sent these holy men that we may imitate them and come to salvation. The patriarchs were 'pillars of perfection' in their own time, sent by God as a corrective to the evil in the world.[2] Christ trained the apostles himself also for this end, that they be our models.[3] The martyrs, too, are meant to be our models, and their proper commemoration consists in the imitation of their perfection.[4] Severus speaks of the monks he has visited and tells us that they live like the angels, they are themselves the living embodiment of the spiritual law and 'for those who see them a law which' regulates our behaviour.[5] It would not be inaccurate to say that the living 'Way' of Christ is seen in the holy men or teachers, who stand in some sort of apostolic succession to him as the original teacher and model.[6]

Many of the holy men exercised great authority and possessed unusual powers, especially the ability to see into the future.[7] They could do this because of their unusual preparation in the virtues and their special purification. In one Homily

---

[1] Homilies LXI (P.O. viii.257–8); C (P.O. xxii.243); XLIX (P.O. xxxv.344); CII (P.O. xxii.280–1); CXVII (P.O. xxvi.346): John the Baptist came to live in the desert of Jordan in imitation of 'the angelic and incorporeal . . . model of the life of Elijah' on Carmel; Hom. CXXIV (P.O. xxix.212); Letter XXXVIII (P.O. xii.294–5).

[2] Hom. XLIX (P.O. xxxv.344).

[3] Hom. CXXIV (P.O. xxix.212). See also *Critique du Tome* (CSCO, vol. 244, p. 104).

[4] Hom. C (P.O. xxii.243).

[5] Hom. LXI (P.O. viii.257).

[6] Cf. also Severus' doctrine of one of the chief origins of sin, viz. the failure of Christian parents to teach their children Christian attitudes and behaviour, both by teaching and by example. Hom. LXII (P.O. viii.276 ff.). (See also Hom. LXXV (P.O. xii), for an example of the mother as teacher.) Thus the hierarchy of teaching ranges from the angels, Christ, and the holy men, down to the Christian teaching of children.

[7] There was general belief in the extraordinary powers of the holy men in this period, as we see both from the church histories and the histories of the monks. Peter Brown in *The World of Late Antiquity*, pp. 102–3, suggests that the particular emphasis this period put upon the authority and power of the holy men is what distinguished the late antique world from the classical world, in which the cult-site played a more important role in people's imagination. See also Hom. XCVIII (P.O. xxv.159–60), in which Severus appears to outline the standard spiritual gifts belonging to one advanced in the Christian life. See also Hom. XLVIII (P.O. xxxv.326–8), for the defeat of the demons by the apostles.

Severus paints a revealing picture of his idea of the role of the preacher, who, like the ancient prophet, sees far enough into the future to be able to anticipate coming disaster, including natural calamities and the attacks of the demons (who are responsible for many of them); his duty is to warn his congregation of what is impending, then 'To prepare, conduct, and direct the events which must spring up. . .'.[1] Severus invests the great teachers, Basil and Gregory of Nazianzus, with such authority, that he says that if he refuses to imitate them in this life, they will be there on the day of judgement as his judges.[2]

These men have, of course, knowledge of God himself and of Christian doctrine. The Holy Spirit, Severus says, appeared at Pentecost to the apostles, not as to servants, but as to friends.[3] Gregory of Nazianzus observed the Uncreated Light of the Trinity with wide open and wide awake eyes, like the angels.[4] The full knowledge of the Trinity was revealed for the first time to the apostles.[5] On a doctrinal level, these men, because of their recognition of God himself, are in a position to teach others, making accurate doctrinal statements. Christ commended Peter not just because he recognized who Christ was, but because he worded his answer accurately.[6] Gregory of Nazianzus' great gift to the world was his theology which was free from error; he could pass this on in an exact manner, because of his enjoyment of the Light of the Trinity, in which he participated.[7]

These teachers are healers of sinners.[8] Severus suggests that

---

[1] Hom. LIII (P.O. iv.24, 27). See also Hom. CXIX (P.O. xxvi), where Mary is called a prophetess because she could see into the future, p. 383.

[2] Hom. CII (P.O. xxii.280–1).   [3] Hom. XLVIII (P.O. xxv.322).

[4] Hom. LXV (P.O. viii.327) (p. 43 above).

[5] Hom. XLVIII (P.O. xxxv.324).   [6] Hom. CXXIV (P.O. xxix.218).

[7] Hom. LXV (P.O. viii.327). See also e.g. Severus' Hymn 132-I-VI (P.O. vi.172), on Mark the Evangelist: 'The divine Mark, the true disciple of great Peter, the chief of the apostles, having with readiness proclaimed or preached to creation day by day the salvation of Christ our God . . . taught the whole of Egypt, which had become drunk in pursuit of the error of demon-worship, not only to believe, but also to proclaim the theology with all accuracy.' Note here too, the role of the teacher in the defeat of the demon worship. See also Hom. XLVIII (P.O. xxxv.326–8): the apostles transformed the earth which was wallowing in drunkenness caused by the demons and woke it up to the knowledge of God, 'and by the fire of pious dogmas they dried up the river of hateful desires which had submerged the world'; at the same time, they taught the ascetic life.

[8] Christ was like a prophet in his concern with the healing of sinners: Hom. CXVIII (P.O. xxvi.362–3).

one of the major causes of trouble in the behaviour of the
Pharisees was their refusal to take their role of spiritual physi-
cian seriously.[1] They could not heal because they could not mix
with sinners. The healing of the woman in the gate of the temple
Severus explains in an allegorical manner: the apostles made
her get up, 'giving her the hand of doctrine', for 'she would
not be able to do any right action or one which led to virtue,
if by their doctrines the apostles had not made her strong
and healed her right and natural power with their teachings'.[2] In this passage salvation comes directly through the
teacher.[3]

While, at their highest, these men illustrate that God does
not ask the impossible of the rest of us,[4] Severus often emphasizes
their humble beginnings. The apostles were ordinary men at
the start, ignorant and unlettered;[5] they quarrelled among
themselves and in general showed great signs of human weakness before reaching their exalted position.[6] This is in line with
Severus' own emphasis on the unity of the salvation[7] offered to
all men in spite of the difference between the routes to perfection:[8] Severus often affirms Christ's love of the ordinary man
who seeks him,[9] and the validity for the life of God which must
be lived in the world. Though he himself clearly prefers the
monastic life, he does not appear to make the common distinction between the two ways. We are all called to the life of
perfection, both by Christ and by the teachers.

[1] Hom. XCII (P.O. xxv.30–3).
[2] Hom. LXXIV (P.O. xii.102–5).
[3] The idea is expressed even more strongly in the passage where Severus says
that it was the apostles who destroyed the drunkenness inflicted upon the world by
the demons. Hom. XLVIII (P.O. xxxv.326–8).
[4] Hom. CXXIII (P.O. xxix.180–4).
[5] Hom. CXXIV (P.O. xxix.212).
[6] Ibid. This quarrelling was to be an example, so that we should be without
excuse for our own lack of progress: we cannot say, 'yes, but the apostles were
perfect', Hom. LXXXII (P.O. xx.372–3).
[7] 'For all there is only one *stadion* of perfection, because, whether for men or for
women, there is only one salvation, one hope, one adoption . . . one gift of the
Spirit', Hom. LXXXIII (P.O. xx.419).
[8] See e.g. Hom. CXIX (P.O. xxvi.375): 'If anyone uses his intelligence following the breadth of the Book inspired by God and especially following that of the
Holy Gospels, he will find many ways of the good life, and that all lead to God,
that they are full of holiness, that they prepare with respect to the future, and invite
to eternal life. . . .'
[9] Hom. CXXIII (P.O. xxix.126).

Christ the Word and the New Creation

In the cosmological realm, Christ is the Second Adam, who has put a new value on human life and begun the work of the New Creation. In the Christian Platonist tradition, generally speaking, it is a less than ideal situation for men to belong to the world of change, or corruptibility and morality, birth and death, sickness and family life. To be in the body symbolizes both difference from God and separation from God, who is immortal and incorruptible, that is, not subject to these 'outside' conditions which determine the life of the human being. The human body in this tradition is at best an embarrassment, at worst the punishment for sin. This denigration of the body is an important element in the Christian Platonic version of the Fall: broadly speaking, God did not create mankind mortal, nor did he intend men to multiply like the animals, nor to be in a state of enmity with their environment. It was through Adam and the Serpent that human dignity was lost, not through the direct plan of God. Through the first Adam, then, came mankind's plunge into the world of change. But through the Second Adam comes a new era in which we are able to leave, as far as is humanly possible, the old world of corruption and decay and re-enter the realm to which we properly belong. For some Christian Platonists, this realm is to be eventually entirely spiritual (see, for example, Origen himself, Evagrius Ponticus, and Stephen Bar Sudaili). For Severus, the realm of the sensible is here to stay, even in the new creation. One aspect of the work of Christ the incarnate Word is the revaluing of the distinctly physical aspect of existence.

First, Christ has restored to us the image of God.[1] We have already seen how he has established the pattern of life on earth which we may follow in order to render ourselves more like what God intends us to be. Christ has also given us

---

[1] There are many elements to the image of God. The mind itself is image. Free will is also part of the image. Hom. LXXXIII (P.O. xx.401); the authority over the wild animals is also part of it (the interpretation acceptable to many modern biblical scholars, working with Gen. 2 and 3), Homilies LXXXVIII (P.O. xx.291–3); LXXI (P.O. xii.69); LXX (P.O. xii.24). The ability to receive righteousness, wisdom, and the other virtues is part, Hom. LXXXI (P.O. xx.355–6). In one place Severus emphasizes that we were made in the image of the Trinity, rather than in the image of the Logos, which is more what we would expect: Hom. LXX (P.O. xii.23–4).

incorruptibility, 'engrafting it into our nature'[1] (we were never incorruptible by anything other than by grace) so that we are no longer subject to death.[2] But that is not all: by his own birth, he has changed the curse which was originally placed on birth into a blessing, and has thus 'blessed our passage into existence'.[3] By his taking of flesh, all human flesh becomes worthy of a new respect: Severus warns people away from the theatre at Daphne by telling them to respect their bodies as the image of God: 'Respect the second divine creation, by which the Word of God in taking a body from the Virgin is associated with you.'[4]

Severus is not advocating the enjoyment of the pleasures of the flesh. Christ has shown us how, by the practice of the virtues, we may belong soul *and body* to the intelligible realm.[5] We are able to do this, not by learning to ignore our bodies, but by making our bodies, especially our senses, serve our souls in such a way that they themselves conform to the image of the soul and become 'intellectual':[6]

. . . the senses of the body, in serving the intellectual operations, are themselves also in some sort rational (*mlîlê*) . . . [Thus] one can proclaim that man has been made in the image of God, himself of soul and body . . . without confusion, a single prosopon, a single hypostasis, a single nature.

Severus similarly insists that the body shares in the pleasure of the *theoria* of the soul, the enjoyment of it penetrating to the bones themselves.[7] We are not surprised, then, at his indignant refusal to equate the sin of Adam and Eve with the sexual one,[8] nor are we surprised to see that he rejects utterly Julian of Halicarnassus' insistence that our bodies as we now

---

[1] See supplementary note, p. 56 below.

[2] Usually Severus says that we have had the grace of immortality restored to us by Christ, as in, e.g., Hom. LXXI (P.O. xii.56). Once he says, however, that Christ has 'engrafted incorruptibility into our nature at the root', when he is talking about the new conditions of our human birth, Hom. XLIX (P.O. xxxv.348–350).

[3] Hom. XLIX (P.O. xxxv.350).   [4] Hom. LIV (P.O. iv.56).

[5] Hom. CXXIII (P.O. xxix.184).   [6] Hom. LXXXI (P.O. xx.355–6).

[7] 'If the eye of the mind (*tar'îthâ*) is purified and if it takes pleasure in upper *theoria* and in the entirely divine revelations . . . this happiness will pass into the bones and penetrate there as a perfume', Hom. LXVIII (P.O. viii.385).

[8] See Hom. CXIX (P.O. xxvi.437).

have them are in any sense a punishment for sin.[1] Our human bodies are neither the punishment for sin, nor are they the cause of the first sin, for the body takes its value from the soul and is the image of the soul.[2]

Severus puts himself firmly within the monastic tradition going back to Athanasius' life of Saint Anthony.[3] The perfect human being alive on this earth possesses not only an abundance of spiritual gifts as the reward of his arduous labours, he also finds himself in a new relationship to creation, similar to that of Adam in Paradise. This new-found relationship is symbolized by his authority over wild animals.[4] Many of the martyrs, for example, were left unharmed by the animals to whom they were thrown. The story of Thecla is a typical example of the lack of animosity between the perfect Christian and the wild beasts. Thecla, 'when she had stripped off the old man and purified her intelligence and learned from Paul, "If any man is in Christ, he is a new creation" . . . was surrounded by a herd of wild animals'.[5] Notice again the relationship between the physical world of the animals and the necessary purification of the intelligence, which results in 'a mind full of *theoria*'. In the case of Anthony, the new creation was also symbolized by a perfect, healthy physique;[6] Anthony came out of his inner desert at last, being neither too fat nor too thin. But Severus does go on to affirm in a non-Platonic but Biblical way that at the end of time, creation itself will be no longer subject to corruption, but restored to its original splendour.[7]

---

[1] Even before the controversy with Julian, Severus argues with Eutyches, Hom. LXIII (P.O. viii.298-9). Our body is not impure. All that soils or renders unclean is sin, so that God is not in any way soiled or touched by sin in his human descent. See Draguet, pp. 100-35.

[2] Severus is explicit: sin issues from the soul or the mind, not the body, Hom. CXXIII (P.O. xxix.180-4). See also Hom. LXVIII (P.O. viii.375). The properness of the relationship between body and soul is expressed by Severus' statement that 'the soul is united to the body by nature', Hom. LVIII (P.O. viii.219).

[3] Hom. LXVIII (P.O. viii.385-6), especially.

[4] According to Vööbus, in the earliest period of Syrian asceticism many of the anchorites lived with wild animals and grazed on grass, not as the symbol of a new harmony with the animals, but as an act of continual mortification and penance (*History of Asceticism in the Syrian Orient*, Part II, pp. 25-8).

[5] Hom. XCVII (P.O. xxv.136).

[6] Severus also believed that Christ was resurrected naked: this symbolizes (among other things) the return of Adam to the primitive state. Hom. LXXVII (P.O. xvi.820-1), preserved in both Syriac and Greek.

[7] Letters XXVII (P.O. xii.248-51); XCVI (P.O. xiv.182-92).

This notion of the basic rightness of the physical creation and its permanence puts Severus far away from the basic value judgements of such a theologian as Evagrius Ponticus, who, with Origen, appeared to believe in the final *apokatastasis* of all things. The point is not so much that Severus was a literal reader of his Bible at this point (as he certainly was not in other places), but that he placed a certain genuine value on the created world. (Gregory of Nyssa, who is a good example of Christian Platonism, did not think of the resurrection body in terms of a physical body: Severus *did* think in these terms; we shall have all our limbs intact, he says, even if they do not function.)[1] The value placed on creation permeates his thought, from the highest reaches of his christology to his condemnation of the cruelty to the horses at the races at Daphne.[2] Though Severus is a monk himself, with a reputation in the ancient sources for asceticism, he affirms the oneness of the salvation open to all men,[3] including those who live in the world. This is in partial contrast to Philoxenus, who, in the Thirteen Homilies, would appear to suggest that the salvation belonging to those who live in the world is of a different order from that to be pursued by the monks. However, the difference in audience—a cathedral full of laymen on the one hand, and a monastery full of monks on the other—might simply account for this apparent difference.

Christ does not simply revalue creation by bestowing on it its original value with the promise of incorruptibility. Christ as God himself incarnate gives a new value to the most vile and humblest of human suffering by the fact that, on the one hand, he suffered in such a humble manner himself, and on the other, that he is the Logos lying behind all things. In a sermon dedicated to the collecting of pieces of cloth from his parishioners for distribution to the suffering lepers of Antioch, Severus calls to mind the words of Jesus when he said that whoever feeds the

---

[1] He both denies the *apokatastasis* and affirms the notion of a literal hell which lasts eternally, Letter XCVIII (P.O. xiv.200–13). The soul at the resurrection will receive a perfect human body with all its members intact, even though they will not be used: the resurrected Christ is the model of what we will be. This state, to which we shall come, will be higher than that of Paradise, Severus says, citing Gregory of Nazianzus and John Chrysostom. Letter XCVI; pp. 182–92.

[2] See e.g. Hom. LXXXI (P.O. xii.69).

[3] Hom. LXXXIII (P.O. xx.419). See also Hymn 333-III-I (P.Q. vii.765–6).

hungry, visits the sick, and cares for those who are in need does it for Christ himself, while the neglect of the needy is also the neglect of Christ.[1] And Severus makes a similar point in other places: we are all in the present in exactly the same position as those who surrounded Christ in his lifetime when it comes to our ability to recognize him and serve him: Joseph of Arimathea served him in a way appropriate to the situation in those days; we, by helping the suffering now serve him in the way appropriate to his present situation.[2] Because of the Incarnation, all human suffering has come to be that of Christ, and it all makes a special demand on the Christian who witnesses it for this reason. This is a very real part of the meaning of the Incarnation, that all human things, no matter how lowly, take on the significance of having belonged and continuing to belong to God himself.

SUPPLEMENTARY NOTES

1. There are several Syriac words meaning 'property' or 'propriety': all are abstracts formed on the root *dyl*, which normally means, with the addition of a personal suffix, 'belonging to——'. See e.g. *dîlāyûth*, *dîlānāythâ*, 'propriety'; *dîlāythâ*, 'property'. Typical statements of Severus as to what propriety is: 'Those who confess one incarnate nature of God the Word, and do not confuse the elements of which he consists, recognize also the propriety of those that were joined in union (and a property is what exists in the form of a manifestation of natural differences) . . . but they recognize the difference only, not admitting a division' Letter I, pp. 177–8; Letter III, p. 194, 'It is not confessing the particularity (*dîlāyûthâ*) of the natures from which Immanuel comes that we avoid . . . but distributing and dividing the properties (*dîlāyāthâ*) to each of the natures'. A propriety indicates 'difference'; '"propriety" means the difference of the natures of those elements that come together to the union', 'First Letter to Sergius', p. 75. The question of what constitutes a propriety and its relationship to the nature or hypostasis to which it belongs occupied a large portion of the correspondence between Sergius and Severus. Sergius sees no way that a propriety can exist without also implying an independent hypostasis and operation (First Letter of Sergius to Severus, pp. 71–2; Severus' 'First Letter to Sergius', pp. 93–4). To Severus, a propriety does not necessarily imply a self-subsistent hypostasis: as there are two proprieties, that of body and that of soul, in a man, there are also two in Christ. A propriety can be the set of properties belonging to a thing that put it within a certain class,

---

[1] Hom. CXXII (P.O. xxix.110–12, 122).

[2] Ibid. 114. Hom. CXV (P.O. xxvi.323): 'Let us blush from the foreign magis, who offered gold to Christ, when he was still a baby according to the economy, while we, even after he has been crucified for us, do not give him a single obole of bronze by the intermediary of a poor man.' See also Hymn 333-III-I: 'For it is not to confessors nor to martyrs, nor to those who have lived and excelled in toils and labours of asceticism only that thou didst promise and guarantee the kingdom of heaven, but to those who . . . fed thee when thou wast hungry and readily gave thee drink when thou wast thirsty . . .', P.O. vii.765–6.

genus, or level of reality, or it can be the set of properties that distinguish the individual member of a class, genus, or level of reality from the other members of the class. The two proprieties in the Incarnation mark off the two levels of reality within Christ, and do not serve to distinguish him either from the other two hypostases in the Trinity, nor from other human beings: by the two proprieties Severus means the characteristics of the uncreated invisible realm on the one hand, and the created, physical, and sometimes intelligible realm on the other. See 'First Letter to Sergius', pp. 76, 79, etc.; Letters I, pp. 182–4; X, p. 201. Severus explicitly rejects in these Letters the notion that the actual elements of which Christ is composed are proprieties which are in some way grouped together around the Word. J. A. Dorner suggested this as an interpretation of Severus' doctrine of the union in *Person Christi*, 1853, p. 76 ff. and was followed by Loofs in *Leontius von Byzantium* and Harnack. Lebon, *Chalkedon*, pp. 516–18, was the first to point out that Severus explicitly rejects this interpretation. For the use of propriety to distinguish one self-subsistent hypostasis from another, see Homily CXXV (P.O. xxix.236); also Homilies LIX (P.O. viii.231); LVIII, pp. 222–3. Lebon, however, sees only one side of the question of Severus' use of the term 'propriety'. For him a propriety is what belongs exclusively to a subject. See *Chalkedon*, p. 535.

2. 'Human nature', referring to what makes us human has two prime aspects for Severus: first, it is the laws governing the physical life-cycle of men: what makes them a species, those things that belong to them all, about which no choice is given, such as intelligence (see e.g. Homilies LXX (P.O. xii.20); LVIII (P.O. viii.219), the soul is united to the body *bakhyānâ*); the Word has flesh and blood in the same way as we, 'in nature and at the same time above nature . . .'; Christ was united with 'the flesh of our nature', Letter LXV (P.O. xiv.30); Christ was one of us by nature and not by sin—sin belongs to the realm of will—*Critique du Tome* (CSCO, vol. 244), p. 45. Mankind was not created immortal 'by nature' but was given immortality as a grace, Hom. XLIX (P.O. xxxv.342), *Critique du Tome* (CSCO, vol. 244), p. 29; Letter XXVII (P.O. xii.250–1). The second aspect of 'human nature' involves the realm of human behaviour—e.g. the new life in Christ is one that 'strengthens and reinforces our nature' so that we may become capable of martyrdom, as we see in the case of St. Drosis (Hom. C (P.O. xxii.237)). Our new behaviour in Christ is 'in' or 'according to nature' (Homilies CXVI (P.O. xxvi.329); LXX (P.O. xii.49), etc.). Severus speaks of us as being capable of 'making violence our nature', Hom. LXVIII (P.O. viii.384). God left 'our nature' with natural law, memory, and conscience after the fall, Hom. LXIX (P.O. xxxv.342–4). In Hom. LXX (P.O. xii.48), acting 'according to nature' means acting according to the laws of righteousness. He says of the ascetic life of Saint Anthony, that to 'be in nature' is to give power to the soul by fasting and works of asceticism, and to nourish the body by immaterial feasts. Hom. LXVIII (P.O. viii.385–6). I. Hausherr, in 'L'Erreur fondamentale et la logique de Messalianisme', p. 70, points out that with the notable exception of Theodoret, 'κατὰ φύσιν is synonymous with virtue, παρὰ φύσιν a synonym of vice in Greek patristic thought'. Christ came to heal our nature, which is sick, Homilies XLIX (P.O. xxxv.342–5); LXXIV (P.O. xii.104–5): the diseased nature means that all behaviour is diseased; Hom. LXII (P.O. viii.276); see also Hom. XCIV (P.O. xxv.53–4), where it is our nature that has fallen.

PART II

PHILOXENUS OF MABBUG

O
UR second monophysite theologian sets out a very different system. Philoxenus' christology and his theory of how we know God are remarkably all of one piece. Christ is God the Word who exists in two modes of being simultaneously, as God, by nature, and as man, by a miracle. We, as baptized believers, also exist in two modes of being, as men by nature, and as sons of God by a miracle. Our true homeland, now that we are baptized, is the country of Christ, whom we perceive to be God, not by any 'natural' perception, but by faith which is given to us in a non-natural manner. Christ's human existence and our saving faith belong to the same order of existence: both are gifts of God, and neither has any practical existence without the other. In the following sections we shall examine in detail, first, Philoxenus' doctrine of the Incarnation, with special attention to the epistemological presuppositions underlying his understanding of it; and second, we shall look at his theory of knowledge, particularly of divine things, beginning with the prerequisites of knowledge, and then looking at its content and character. In the end, we shall draw what epistemological and christological conclusions seem fit.

The Double Being: Being By Nature and Being By a Miracle

Jesus Christ is God by nature, man by a miracle of his will: he has one nature or hypostasis, the divine, but he has two modes of existence, a natural one, and a non-natural one.

To be God, or man, by nature means to be God or man inalterably and involuntarily: what Philoxenus means by the 'nature' of a man or God in this sense includes the basic unchangeable characteristics that belong to him by virtue of his membership in his species. In the case of God, the inalterable nature includes such qualities as impassibility, immortality, incorporeality, simplicity, incomprehensibility, and all the other characteristics along this line which God possesses.[1] To be a man by nature means to be mortal, passible, visible, corporeal, limited, rational, and so forth. What we are by nature is outside the realm of our control :[2] neither we nor God change or lose these characteristics of our nature : our identity depends upon them. This is the first mode of existence in the Incarnation : God remains, in the Incarnation, *God by nature*, impassible, immortal, invisible, intangible, and so forth, in spite of birth from the virgin, suffering, death, tangibility.

In the Incarnation, however, God also comes into another mode of being : the divine hypostasis of the Word becomes a man *by a miracle*, which takes place through the action of God's will[3]

---

[1] God is immortal 'by nature': this means that if he were actually to cease to be immortal, he would cease to be God. Thus, God remains immortal in the Incarnation, while nevertheless dying, in so far as he is a man. For typical statements of the unalterability of the divine nature, see e.g. 'The Letter to Zeno', pp. 164; 170-1, in *Three Letters of Philoxenus Bishop of Mabbogh*, trans. and ed. A. Vaschalde, 1902; *Philoxeni Mabbugensis: Tractus tres de Trinitate et Incarnatione*, ed. A. Vaschalde, CSCO, vol. 9 (Louvain, 1961), 67-8; 89, 250, etc.

[2] While we become sons of God by a miracle at baptism, we still remain men 'by nature', i.e. we do not change the fact that we are still men having human needs and human limitations—we still grow hungry, need sleep, and so forth. A monk is said to dwell in the realm of the Spirit, and is thus called an angel, but he 'is called an angel instead of a man because of his service and manner of life, and not because of his nature', Hom. VII, pp. 192-3, *The Discourses of Philoxenus*, vol. I, trans. and ed. E. A. Wallis Budge; see also *Tres tract.*, pp. 134, 222; 'Letter to Zeno', p. 165.

[3] The Word has two modes of being in the Incarnation, and Philoxenus describes them most frequently in terms of God's 'being' as he remains in his nature without change, and God's 'coming into existence' as a man through an act of his will; this coming into existence, however, is not simply an ordinary act of God's will, for all creatures come into being through God's will. A. de Halleux, in his massive *Philoxène de Mabbog: sa vie, ses ecrits, sa theologie*, sees in the theme of the 'divine coming into existence' the most basic thread which runs through Philoxenus' entire theological system, and describes at some length the relationship between God's will and his nature within the Incarnation (pp. 341-9). Though de Halleux spends a considerable amount of time relating the divinization of the Christian to the Incarnation, he tends to ignore the aspect of the *double* being of both Christ and Christian as it accounts for two *simultaneous* existences, one of which is a miracle, and the other of which is 'natural'. To stress the 'miraculous' nature of the Incarnation in this way is to introduce a real duality into the Christian's life, and into the person of Christ as well.

The two terms for the two types of existence of the Word in the Incarnation are seen in the prologue to John: the Word 'became flesh', *hwâ bhesrâ*; see *Tres tract.*, pp. 46, 52, 56, 206, etc.; *Letter to Monks of Senoun*, p. 61 etc.; 'he was' or 'he existed' beforehand without flesh, and continued to exist in the Incarnate Christ as God: this verb is expressed by *'ithaw*, a suffix attached to the particle, *'ith*, which expresses existence, but which carries no tense, other than the one within the hypostasis of the Word himself.[1] To explain what he means by this second mode of being, which exists simultaneously with the first, Philoxenus gives us several extremely important parallels to the Incarnation. The first and most important is the double being of the baptized believer :[2] a man who is baptized becomes an adopted son of God ; having received the Spirit, he comes into a whole new mode of life at all levels, religious, psychological, and physical. He truly becomes a 'new man' who has experienced a new birth, and he is 'born' into a 'new country'.[3] The man in question is no longer an enemy of God, one who is bound to the world and unable to perceive the whole spiritual realm which both encompasses and lies behind the visible creation. The new man is a new inhabitant of the realm of the Spirit.

Philoxenus does not regard the shift from being a bodily man to being a spiritual man as a change (*shûḥlāphâ*) from one state to its opposite : to become a spiritual man is to take on a new mode of being *in addition to* the first mode. Thus, the new man is born again and exists in the spiritual realm by a miracle (*bthedhmûrtâ*) while he continues simultaneously to retain his 'nature' :[4] hence he becomes impassible, yet he grows old and

that it picks up from the verbs around it (*Tres tract.*, p. 206 etc.). Both *hwâ* and *'îth* are common Syriac verbs, both of which normally express the verb 'to be'.

The 'miraculous' nature of the Incarnation is found in two typical statements: the Incarnation is 'a miracle and not a natural thing. For this reason, we receive it by faith alone . . .', *Tres tract.*, p. 83. 'It is not only inasmuch as he is Son of God that one must think his actions are miraculous, but especially inasmuch as he became man, because to be and to have is natural [for God] but to become and to acquire, supernatural', *Letter to the Monks of Senoun*, p. 62; see also e.g. *Tres tract.*, pp. 173, 206, etc.; 'Letter to Zeno', p. 170. The Syriac word for 'miracle' Philoxenus uses most often is *tedhmûrtâ*; see e.g. *Tres tract.*, pp. 83, 116, 117, 131, 206, etc.; *Monks of Senoun*, pp. 9, 62, 'Letter to Zeno', p. 170 etc. He also occasionally uses the term *dûmārâ*, from the same root; see e.g. *Monks of Senoun*, p. 62; *Tres tract.*, p. 221.

[1] *Letter to the Monks of Senoun*, p. 9; see also p. 57; *Tres tract.*, p. 173.
[2] 'However the old man, when he is born from baptism becomes the new, not by means of change, but by power and by a miracle. . . . Thus is God, who, on our behalf and because of us, became a man', *Tres tract.*, p. 131; see also pp. 134, 119–20.
[3] *Thirteen Homilies*, II. 31; VII. 191–2, etc. Sometimes Philoxenus calls the 'old man' the 'old nature', and the 'new man' the 'new nature', as he does in Homily IX, p. 303. Philoxenus does not use the word 'nature' in only one sense.
[4] *Tres tract.*, pp. 132, 134, 222, etc. In the Incarnation, 'The Word, therefore, became something he was not, and remained something we were not, that is,

dies; he lives in the invisible realm of the angels, yet he is visible and tangible to other men.[1] He remains a man *by nature* while becoming a son of God *by a miracle*. Philoxenus explicitly links our new being following baptism with the humanity of Christ in the Incarnation. John the Evangelist, according to Philoxenus, binds the Incarnation with the new birth in such a way that one cannot be understood or even discussed without the other.[2]

If a man should try to ask how God is born a man from a woman, he will learn what is set next to it, how each one of us, when he is *by nature* a man, is born a son of God by baptism. And the explanation will be incomprehensible—how the Word was born [as] flesh from the Virgin, and how a bodily man is born a spiritual man from the waters and the Spirit.

This double existence of the same subject is further illuminated by Philoxenus' use of the examples of the miracles of the burning bush[3] and Moses' staff which became a snake when

sons of God . . . We became sons of God, although our nature was not changed, and he became a man by his mercy, although his essence was not changed', 'Letter to Zeno', pp. 164, 165.

[1] A remarkable passage in the ninth homily of the *Thirteen Homilies*, pp. 287–91, describes the new state of existence in the realm of the angels.

[2] *Tres tract.*, p. 120.

[3] See Philoxenus' companion of the miracles of the Exodus with the Incarnation, in *Tres tract.*, pp. 113 ff. Moses saw the burning bush; 'the same one was entirely as fire, and entirely as a bush, in that not only was the fire surrounding the bush on the outside, but it seized it and set it on fire, and it was seen that the same one was both of them—bush and flame. For this Scripture hints that the bush was as the fire which seized it entirely and did not destroy or finish it off . . . but it was in its appearance both of them—bush and flame . . . For thus it is written that Moses saw the bush in which the fire was kindled and the bush was not burned up. . . But not at this alone did Moses wonder, that he saw that the fire was in the bush, but also that the bush was not burned up, or changed from its greenness. . . And that occurrence was not only a miracle, but also a type (*ṭûpsâ*)—a miracle with respect to the vision of Moses, and a mystery (*râzâ*) with respect to what was to be, for in place of the fire which dwelt in the bush, the Virgin received God, and as there, in the case of that fire which dwelt upon the bush, the same one was seen to be them both, fire and bush, thus also was God who came to the Virgin and was made man from her: the same one is believed to be God and man; the man was visible to the eye, and God, to the mind. He was tangible as a man, and the same one was intangible as God. Again, all of him was in every place as God, and all of him was in the Virgin as a man. . . And with respect to the fact that he remained God, so also the bush was entirely wood *by reason of its nature*, and all of it fire, *as by a miracle* . . .'. Philoxenus also makes use of this analogy in his Commentary on John 1: 1–17, ff. 77–87; cf. de Halleux, p. 325, no. 40.

he threw it down in front of the Egyptian sorcerers.[1] We might be tempted, if it were not for these specific examples Philoxenus uses to illustrate the Incarnation, to see in him some sort of phantasiast who denied the reality of the flesh and blood of Christ. But this is not possible : it is perfectly clear from Philoxenus' language that while the *nature* of the burning bush remained the 'green and juicy bush', and the nature of the staff continued to be a staff, and only by a miracle the bush burned and the staff was a snake, Moses could have burned himself on the bush, and the sorcerers could easily have died of snake-bite. The snake, the fire, and the new man exist, then, in Philoxenus' words, 'in power'.[2]

The final example drawn from human experience which Philoxenus uses to illustrate the dual mode of existence of the single hypostasis of God the Word in the Incarnation is that of the bread and wine in the Eucharist : The bread and wine remain *by nature* simply bread and wine, but 'in power' by a miracle they become in truth the body and blood of Christ. The bread and wine remain 'entirely' bread and wine, while at the very same time they become by a miracle to the eyes of faith the body and blood of Christ.[3] In the same way, Christ is a man by a miracle, while he is simultaneously God by nature. The same hypostasis of Christ, therefore, appears to fleshly eyes as that of the man, Jesus, as it in fact is ; but it also appears to the eyes of faith as it is in its nature, that of God the Word.

All these examples illustrate how it is that Philoxenus can

[1] *Tres tract.*, pp. 158–9. The staff became a snake 'in truth' when Moses threw it down. When the staff became a snake, furthermore, to the Egyptians, the snake was only a snake, but Moses saw it for what it really was, simultaneously staff and snake, not 'in two genera', but in one, 'a staff by nature, and a snake by a miracle (*bthedhmûrtâ*)'. The other miracles of the Exodus, such as the water which turned into blood, are treated in the same manner. The important thing to note both here and in the account of the burning bush is not only the two modes of existence, by nature and by miracle, but the two modes of perception which correspond to them, i.e. by the senses, and non-sensually, either by the 'mind' or by faith.

[2] *bhaylâ* (*Tres tract.*, p. 131). The new man, as well as the bread and wine of the Eucharist, 'by means of the fact that the Spirit is united to them, become *in power* the things we believe them to be. Thus also is the Word of God: He did not become flesh by means of change, and so become a man, but by means of the union to the flesh and blood which are ours ...'. To be in or by 'power' is, then, contrasted not only with being 'by nature': it is also an alternative to being something by a *change* of nature. Christ was also a man, 'in' or 'with' power, *Thirteen Homilies*, IX. 303.

[3] *Tres tract.*, pp. 130–1; see also pp. 118 ff.

insist that God could become a man without changing from what he was before the Incarnation: God by nature. It is interesting to note that this key word, *shûḥlāphâ*, has such different meanings in the theologies of Philoxenus and Severus. In the Syriac translators of Severus it meant the 'difference' between the humanity and the divinity which was preserved in the hypostatic union. For Philoxenus *shûḥlāphâ* has an almost exclusively negative meaning: it means 'change' in the sense of loss of identity. To apply it to either the humanity or the divinity in the Incarnation is to say that the humanity ceased to be humanity or the divinity, divinity.[1]

The Two Births

Philoxenus often expresses this basic idea of the double mode of being of the single hypostasis of the Word in terms of the two births, the birth of the Word from the Father, and the birth of the humanity from Mary. When he talks about the two births, he stresses first, that the coming into being of the humanity of Christ was *not* basically like the coming into being of ordinary men, and second, that although he talks in terms of the simplicity[2] of the Word, even in the Incarnation, he wishes to

---

[1] de Halleux lays out Philoxenus' basic arguments to demonstrate how the divine nature did not change in the Economy, *Philoxène*, pp. 341 ff. God came into being without change, first because he exists without having become; second, because he did it for us and not for himself; third, 'because he came into being by will and not by nature'.

[2] Often Philoxenus indicates that the Word remains 'simple' (*pshîṭâ*) even within the Incarnation (cf. *Tres tract.*, pp. 190, 192). At other times, however, he will say that the Word 'took all our composition upon him' (*nsabh 'alaw(hî) koleh rûkhābhan*) or 'became composite'. (*Tres tract.*, p. 183; *Monks of Senoun*, p. 65.) After explaining that one recognizes a single Father both in the acts of begetting and creation, Philoxenus goes on to say that, 'Just as the Father is one in his simplicity, thus one confesses that the Son is one with respect to the fact that he was composite (*'ethrakebh*) with the flesh', *Monks of Senoun*, p. 65. The answer to the problem of the apparent contradiction appears to be this: The concept of simplicity implies primarily unity or oneness; sometimes, in the case of the Father, it also implies freedom from physical 'composition', but it does not need to. The Father's *nature* is simple, says Philoxenus in one place, even though he has many different activities: *Tres tract.*, p. 31. The Incarnate Word is simple, in so far as there is only one identity, one subject, but he is composite in the same way that we are composite: *Tres tract.*, pp. 41, 255. As simplicity is a prerequisite of knowledge of God, and is an aspect of faith, it is a quality of mind which cannot see evil in anything, and which looks directly at the spiritual realm without being torn by doubts: a simple mind is one basically motivated toward one thing. Philoxenus devotes two of the *Thirteen Homilies* to this subject, IV and V.

make a firm distinction between what belongs to Jesus by virtue of his humanity, and what belongs to him by virtue of his divinity.

When we look at Christ, we see both a human hypostasis and divine hypostasis, depending upon the angle from which we view the one single hypostasis of the Incarnate Christ.[1] In the same way, when we look at the origins of the single hypostasis, we encounter two births.[2] The birth from the Father is beyond our comprehension, and inaccessible to reason, although we may say of it that it is eternal, and outside the realm of time. The birth of the hypostasis of the Word from the mother is not eternal, but temporal, and to all appearances, it ought to be like the birth of ordinary men from ordinary mothers.[3] But this is not the case,[4] for an ordinary man comes into existence from nothing, moving, therefore, from one state to its opposite, namely, something. In the same way, when an ordinary man dies, he moves back from something into nothing.[5] But this is

In Hom. IV, p. 81, he says: 'That name, which is suitable to God, simplicity has received, for we also call God simple . . . for there are no composites or parts of the body in him. Thus in our ordinary speech, a man who is not cunning in wickedness is called simple by us, because he does not have the anxious trepidations of evil things'. And concerning 'composition' as a psychological term, from the *Letter to Patricius*: Being 'in composition', *brukābhâ*, is the opposite of being 'in quiet', *bshelyâ*: 'If a multiplicity of thoughts is inherent to composition, it is evident that unity is inherent to simplicity, in such a way that outside composition is found simplicity, and outside thoughts, *theoria* of unity,' par. 62, p. 810. To say that the Word remains 'simple' within the Incarnation is not to make a statement about the 'radical transcendence of God', nor does it say anything about the materiality or lack of materiality in the union; the Word remains 'simple' because there is only one 'being' in the Incarnation, though within the Incarnation, that being is composite. But see de Halleux, p. 380, n. 7.

[1] 'Letter to Zeno', p. 165. We see a human hypostasis with the eye of the body, and if we can look at Christ through the eye of faith, we see the divine hypostasis of the Word. Without faith, we see only a man; with it, we see, not a separate human hypostasis, and alongside of it, the hypostasis of the Word, but the Word in which the human hypostasis receives its constitution. See e.g. *Monks of Senoun*, pp. 43–4.

[2] 'Letter to the Monks of Beth Gaugal', in *Three Letters*, p. 151; *Tres tract.*, pp. 240, 255, etc. The Virgin gave birth both naturally and non-naturally: 'naturally, because she bore flesh; above nature, because she gave birth to the Word enfleshed'. Both activities in her giving birth are miracles (*Tres tract.*, p. 255); neither is comprehensible (*Tres tract.*, p. 70).

[3] Both births are incomprehensible to reason, the first, for obvious reasons, the second, because it is a miracle, and is done 'in the hypostasis of the Word', *Monks of Senoun*, p. 9; *Tres tract.*, p. 83, etc.

[4] *Tres tract.*, p. 182; see also p. 96.

[5] *Tres tract.*, pp. 62–3; 66; 200; 201, etc.

not true of Christ: even in his coming into existence in the
realm of time, the Word did not go from one state to its opposite, for even before he came into being he existed, and even
when he died he continued to be immortal as God.[1] Even as a
human being, the basic framework of human life did not apply
to him, because his existence was not defined by these limits of
nothing and something. Because he continued his divine existence even though he was incarnate, he was not basically like
other men; he came into being 'without changing from what
he had been' before the Incarnation, that is, God the Word.[2]

Philoxenus strengthens his argument that the coming into
being of the Word was not like that of other men by using a
similar argument to the one Severus uses. All ordinary men
come into being 'for themselves', that is, they do not come into
being simply for the purpose of bringing about the new life of
beings outside themselves. In the case of ordinary men, their
telos is their own participation in God. But this was not true of
the coming into being of the Word. He did not come into being
in order to participate in God, but to bring us into a new
being; he came to make us sons of God, to bestow on us the
Holy Spirit through baptism.[3] Everything about the humanity
of Jesus belongs to the realm of miracle, not the realm of nature.

The second point which he continually makes about the
two births is this: just as Christ was born of the Father only in

---

[1] He did not go from one state to its opposite: *Tres tract.*, pp. 62, 63, 66, 200,
201, 217, etc. He continued to be immortal in death: 'The immortality of God
does not prevent us from believing in his death, nor does his death oblige us to
deny his immortality. God was tried by death ... [But] as spirits cannot die,
he did not die spiritually; besides, his nature is immortal. But, since the body
is subject to the power of death, he was tried by death corporally ... He was
dissolved as a man', 'Letter to Zeno', pp. 170–1. See de Halleux, pp. 490 ff.
Philoxenus shared the common idea of the ancient world that death was the
separation of the soul from the body, rather than the notion that death was the
destruction of the person in terms of personal identity. It is obvious that, if death
is only the separation of soul and body, one does not have a paradox at all when
one says that the immortal God died on a cross: He died, in so far as soul was
separated from body; he was immortal, in that, in so far as he is a 'spirit', his
existence did not depend upon the union of body and soul. Philoxenus emphasizes
that while God is immortal and impassible *by nature*, he became passible and mortal
through his *will* (*Tres tract.*, p. 89, etc.), but we must understand this as he meant
it, i.e. he became mortal and passible in so far as he became a man by his will,
or by a miracle.

[2] *Tres tract.*, pp. 67, 68, 131, 200, 201, 217; 'Letter to Zeno', pp. 164–6.

[3] *Tres tract.*, pp. 62, 63; 87, 88, 120, 207, 221.

so far as he was God, he was born of the mother only with respect to his humanity.[1] We say that the Word was 'born' because the humanity actually belonged to him as the flesh of an ordinary man belongs to him.[2] But we do not say that the Word went from a state of nothing to something: only the humanity did this. In the same way we can say that the Immortal one died, or the impassible one suffered, or we can make any of the seemingly paradoxical statements Philoxenus loved to make. In spite of his extreme dislike for the language of the separate proprieties, Philoxenus puts the concept to a very basic use.[3] The notion, in fact, underlies the whole of his theological structure. Philoxenus does not intend to confuse the humanity and divinity in Christ.

The Concept of Mixture

Although Philoxenus' intention certainly was not to confuse the humanity and divinity in the sense we would regard as

---

[1] *Tres tract.*, pp. 253–5; 'Letter to Zeno', pp. 168–9.

[2] *Monks of Senoun*, p. 64: 'It is written that the Word became flesh, because the flesh which he became belonged to the Word himself, and it was not that of another man.' See also p. 5 etc. Even though the flesh belonged to him as his own and was taken into the hypostasis of the Word, the flesh was not changed into the divinity, any more than the divinity was changed into humanity: 'Just as his own nature was not changed into flesh when it came into being, the flesh was not [changed] into the nature of the divinity when it was divinized. If his flesh had been changed into the nature of his divinity, it would have been intangible and invisible; and on the other hand, if his divinity had been converted into the nature of the flesh, it would not have been able to exercise the power which belonged to God, nor spoken or acted as belongs to God', *Monks of Senoun*, p. 52. See also *Tres tract.*, p. 203.

[3] Philoxenus does make a distinction between what is appropriate to the humanity and what is appropriate to the divinity within the Incarnation—e.g. stating that God died in so far as he was a man, and therefore was mortal, while he remained immortal in his divinity. When he does this, he is using the concept of the two proprieties as Severus used it (Severus believed that one self-subsistent hypostasis may have more than one, or even more than two, proprieties). Philoxenus does not know, apparently, of such a concept of propriety as Severus came to use; he rejects the notion of two proprieties as it was expressed at Chalcedon, because to him, two proprieties means necessarily two separate hypostases or natures (see e.g. *Monks of Senoun*, p. 22). Philoxenus says, explaining the passage 'the Word became flesh', that 'the flesh does not have any individuality which is not also that of the Word; and again, there is no property which one may not think is also that of the flesh . . . After the Word became flesh, his own properties and those of the flesh we confess to be one, because the one who became is the one who is, and the one who is is also recognized as the one who became and not another', *Monks of Senoun*, pp. 62–3.

condemned by Chalcedon, from his tradition he had inherited a practice of speaking of the union between the manhood and the Godhood as a 'mixture'. In this section we discuss the difficulties in which he involved himself as a result.

The concept of 'mixture' is a key concept in Philoxenus' theology : he uses the word to describe not only the union of the believer with the Holy Spirit, the union of the believer with Jesus, and even the union of soul and body ;[1] he also uses it to describe the union of humanity and divinity in Christ, using the analogy of the mixture of blood and semen in the womb of an ordinary mother.

In Philoxenus' theory on the formation of babies in the womb, father and mother both contribute equally to the new child ; the semen from the father and the blood from the mother are united indissolubly and thus produce the child.[2] Philoxenus

[1] There are two basic 'mixing' words, which in Philoxenus' system generally carry a positive connotation, as verbs or as noun derivatives: words formed from the root *mzg*, and words from the root *ḥlṭ*. The first is far more common. Examples of 'mixtures': If one is in the wilderness and has made all the necessary sacrifices, then God's 'glory arises in your soul, and he mixes (*māzeg*) you with the Spirit itself . . .', Hom. IX, p. 317. 'Your own union with Jesus today is in deed, in that he has mixed you (*mazeghākh*) in the life of the Spirit by baptism . . . You, today, in deed, he has mixed (*ḥalṭākh*) in his hypostasis', Hom. IX, p. 324. The 'hot fire of Jesus' is 'mixed' in our souls, Hom. XII, p. 497. In a negative sense, the soul is 'mingled' (*ḥlîṭâ*) with the body, Hom. XIII, p. 511. The lust of the soul is to be mixed with the lust of the Spirit, Hom. XIII, p. 526. The soul and body, in their proper relation to each other are 'luminous' and 'mingled' together, Hom. X, p. 408; see also Homilies X, p. 358; XI, p. 467; XIII, pp. 570, 571, 577.

[2] A large part of *Tres tract.* (pp. 197-9) is devoted to the working out of this analogy; see also p. 73. Philoxenus used this analogy of the mixture of blood and semen to form a baby, to argue against both the Eutycheans and the Nestorians. He felt that neither group conceived of the union in such a way that there was a real union between the humanity and divinity in Christ. To him, the Nestorian union was at best a loose 'indwelling' of God in a man, and the Eutychean union in its own way was just as bad: the Word simply used Mary as a receptacle, forming his own flesh within her, but taking nothing from her, neither flesh nor blood. The Eutycheans, according to Philoxenus, based this understanding of the Incarnation on a mistaken notion of what is contributed by each parent to the formation of a new child in the womb, the father contributing everything, the mother simply providing the place where the father's semen can grow and become a baby, *Tres tract.*, pp. 203, 204. Philoxenus implies that his own alternative position was repugnant to the Eutycheans because an addition to the hypostasis of the Word, in the form of the humanity, necessarily meant an addition to the nature of God himself. His argument in return is not very strong: the Eutycheans 'were not able to understand the power of the union, and to know that God is able to do everything, and that as he is one in nature with the Father, it is possible for him to be one in hypostasis also with his flesh', *Tres tract.*, p. 205.

uses this physiological theory to explain how it is that Jesus is 'from the nature'[1] of Mary, and at the same time, 'from the nature' of God, while he himself is only one being, and not two. One cannot separate the elements in a natural child, identifying the parts of the child that came from the father and those that came from the mother. The properties of a child cannot be divided up and portioned out to the parents, so that one would say, and really mean it, 'he has his mother's eyes'. In this same way, Philoxenus says, the humanity and divinity in Christ are inseparably united.[2] When Philoxenus talks about Jesus coming from 'the nature' of Mary, he means two things : first, the collective human nature we all come from and in which we all participate,[3] and second, the actual physical body of Mary.[4] Mary's 'nature'—what she contributed to the formation of Jesus—was not just the blood, as it would have been in the formation of an ordinary child, but also flesh, which then combined with the Word in the place of semen.[5]

In the formation of an ordinary baby, the mixture of the two elements takes place in such a way that the new baby is created through the *change* which takes place when the blood and semen are united. But Philoxenus explicitly denies the idea that the humanity or divinity in Christ suffers any change when united to produce the Incarnate Christ.[6] He uses the

---

[1] *Tres tract.*, p. 140. Philoxenus uses several expressions when he is talking about the way in which Christ is related to human nature: Jesus was 'homoousios' with us or our humanity: 'homoousios' in Syriac is expressed as *bar kyānâ*, 'member of the nature'; e.g. *Tres tract.*, pp. 251, 267. Christ inhabited or took upon himself our 'common nature', *kyānâ dhgawâ*, *Tres tract.*, pp. 168, 170-1, 182. Jesus is a man 'by nature', *bakhyānâ*, *Tres tract.*, p. 49. God became man 'from human nature', *men kyānâ 'nāshāyâ*, *Tres tract.*, p. 42. He is 'from our nature', *Tres tract.*, p. 97 etc.

[2] *Tres tract.*, p. 199.   [3] *Tres tract.*, pp. 168, 170, 171, 182.

[4] Philoxenus' language sometimes suggests that he may be thinking in terms of a kind of 'stockpile' of the raw material out of which all human beings are formed. He says not only that the Word was incarnate 'from our nature', but also that he is incarnate 'from our body', which means the same thing: see e.g. *Tres tract.*, pp. 60, 144, etc. For a similar idea of human nature as the raw material out of which all human beings come, see the early Jewish legend that Adam originally filled all heaven and earth and was completely formless; from him came all later men, conceived in terms of their bodies; see the Midrash on Genesis, *Bereshith Rabba*, 24:2.

[5] 'The Word from the Father instead of semen from the man, and flesh from the mother in place of blood from the woman: from the two of them in the union' comes the one Christ, *Tres tract.*, p. 197.

[6] *Tres tract.*, pp. 198, 199.

example of ordinary human conception only to demonstrate how inseparable the union is, as well as the fact that one cannot distinguish between what belongs to the man and what to the Word.[1] His only answer to the question of how it is that there is no change in either the humanity or divinity within the union is that it is a miracle and cannot be understood. Since the union takes place 'above nature',[2] it does not fall under the normal law of the creation of babies. The problem is that the metaphor seems scarcely intelligible any more after Philoxenus denies the offending consequences : it no longer illuminates but confuses the reader.

Looking at the analogy of the union of blood and semen from within the context of ancient philosophical discussions on the concept of mixture, one would assume that Philoxenus is thinking of the union of humanity and divinity in terms of the mixture of liquids. But he rejects most emphatically the idea that the union of the Word and his body is to be understood in this way :[3]

The Word was not changed into flesh when he was embodied from it, nor was the flesh turned into nature of the Word when he was united to it. Nor again were the natures mixed with each other like water in wine—those things that by means of their mixture destroy their natures—or like colours and darkness.

We see, then, that Philoxenus explicitly rejects the idea that the humanity and the divinity lose their characteristics within the union. The words which to Philoxenus convey this forbidden meaning are *bûlbālâ*, 'confusion', and, *ḥbhûkhyâ*, 'commingling'.[4]

Perhaps Philoxenus is thinking of a union like that of the Stoic κρᾶσις δι᾽ὅλων. Like the Stoics, Philoxenus was a materialist : he believed that not only were bodies material, but souls and spirits, too.[5] Like the Stoics, he did conceive of the union

---

[1] Ibid., pp. 197–9.   [2] Ibid., pp. 199, 255.

[3] *Tres tract.*, p. 151 ; *Monks of Senoun*, p. 51.

[4] *Monks of Senoun*, pp. 9, 15 ; *Tres tract.*, pp. 148, 151, 201.

[5] Philoxenus constantly uses the two adjectives, 'subtle' or 'thin' (*qaṭînâ*) and 'dense' or 'thick' (*'abhyâ*), to describe the relationships between the body, the soul, members of the spiritual realm, and God himself. In the hierarchy of things, the body is densest, the soul and angels more subtle, and God most subtle of all. 'The mind (*madh‘â*) with respect to [God's] subtlety (*qaṭînûthâ*) is dense (*'abhyâ*), and the soul is [like] the body compared to his spirituality', *Tres tract.*, p. 11 ;

of body and soul as the union of two material substances occupying the same place at the same time.

While the mother and father provide the raw material, so to speak, in the formation of an ordinary child, they do not provide the soul; technically, the parents are parents only of the child's *body*. In the same way, Mary is not the mother of the human soul of Christ.[1] Our discussion thus far, therefore, has not given us any information about the way in which the human *soul* of Christ was united with the divinity.

In concluding this section, we may ask whether Philoxenus violated the intent of the Chalcedonian adverbs—specifically, the two in which the council's Definition asserted that the humanity and divinity of Christ were united 'without confusion' and 'without change'. Did he conceive of the union in such a way that the humanity and divinity were 'mixed' in an unacceptable manner? In answer, we must say that Philoxenus himself was very much aware that he was using a dangerous analogy when he talked about the mixture of blood and semen. He understood that if one did not look at his qualifying remarks, one could not fail to be misled by the analogy. He excuses himself for using the language of mixture on the grounds that he has inherited the language of St. Ephraim;[2] nevertheless, the whole concept of 'mixture' runs through Philoxenus' theology. One can only conclude that, while he did *intend* a doctrine which the Chalcedonians would have found orthodox, the use of this particular analogy is highly suspect. The fact that the notion of union by mixture is found in so many places outside the specific christological one also tends to affirm that Philoxenus does not use the language in

see also p. 22. The body can be made lighter and more spiritual, both by eating less and by spiritual discipline; conversely, the soul can be made so 'dense' that it loses its spiritual character, Hom. X, pp. 358; 407–8; etc. God sent his son to 'make us spirits and subtle beings (*rûḥānê wqaṭînê*) and raise us up from the density ('*abhîûthâ*) of the flesh and its passions', *Tres tract.*, p. 220.

[1] *Tres tract.*, pp. 253–4.

[2] Ephraim only uses the language of 'mixture', says Philoxenus, because Syriac, at the time when Ephraim wrote, had no proper technical vocabulary (*Monks of Senoun*, pp. 54–5). Philoxenus realizes that from Ephraim's language one might assume that he is thinking of the mixture of divinity and humanity in terms suggestive of the way in which liquids are mixed; Philoxenus denies it, *Monks of Senoun*, p. 51.

this context accidentally; the concept of 'mixture' is indigenous to his thought.[1]

Soul and Body

Proceeding to a different aspect of Philoxenus' christology, the relationship between the soul and body of Jesus, we shall begin with the relationship between soul and body in ordinary men.

To Philoxenus the soul and body of each man are two warring 'natures', two opposing 'wills' which struggle for mastery over each other.[2] Depending upon which of the two gains the mastery, a man is, then, either a 'spiritual' or a 'bodily' man. If we understand what Philoxenus means by these words, 'body', 'soul', 'will', and 'nature' in this context, and if we also understand his views on the nature of the union between body and soul, we shall be in a good position to go on to a discussion of the problem of the humanity of Christ, in terms of the presence or absence of a human hypostasis, a human will, and human nature.

The word 'body' can, for Philoxenus, refer simply to the flesh a human being carries around with him—hair, bones, blood, finger-nails, and so forth.[3] At times he makes use of this more 'Greek' division between body and soul, where 'soul' is the rational, thinking part of a man, in contrast to the body, which cannot think and has no 'will' of its own. Generally, however, 'body' means more than the actual visible element of a man.

In the context of the relationship between soul and body, 'body' is the term Philoxenus uses to describe the reality which opposes the soul. Soul and body are, then, individual representatives of the principles of life in the world of the Spirit and life in the material and visible world of ordinary human affairs. The 'body' includes all the physical, non-rational elements

[1] de Halleux disagrees, and takes Philoxenus at his word, that he only uses it because he finds it in Ephraim, *Philoxène*, p. 387.

[2] The soul and body are at constant war with each other 'and as their *natures* are contrary to each other, even so also are their wills', Hom. XI, p. 465; see also Hom. XII, p. 540. He says of the soul and body, 'each of these, whether it be the body or the soul, draws the other to its own will, because they are contrary to each other in their natures (*bakhyānayhôn*) and also in their wills (*bṣebhyānayhôn*)', Hom. X, p. 358.

[3] Cf. *Tres tract.*, pp. 73–4, Hom. XIII, pp. 578–91.

that belong to an individual man, but it also includes all his drives toward participation in the life of the world[1]—sometimes even his thoughts and plans which involve life in the world.[2] In this respect, then, the body is 'rational'. Philoxenus hints that rational knowledge, the knowledge of how things work, the study of medicine and astronomy and science, are bound to the life of the world.[3] The 'nature' of the body which opposes the 'nature' of the soul includes the properties of the sensible, visible world which come to the body through birth and make it what it is, namely, mortal, visible, subject to human needs for sleep and food, and so forth. The 'will' of the body is the inherent drive toward participation in the ordinary life of the world which each man contains in himself.[4]

The element opposed to this in each man is his soul. As in the case of the body, this term includes far more than simply the human capacity for higher thought, and the immortal element in each man. It is the portion of each man that can participate in the life of the Spirit,[5] which should take its place in the 'country' of spiritual beings, the realm of the angels.[6] While the realm of body is the realm of knowledge gained through the analysis of raw data fed in by the senses, the realm of soul is that of direct apprehension, through faith and the Holy Spirit,[7] of all

[1] Hom. XI, pp. 466–7. The drive toward participation in the life within the world is often called 'the lust of the body'; this is opposed to the 'lust of the soul', see e.g. Homilies XII, pp. 514, 526; XIII, pp. 570–1, etc.

[2] See especially Hom. XI, pp. 466–7. 'Do not destroy the work of the soul by the works of the body [and] the thoughts [of the soul] by the thoughts [of the body]. Save the life of your soul from your body as if from a fire', 'A Letter of Philoxenus of Mabbug sent to a Novice', ed. Gunnar Olindar, p. 11 : 'Do not take upon yourself the customary habit of the thoughts of the body when you hear about incorporeal countries, and do not fashion imaginary forms out of your heart...', Hom. II, p. 31.

[3] *Tres tract.*, pp. 73 ff., pp. 104 ff.

[4] The 'lust of the body' is the will of the body, within a person, driving him to indulge the body's appetites, first and foremost the 'lust' for food, and then for all other things of the world, including even the desire for learning and teaching, Hom. IX, pp. 459 ff. See also Homilies XI, pp. 465–7; XIII, p. 577, XII, p. 497. The counterpart of the will of the soul is the 'lust of the spirit', Homilies XIII, p. 572; XII, p. 514, etc.

[5] Hom. IX, pp. 260–2, etc.

[6] See Hom. IX, pp. 264 ff.; especially pp. 288 ff.

[7] 'Outside these five senses ... a man can neither perceive anything of the corporeal world, nor does the world exist to him outside these senses. And the remainder of everything which is spiritual, whether it be what exists of itself, or whether it be things that are created, cannot be subjected to one of these five

knowledge of divine things. It is outside the realm governed by the laws of nature : it is 'above nature'.[1] This is the realm in which the Incarnation not only takes place, but is perceived and understood. It is the soul, united to the Holy Spirit, then, that understands, through a direct perception, i.e. faith, the reality lying under the visible world, that sees the new man who comes into existence through baptism, that understands that the bread and wine in the eucharist are the body and blood of God, that can see the nature of the staff in Moses' transformed snake.[2] The 'nature', then, of the soul includes its immortality, its 'thinness' (to use Philoxenus' materialistic language), and its belonging to the life of the spirit, that is, all those things that make it definably what it is and not body. Its 'will' is its drive toward participation in the life of the spirit. Like the body, it has its own drives and lusts.[3]

Philoxenus conceives of both body and soul as material, and he regards both as being small 'pieces' (*mnawāthā*) of larger wholes. In one place he says, speaking of the relationship between soul and body, 'by a wise dispensation, a portion of the spirit was placed in a portion of the body'.[4] It is not clear in

forms, neither can it be experienced by any one of these five senses... For this reason also when our Lord gave us this blessing of perceiving him, he delivered to us first of all, faith, with which we might perceive him...', *Thirteen Homilies*, Hom. II, p. 36. See below, pp. 87 ff.

[1] Hom. XI, pp. 425, 427, 428. Philoxenus distinguishes between genuine needs of 'nature' and needs that are not genuine—e.g. he explains that hunger that may be endured and vanquished by patience is not 'natural', i.e. is not a need that must be filled for the sake of the health of the body. What we call 'natural' needs ought to be filled, and the body ought to be kept healthy (*Lettre à Patricius*, p. 780. See especially Prologue to the *Thirteen Homilies*, pp. 20–1). Nevertheless, what the body needs is the most unappetizing of food, and as little of it as possible, Hom. XI, p. 464. It is not surprising that, given Philoxenus' materialistic view of body and soul, the heaviness or 'fatness' of the body, caused by overindulgence in eating, means, first of all, the destruction of the 'lightness' of the soul: 'as the body is nourished, the soul becomes enfeebled . . . and as the body adds to the strength and vigour of its stature, the stature of the soul bows down. . .'. See also Hom. X, pp. 407, 408. The whole life of the spirit is 'above nature' : Hom. XII, pp. 496 ff. Prologue, pp. 17, 18, etc.

[2] *Tres tract.*, pp. 118–20 ; 'Letter to Zeno', p. 165, etc.

[3] Hom. IX, p. 358, etc. See also Hom. XI, p. 434.

[4] Hom. IX, pp. 357–8 : 'Since a light and spiritual nature (*kyānā ruḥānā wqalīlā*) is mingled in us, the body should seek spirituality and lightness. . . Now by a wise dispensation, a portion of the spirit (*mnāthā dhrūḥā*) was placed in a portion of the body (*bamnāthā dhphagrā*), and as the body becomes heavy with food, it draws and brings down the soul to it, and hangs its own weight on it, and ties and fetters the wings of the thoughts of the soul. But if the life of the body be maintained con-

either case what the little pieces of body and spirit are thought to come from. In the case of the body, he may be thinking of human nature in general : we know from other places that he conceived of human nature as a kind of concrete collective, made up of all men, or at least being the source from which all human beings are drawn.[1] This was a common notion in the ancient world ; Gregory of Nyssa, for example, draws upon it in his treatise 'On Why Not Three Gods' to prove that the Oneness of God is as real as the Threeness.[2] What is usually called the 'physical' theory of atonement is based on this notion of collective human nature. The other possibility for what Philoxenus had in mind, when he said that the body was part of a larger body, is that 'body' includes not only the sum total of human bodies, but also all matter that goes to make up the world of 'nature', i.e. the visible world. This would be in keeping with the notion that 'body' itself represents a principle opposed to the realms of God and the spirit.

It is also not clear how Philoxenus visualized the Spirit, from which the portions of the spirit come, to be combined with bodies.[3] It is possible that he had some idea of the spirit, in this sense, akin to the Stoic idea of the world-spirit from which individual spirits come. It is also possible that 'spirit' in this usage refers in a collective sense to all the members of the spiritual realm, including angels and men. He has told us elsewhere that, in the hierarchy of being, bodies are the heaviest, souls and members of the spiritual realm are light and thin, and God the thinnest and lightest of all. In this case, then, he would be saying in this passage only that soul and body come from two different layers of reality. The third

---

stantly by a sparing use of food, it becomes light and purified and refined and the heaviness of its nature dwindles away and makes bright the soul which is in it and makes it glad, and is, moreover, itself obedient readily to its will. . . For each of these, whether it be the body or the soul, draws the other to its own will, because they are contrary to each other in their natures, and also in their wills.'

[1] de Halleux, pp. 390–1.

[2] P. G. 45, 120.

[3] e.g. as in Hom. IX, pp. 358, 263–4, 295, etc. The problem is complicated by the fact that 'soul' and 'spirit' are sometimes synonyms and at other times not : sometimes the soul is to be 'mixed' with the Spirit (Homilies IX, p. 317; XII, pp. 569–70) ; at other times there seems to be no distinction between soul and spirit, or else Philoxenus talks about the soul without talking about the spirit : Homilies IX, pp. 322–3; XI, pp. 465–7; XII, pp. 513–14.

possibility is that the 'spirit' in question is really the Holy
Spirit. In this case, he would be saying that each man actually
has, as part of his composition, a 'piece' of the Holy Spirit.
Philoxenus certainly believes this to be true of each man who
has been baptized,[1] but this is probably not what he means in
this context : the human soul is generally conceived of as being
a separate element from God who is present in the individual
as 'spirit'. Nevertheless, the question of the exact relationship
of the realm of the Spirit to the Holy Spirit is unclear in
Philoxenus' over-all theological system.

Soul and body are not naturally joined to each other.
Philoxenus warns us :[2]

You must not think that the soul and body are linked together
(*nqîphîn*) and that one is mixed (*mmazgîn*) with the other naturally
(*kyanâîth*), for there is much room between them, and it is a terrible
depth which not every man is able to search out and pass over . . .

Each man who is interested in leading the life of the Spirit
must aid his soul in the defeat of the body, so that the body
may be joined properly to the soul, and made its ally.[3]

As the soul and body are locked in mortal combat, they are
'mixed'[4] together in a bad sense, and the soul is sometimes over-
powered by the body. Gradually it withers up and becomes a
slave to the body : all its energies and resources serve the body.[5]
All knowledge of the realm of the spirit is lost, and the soul is
said to be dead, though the body lives on in its life in the
world.[6] This can happen when the physical body is indulged
by excess food : Philoxenus regards gluttony as the root sin
from which all others spring, because it makes the soul itself

---

[1] See especially 'Memra de Philoxène de Mabboug sur l'inhabitation du Saint-
Esprit,' *Le Muséon*, 1, 2 (1960), 39–71, ed. A. Tanghe. This entire treatise is on the
relationship of the baptized believer to the Holy Spirit which dwells within him.
See also Hom. IX, pp. 260–2.

[2] Hom. IX, pp. 322–3.

[3] Homilies XIII, p. 580; X, pp. 407–8; XIII, pp. 576, 577; XI, p. 467.

[4] 'So long as the soul is mixed (*ḥlîṭâ*) with the body in its thoughts it cannot
direct the body. . .', Hom. XII, p. 511; 'Unless the mind stand in its solitary
nature it cannot gather to itself the power of its nature, for so long as it is mingled
with the body its power is stolen away and dissipated on the members of the body
. . . and it becomes a being who is under orders, and not one who gives them',
Hom. XII, p. 513.

[5] Ibid.   [6] Hom. XI, pp. 466–7.

heavy and dull.[1] 'As the body becomes heavy with food, it
draws and brings down the soul to it, and it hangs its own
weight upon it, and it ties and fetters the wings of the thoughts
of the soul. . .' Philoxenus also speaks of this mastery of the
soul by the body as a kind of adultery or perversion of the
relationship that ought to exist between soul and body.[2]

The soul and body must, then, be removed from each other
when they are in this wrong relationship,[3] and the thoughts of
each must be separated from the other, and mixture, in this
sense, avoided.

The ultimate proper relationship of soul and body is also a
union, but a union in which the soul dominates the body and
changes it, so that the body in a sense also becomes spiritual.
He tells the monks to whom he writes to[4] 'lift up the power of
your body upon your soul, and change and mingle the life of
it with the life of your soul, that its mortal life be preserved
with its immortal life, and its feeble power be mixed with the
might of its spiritual power'. This union Philoxenus compares
to the proper and lawful sexual relationship of a man and his
wife, which can occur when the soul has already begun to
recognize its union with the Holy Spirit after baptism. This is
the ultimate goal of both soul and body, for 'when the body
has intercourse with the soul and the soul with the Spirit, and
through the Spirit with the Trinity, in very deed are accom-
plished the words, "the Lord is over all and in us all"'.[5] The
body and its power are to be 'mixed' with the soul, and ultimately with the Trinity itself, but the thoughts and 'lusts' and
drive of the body toward the life of the world are not to be mixed
with the soul, but are to be weakened and lost so far as possible.

The Soul and Body of Jesus

What does Philoxenus mean by the body of Jesus ? In the
Thirteen Homilies, where he lays out his major views on soul and

---

[1] Hom. IX, pp. 357–8.

[2] 'When the soul is joined to (*teshtawtaph*) the body, this union is adultery and
fornication ; but if the body is united to (*nethnaqaph*) the soul in one agreement,
and is raised above from below in a right union, it is the union that is according to
the law that is implanted naturally in the hypostasis of each one of us by the
Creator. . .', Hom. XII, pp. 522–3. This 'fornication' and 'adultery' take place
when the 'remembrance of God' is removed from the soul, pp. 525–6.

[3] Hom. XII, pp. 511–14.   [4] Hom. XI, p. 467.   [5] Hom. XII, p. 524.

body and their relationship to each other, Philoxenus indicates
that Jesus not only possessed a body in the mere physical sense
of the term : he was united to a body in the broader sense of the
term as well, natural physical body, natural appetites and
emotions, and the mental faculties necessary for participation
in the life of the world.[1] One of the greatest works of the Word
as he revealed himself to the world was that of demonstrating
'in his own hypostasis' the means of growth into the new life
of the Spirit, which ought to follow baptism.[2] From Philoxenus'
description of Christ's pioneering efforts to do this, it is clear
that Jesus was not simply a man in appearance only :[3]

[Jesus] began first of all the war which was against the greediness
of the belly, and he overcame this lust by the patient endurance of

---

[1] Hom. XI, pp. 479–80 ; 482 ; see also *Tres tract.*, pp. 56, 167, 181, 186, 187, 190.
de Halleux notes Philoxenus' distinction between 'passions' and 'needs', and
'lusts'. Passions and needs as they were assumed by the Word, not only include
suffering and death, but also the 'emotions of the soul of the Incarnate Word'.
Lusts, on the other hand, are 'unnatural' appetites, as opposed to actual needs.
'The Incarnate Word [then], destroyed without assuming them, sin and lust ; on
the one hand, he personally assumed needs and passions, but he assumed them
voluntarily, or according to the economy, i.e. freely', *Philoxène*, p. 466. See also
pp. 459–83. Philoxenus does, however, on occasion, talk in terms of 'lust' with
respect to Jesus, as he does in the passage quoted below, in which Jesus has to
conquer the 'lust of the belly', the love of money, boasting, and vain-glory. But as
de Halleux points out, Philoxenus' notion that Jesus was not subject to death is
based on the notion that death is a direct product of lust, as it is transmitted
through physical procreation : see e.g. Hom. XI, p. 447 ; *Tres tract.*, p. 253. In the
Commentary on John, Philoxenus explains the birth of lust in Adam, following the
'Evagrian theory of the "three movements of the intellect"' : in the first stage,
there is no lust ; in the second stage, from the time of the commandment not to
eat the fruit until the transgresssion, lust was present, but somehow exterior to
Adam ; from the time of the fall, it has been part of his very nature—'mixed' with
it. See de Halleux, p. 463. Jesus, apparently, was subject to lust in the same way
as Adam before the fall : lust was present to him, but not yet part of his nature :
Commentary on John III, 13, f. 216 ʳb, de Halleux, p. 468, n. 27.
    Philoxenus often uses the term 'body' or 'bodyhood' to refer to what Severus calls
the 'humanity' of Jesus. The terms 'body', 'flesh', and 'body-hood' all signify what
the Word took on to become man. *Tres tract.*, p. 251 : 'The bodyhood (*pagrānûthâ*)
is rightly considered to be that of God'. See also *Tres tract.*, p. 56, where Philoxenus
states that referring to the body of Jesus automatically implies the soul which is in
it ; p. 50, where 'nāshûthâ and *pagrānûthâ* are in parallel ; 'Letter to the Monks of
Beth Gaugal', pp. 149–50. When the gospel says that the Word became flesh, it
means that Jesus 'grew in the flesh in stature, and hungered and thirsted and
worked and rested and slept *and grieved and was disheartened and was afraid, and was
troubled,* and was seized by crucifiers. . .', *Tres. tract.*, p. 167.
    [2] Homilies IX, pp. 303 ff.; VIII, pp. 222–4; 236.
    [3] Hom. XI, pp. 479–80.

fasting, that he might also give us an example and lay down the law for us, so that we, if we desired to enter a spiritual rule of life and conduct, might begin with fasting . . . Our Lord first of all defeated the lust of the belly, and after it, the love of money, and the empty boasting of the world . . . And after these things, he conquered vain-glory . . . and by these three he overcame and brought to nothing all the passions which cling to them, and he began to preach the kingdom of his Father with power, and to deliver the doctrine of perfection to the children of men.

Christ, then, was said to suffer human passions and desires in an ordinary human manner.[1] In other places, too, Philoxenus indicates that Jesus suffered all human things, and to a greater degree than other men: he suffered intensely from thirst and hunger; the devil tempted him harder than anyone else; his death and burial were more agonizing than other men's deaths. Jesus was even more afraid than other men; his terror was so great in the garden of Gethsemane that he sweated drops of blood.[2] Philoxenus' language is unambiguous: he is not depicting the humanity of Jesus in any phantasiast sense, nor is he thinking of Jesus as allowing his body to grow hungry or thirsty on some occasions, so that the divinity can be said to experience human things. Jesus overcame the body's lust for food only by painful fasting.

Philoxenus never talks as though Jesus on a particular occasion assumed a particular need which he then abandoned later. When the Word put on our humanity, he put on all its requirements (with the exception of sin) though he did it voluntarily. To demonstrate how completely Jesus was a man, Philoxenus emphasizes that he came under the law (*Tres tract.*, pp. 182–4). Christ had to keep the law, since he was a bodily creation who had 'become by his will a man who served the law' (p. 184). On the other hand, if Jesus had had to fight the lust for food 'according to his own strength, he would never have hungered at all, for the nature of his *spirituality* was not to hunger; but he

---

[1] Though de Halleux is right in emphasizing that, while Jesus underwent all human things, he suffered them voluntarily, rather than naturally (*Philoxène*, p. 466). Christ 'suffered passions and death on our behalf by his will when he is in his nature immortal and invisible', *Tres tract.*, p. 89; Hom. XI, p. 447, etc. We remember that this non-natural realm is the realm of miracle: 'All things that concern him are miraculous and not natural and ordinary matters, for it is necessary that all things that God does be miracles', *Monks of Senoun*, p. 61.

[2] *Tres tract.*, pp. 186, 187, 190.

fasted according to the body, according to the capacity of the power of carnal beings, and he brought himself down to us, and revealed to us the limits of his natural endurance'.[1]

There is also no doubt about the fact that Philoxenus understood Jesus to have the same type of thinking faculties as all men have.[2] He criticizes the Apollinarians on this point, using the old argument that if the Word did not assume a human mind, then the human mind would not be saved, but only the human body.[3] Philoxenus says frequently that the Word took upon himself all human things, with the exception of sin. At other times he says that the Word took from us all things necessary to the formation of a man.[4] Jesus had a human understanding, ma'dâ.[5]

As we have also seen, Jesus participated fully in the life of the Spirit.[6] Philoxenus even speaks of the fact that Jesus was born anew by baptism, before he went out into the wilderness accompanied by the Holy Spirit.[7] On the other hand, Philoxenus says that Jesus did not need to be accompanied by the Holy Spirit, since he was God the Word; but the Holy Spirit went with him because Jesus' sojourn in the wilderness was to be a perfect model for the ascetic life of perfection.[8]

The Human Hypostasis of Jesus

If we go on to ask whether Jesus' body and soul had a hypostasis, we find that they did in fact have one, but an independent

[1] Hom. XI, p. 481.
[2] Jesus possessed his body in the same way as everyone else does, 'and he possessed its life and power and operation, and as everybody [else], the soul which dwells in it', *Tres tract.*, p. 56. This soul was 'not without understanding', p. 181, see also pp. 174–5.
[3] *Monks of Senoun*, p. 9; *Tres tract.*, p. 222.
[4] *Tres tract.*, pp. 174–5; see also pp. 131, 241. Philoxenus frequently affirms that Jesus became a 'complete' or 'perfect' man, *Tres tract.*, pp. 170, 183, etc.
[5] *Tres tract.*, p. 181.
[6] That is, Jesus himself went out into the wilderness and inaugurated the life of the Spirit by demonstrating it completely 'in his own hypostasis'.
[7] 'In baptism, then, our Lord fulfilled the way of the righteousness of the law; and from the Jordan he made the beginning of the way of his own rule of life; for until the Jordan ... he was subject to the law as a servant, but from the Jordan ... his life and conduct were in the freedom which he delivered, and not in the commandments of the law. *For Jesus was born again by baptism,* and from the womb of the law, the spiritual country received him ...', Hom. IX, p. 258.
[8] Ibid.

hypostasis which could exist apart from the Word, or which could be counted as a second entity within the union :[1] 'If soul and body are not counted as another hypostasis along with the hypostasis of the Word, *because their hypostasis was in the hypostasis of the Word,* then another nature is not counted along with the nature of the Word . . .' It is of great importance that, after the union, one is left with only one countable being,[2] namely, the incarnate Word. However Philoxenus speaks of body and soul having 'their hypostasis . . . in the hypostasis of the Word'. Body and soul are united and become human within the Word himself,[3] and thus come to have their own hypostasis which depends, for its existence, on its intimate union with the Word. 'Hypostasis' understood within this context, might almost be translated as 'identity'.

Everything belonging to Jesus as the incarnate Word, Philoxenus says, belongs to, or was taken up into, the hypostasis of the Word.[4] The union of flesh and soul took place

---

[1] 'Against Nestorius', included in the introductory material to the *Thirteen Homilies*, Vol. II, p. cxxvii. See also *Tres tract.*, p. 58: 'He did not take another, but his [own] hypostasis', and *Letter to the Monks of Senoun*, p. 57. Philoxenus did, on occasion, use the language belonging to the Cyrillian-Alexandrine tradition to which Severus also belonged (as Lebon documents in 'La Christologie du monophysme syrien', *Chalkedon*, I. 425–580). Lebon does not interest himself in a study of Philoxenus' christology as it is expressed in different terms from Severus'; he is instead, interested in it only as it is related to a Severan-Cyrillian type of christology. A reading of Lebon would suggest, erroneously, that Philoxenus attempted to work out a solution to the christological problem along lines essentially the same as Severus', only where Severus was 'profound and speculative', Philoxenus was 'simple' and 'straightforward' (p. 428). This is to fail to see that Philoxenus did attempt the construction of a christology on quite different lines, though he could use the language of the Severan tradition when he wanted to. Nevertheless, Lebon's work is tremendously valuable in cataloguing what Philoxenus was and was not willing to state in Severan terms. de Halleux discusses the various meanings of the terms 'hypostasis' and 'nature': see pp. 351–2; 356; 375, n. 45.

[2] Philoxenus explains how the term 'union'—in Syriac, *ḥdhāyûthâ*, an abstract noun from the root meaning 'one'—actually means 'oneness', *Letter to the Monks of Senoun*, p. 54; *Tres tract.*, p. 251. See de Halleux, *Philoxène*, p. 385, notes 21–2.

[3] 'In the very Word was the composition of the two of them, soul and body . . . And in the same way, when these are released by death and sent far from each other, they were not outside him, and he was not thought to be outside them [as though he were] another hypostasis or nature; thus also when they were in him, by the fact he was made man and was ensouled—but this means they had their composition in him—they were not known apart from him, and therefore, they were taken up and were his, or rather, were in him', *Monks of Senoun*, pp. 57–8.

[4] Some typical statements: 'If . . . we believe that the body belongs to him,

within the hypostasis of the Word. Everything Jesus did during
his lifetime was done by the hypostasis of the Word.[1] What
Jesus said was spoken by the Word himself. The hypostasis of
the Word in all these cases means 'the Word himself'. What
belongs to, or is done in or by, or is spoken by 'the hypostasis
of the Word, is what belongs to, or is done in or by, or is spoken
by the very Word himself, appearing and acting and speaking
directly, and not through the means of a man who, as a
separate entity, acts for him'.[2] Thus Philoxenus uses the word
qnômâ in this way to emphasize two points : first, that everything we say about Jesus, we are, in fact, saying about the Word
himself, in so far as he is incarnate, and second, that the Word
acted directly in all things, and not through an independent
human agent. Further, by the 'hypostatic union', Philoxenus
means first, that the flesh belonged 'hypostatically' to the
Word, i.e. as his very own, and not as anyone else's. Conversely, the term 'hypostatic union' means to Philoxenus that
the human soul and body of Jesus did not exist separately and
apart from the Word at any time before they were united to
him.[3] Second, it means that the humanity belonged to the
Word himself, and was not simply related to the Word by an
act of his will.[4]

Philoxenus sometimes uses the word 'hypostasis' in another
way, as an equivalent or near equivalent of soul, where 'soul'
is that part of a man capable of participating in the life of the

because he was made man, then corporeity is the property of the hypostasis of
God, and not of another human hypostasis', 'Letter to Zeno', p. 166. 'Truly
the body was his own, but this means, "of his hypostasis"', *Tres tract.*, p. 256, etc.

[1] 'What the master wished the disciples to be, he depicted and showed them
in his own hypostasis . . . These were the fair deeds and excellent manner of life
which he demonstrated in his own hypostasis . . .', Hom. VIII, p. 243; 'In his
own hypostasis he became a law for us', Hom. VIII, p. 222; see also p. 249.

[2] 'Letter to Zeno', pp. 165–6.

[3] *Tres tract.*, pp. 57–8; 144. 'The body is not counted as another hypostasis
by itself and from itself, and belonging to him, but it is the property of God
who is known to be embodied by nature', *Tres tract.*, p. 51. '[The Word] hypostatically became flesh; another did not become flesh, and then he adhered to
it', p. 179. See also pp. 62, 97, 256; 'Letter to Zeno', pp. 165–6; *Monks of Senoun*,
pp. 62–3. Philoxenus uses 'naturally' and 'hypostatically' as synonyms when
talking about the union, see e.g. *Monks of Senoun*, pp. 43–4.

[4] Union 'hypostatically' is also contrasted on occasion with the activity of
God's will alone in other places: 'While in other wombs his *will* forms babies,
in the womb of the virgin he was hypostatically enwombed . . .', *Tres tract.*, p. 61;
see also pp. 99, 219–20.

Spirit. For example, in the *Thirteen Homilies*, warning against the dangers of gluttony, he says,[1]

Do not be . . . in your life a grave to your soul, and do not yourself destroy your hypostasis within you before it be destroyed in the natural grave. Look! Your soul is buried in your body as the body in a grave. The body was established by the Creator as a glorious instrument to belong to the soul and as a partner in all good things. Why have you made it a grave?

The human hypostasis, then, in this sense, does not include the body, but belongs, with the soul, to the realm of the Spirit, rather than to the natural realm. Note that the body is said to be able to live without soul or hypostasis. This idea of a human body living on without its soul or hypostasis calls to mind again the puzzling passage in Theodore of Mopsuestia's *Catechetical Homilies*, in which he speaks of the fact that animals do not have hypostases. If we understand 'hypostasis' to refer to the element in a living being which is able to participate in the life of the Spirit, the passage makes sense: Animals do not participate in the life of the Spirit; only men, among all the members of the natural world, are able to do this. Since Philoxenus is quite sure that Jesus had a human soul, Jesus would have to have a human hypostasis in this particular sense of the word; nevertheless, his hypostasis would be incorporated within the hypostasis of the Word, just as his body was.

The Concept of Indwelling

To Philoxenus, the verse from John, 'The Word became flesh and dwelt in us', makes two different theological points. The first half of the verse tells us something about the relationship between the Word and his own human flesh and soul, and the second something about the relationship between the Word and the rest of us. The concept of the union that Philoxenus understood his 'two-nature' opponents to have, not only destroyed the distinction between the two halves of the verse; it also conceived of the union in such a way that it removed the possibility of human salvation for anyone but the man Jesus. In this section, then, let us examine the concept of 'indwelling'

[1] Hom. IX, p. 383. See also Homilies X, p. 418; XII, p. 534; 525. *Tres tract.*, p. 121, speaks of the hypostasis of each man being poured out and renewed at baptism.

in the senses in which it was rejected, and accepted, by Philoxenus.

Philoxenus believed that the two-nature theologians used
the term 'indwelling' to describe the Incarnation in such a
way that it necessarily implied only a prosopic union.[1] If the
verse in John is interpreted to mean, not that the Word
dwelt in all of us, but that he indwelt specifically in Jesus, then
the union was only one of love or honour or authority or will.
This is the way that the Holy Spirit was present in the prophets
and holy men of the Bible, but Jesus was more than a prophet
or holy man. This could not be the way that the Word was
present in Jesus. Even though the Holy Spirit could inhabit a
prophet or holy man, Philoxenus says, from before birth, as
was true of Jeremiah and John the Baptist and many others,[2]
one does not say that the Holy Spirit *became* flesh when talking
about Jeremiah or John,[3] because even though the Spirit was
said to be present in them from before birth to their very death,
there were still two self-subsistent hypostases, two sources of
activity: Jeremiah and John acted in the name of God, or
spoke for God prophetically through a gift of God.[4] They acted
through themselves, through their own will; when they acted,
it was not God acting directly. When Philoxenus rejects the
language of Chalcedon, it is always because he interprets their
language in this way: two natures means two hypostases,[5] and

---

[1] See e.g. *Tres tract.*, p. 140. The union of humanity and divinity in Christ was
not like that of 'Paul and Peter who were two in number and one in the will
of faith', nor were the humanity and divinity united by honour and authority;
instead, the union is 'natural', p. 196. Philoxenus also rejects the notion that Christ
put on the humanity as a man puts on a piece of clothing: 'The Word did not
weave himself a garment and put it on, nor build himself a palace and live in
it, nor did he make a house and dwell in it . . .', p. 46. See also 'Against Nestorius',
p. cxxv.

[2] *Letter to the Monks of Senoun*, p. 25; *Tres tract.*, pp. 210 ff., 262.

[3] *Tres tract.*, p. 258; see also p. 210.

[4] *Tres tract.*, p. 262. The gift is 'the gift of the Spirit', *mawhabhtâ dhrûhâ*, or
'the grace of prophecy', *taybûthâ dhanbhîûthâ*.

[5] 'The council [of Chalcedon] established the doctrines of Nestorius . . . For
it also said, like Nestorius, "two natures", to each one of which belongs its own
proprieties. But this means, to God, the miracles, and to the man, the passions,
and two natures, to which belong individual operations. But they are also manifestly hypostases and not just *prosopa*', *Monks of Senoun*, p. 22; see also p. 15. 'If
we admit [in him] nature and nature, we must necessarily acknowledge hypostasis
and hypostasis, and consequently we must acknowledge two sons and two Gods',
'Letter to Zeno', p. 167; see also 'Against Nestorius', pp. cxxvi ff.

two hypostases means a union identical to the union between the Holy Spirit and a holy man or prophet.

To get Philoxenus' second objection to this particular interpretation of the verse, such a concept of indwelling does not permit any notion of the Word dwelling in the rest of us.[1] When Philoxenus reads the passage in John that says 'the Word became flesh and dwelt *ban* [original Greek, ἐν ἡμῖν]', he reads this last phrase as 'in us', not 'among us'.[2] That is, the passage, to Philoxenus, does not say that the enfleshed Logos lived as a man in the company of other men, but that after the Incarnation had made it possible, the Logos was able to indwell in any member of the human race. It is only through this 'indwelling' of the rest of us that the salvation of any of us occurs. Philoxenus supports his reading of the text by citing the name given to Jesus, 'Immanuel' : 'Immanuel' means, not 'God is with *him*', but 'God is with *us*'.[3]

There are two different ways in which Philoxenus thinks of the indwelling in us. The first way we have already briefly looked at in passing in our discussion of Jesus' human body. In this sense, Jesus is said either to be 'in the common nature' (*bakhyānâ dhgawâ*), or to be 'from our nature', or 'from the nature of Mary' or *bar kyānan*, a term which generally renders the expression 'homoousios to us'.[4] Philoxenus appears to be talking of human nature here either as a collective made up of the sum total of all men, or possibly as a kind of raw material from which all human bodies have been made. Sometimes Jesus' taking on of human nature is seen in terms of the Word's taking on all the characteristics and properties that make up a human being.[5] In this way of looking at it, the 'indwelling' in

---

[1] See de Halleux, pp. 332–3; 421. The Word did not dwell in one man alone, because it is impossible that 'flesh dwell in flesh'. 'Thus, by his coming into being, he appeared on earth and lived with men, and by his immutability, he resided in us, as God, in temples, by the Spirit . . .', *Monks of Senoun*, p. 5.

[2] 'For the Word did not dwell in a man, as they rave, but in us—in men— he dwelt', *Tres tract.*, p. 168. 'We are his temples, as Paul says, and not another human being who is known outside of him', *Tres tract.*, p. 241.

[3] *Tres tract.*, p. 169.

[4] 'In the common nature', *Tres tract.*, p. 168. He is 'from our own nature', *bar kyānā dhîlan, Tres tract.*, p. 55, see also p. 251. Jesus is related to the Virgin 'by nature', and *bar kyānā*, homoousios to her, *Tres tract.*, pp. 260, 262, 267; he is 'from the nature of the Virgin', p. 140. He was made man 'from us', p. 50.

[5] The Word was joined to 'those things from which a human nature is constituted . . . and not to the hypostasis of a man, by which he confers honour on

us began from the moment in which the Word entered the womb of Mary, and our salvation began from that point. Human nature was taken up into the very hypostasis of the Word and renewed there,[1] and death and corruption and the rule of the demons were overcome.

Philoxenus' second way of thinking of the indwelling of the Word in us is not in terms of *all* human beings, but only of the baptized. In the *Monks of Senoun* he says :[2]

We understand that it is in us that he has dwelt as God, by his grace, because it is we who have become his temples . . . The temple of God is, then, *each baptized one*, in whom the Spirit of God dwells, who has received baptism, and by the intermediary of which he has also received Christ who gives the Spirit . . . There, where the Spirit is which he gives, in him also he dwells, by his Spirit.

In another passage, this time from the *Three Treatises*, Philoxenus explicitly draws the link between the presence of Christ through the Spirit in each baptized man and his indwelling in the common human nature. In this passage, it would appear that the Word's taking on of the common human nature perhaps acted in such a way that it rendered each man capable of receiving the presence of Christ through the Spirit by baptism :[3]

The flesh which is common is his, and not that of the righteous alone, for he was enfleshed from the nature of humanity by means of the virgin, and became a man. Thus, he also dwells in all of us, in anyone willing to be baptized and be born anew. 'You are temples of God and the Spirit of God dwells in you.' The Word dwells in us, therefore, by means of his Spirit. And our nature became a temple for him by means of his having been emptied out and made flesh from us.

the nature of man . . . and it was human nature (*kyānā 'nāshāyâ*) that he made worthy to be set as sons, and not just one man . . .', *Tres tract.*, pp. 241, 242. He was joined to 'what belongs to us', p. 57.

[1] No one is able to explain how the hypostasis of each man is poured out and renewed in baptism, or how the Word could create in the virgin 'simultaneously the whole nature of humanity', *Tres tract.*, p. 121. 'Now Christ, he who has performed the renewal of our nature in his hypostasis and in secret ineffably has united us (*rakebhan*) as limbs in his body, has wanted to give life to his limbs, not by gift but in deed by nature . . .', *Lettre à Patricius*, p. 830; see also p. 838.

[2] *Monks of Senoun*, pp. 3, 4.   [3] *Tres tract.*, pp. 168–9.

In Philoxenus' over-all view of human salvation it is baptism that plays the most crucial role, rather than a doctrine of the atonement expressed in terms of the redemptive value of Christ's death (though this is certainly an important concept to him). Through baptism we come to receive the presence of the Holy Spirit, which from this point is linked to our soul permanently, even when we sin.[1] Only from the time of baptism can we come to dwell in the realm of the Spirit.

Three Ways of Life

Christ came to bring us knowledge of God. But in Philoxenus' system, not all men are able to enjoy this knowledge. There are three ways of life, the life of the Old Man, which is directed entirely toward the world and its non-spiritual goals, the life of righteousness within the world, and the life of perfection. The first way is the way of death. The second two were given to us by Christ, the way of righteousness for the weak, and the way of perfection for the strong. Only in the last two is real knowledge of God available to us.

The life of the Old Man we talked about indirectly when we talked about Philoxenus's use of the concept of 'body'.[2] To live the life of the body, or the life of the old man, means to live tied to earthly values of money, family, and reputation. It entails being a slave to the physical drives of hunger, sex, and all the passions of anger, covetousness, and pride. It means seeing all of reality in terms of one level of the literal. To the man who lives like this, for all practical purposes, nothing exists outside what he can perceive with his five senses.[3]

The second type of life is the life of righteousness. It was instituted by Jesus for the weak, for those who were unable to move on to the life of perfection.[4] This is still life in the world, but it is directed toward God. This is the life of obedience to

[1] 'Memra de Philoxène de Mabboug sur l'inhabitation du Saint-Esprit', ed. A. Tanghe, Le Muséon, 1, 2 (1960), 39–71. The permanent presence in the soul of the Holy Spirit is the major topic of Philoxenus' essay.

[2] Philoxenus, in fact, calls the Old Man 'bodily man' a great deal of the time. See Tres tract., p. 132, for both.

[3] The Old Man is fallen man as he is bound to the world; he lives without faith, Hom. II, pp. 36–7. To him, the visible is reality, while what he cannot see does not exist, cf. Hom. IX, p. 296.

[4] Hom. VIII, pp. 223–4.

the law, and its culmination is perfect obedience and perfect righteousness defined in terms of the law.[1] In it a man may be justified, but not made perfect.[2] At best, Philoxenus regards it as the lowest form of Christian life in which a man may participate and still achieve salvation. It is, however a proper preparation for the real life of perfection.[3] It is unclear whether Philoxenus believed that those participating in the Christian life at this level should be baptized or not; presumably, he would not reserve baptism for those alone who leave the world for the monastic life.[4] It is also unclear to what extent Philoxenus thought that one leading the life of righteousness could participate in the life of the Spirit, how far he could go toward a higher knowledge of God. The higher levels of participation in the life of the Spirit are definitely closed. Nevertheless, this man is 'justified'.

The third way of life, the life of perfection, was given to mankind by the Word himself, in his own hypostasis. This is one of his chief works in the Incarnation. Through the assimilation of this revelation we are allowed to participate fully in the divine life, not just in fits and starts on certain occasions, as the

---

[1] 'The righteousness of the law may be thus described: a man should labour while he is in the world, whether to clothe the naked, or relieve the afflicted, or receive strangers into his house, or visit the sick . . .', Hom. VIII, p. 255. Gribomont objects to the translation of *zadîqûthâ nāmôsāythâ* as 'the righteousness of the law'; he finds in it a pleonastic construction, which he would prefer to translate something like 'the rectitude of the law', since, as he says, 'the righteousness of the law' calls to mind the Old Testament law, rather than the New Testament law which Philoxenus had in mind. 'Les Homélies de Philoxène de Mabboug et l'écho du Messalianisme,' *l'Orient syrien* (1957), 426.

[2] 'For I do not say that those who are in the world cannot be justified, but that it is not possible for them to arrive at perfection', Hom. VIII, p. 223.

[3] Philoxenus often describes our growth in the life of righteousness as similar to the growth of the embryo in the womb: When we arrive at our full embryonic growth within the womb of the world, and we have achieved the highest level of righteousness, then, by the embracing of poverty, we can go out of the world and be born again into a new order of existence, Homilies II, p. 29; IX, pp. 262–264, etc.

[4] Baptism is the entry into the spiritual way of life : Jesus' baptism was a model for us; his baptism was immediately followed by the going into the wilderness accompanied only by the Holy Spirit, Hom. IX, pp. 274–5 ; see also pp. 257–9 ; 262. In the case of Jesus, who is our model, his baptism came after he had perfectly fulfilled all the requirements of the life of righteousness, Hom. VIII, p. 251. On the other hand, Philoxenus sometimes distinguishes between baptism and the new birth which comes about as a result of leaving the world, *Lettre à Patricius*, pp. 840–2. Salvation itself is a result of baptism, *Tres tract.*, pp. 120–1, etc., and certainly not restricted to the perfect alone.

righteous men of the past did, but all the time.[1] The life of
perfection is the life of monasticism, or asceticism :[2] it is the life
a man takes up when he renounces the world and all it stands
for, the life of the Spirit, as opposed to the life of the body. At
its peak, it is the life of perfect freedom—from the passions,
from all earthly ties and attachments, and even freedom from
the law. The life of perfection is the life of perfect knowledge.[3]
At its height, it is a life totally dominated by love.[4] One enters
on the way of perfection, first through baptism, and second
through the leaving of the world. This is the second birth, in
which one is born as a baby, spiritually speaking, into the
'countries of the Spirit'.

Faith

Whether we would live the Christian life of righteousness or
the life of perfection, without faith we cannot even begin. Faith
is the first essential prerequisite to any Christian life. It is so
important that one might say that Philoxenus' doctrine of faith
stands at the very heart of his whole theological system.

Faith is first of all a kind of sixth sense,[5] an organ of perception by means of which we are able to experience the whole
realm of the Spirit which lies invisibly beyond or within the
natural realm. Philoxenus himself prefers to compare it most
often with the faculty of sight. As the healthy eye simply needs
to be open, to be facing the thing at which it is looking, and to
have adequate light in order to see, so does healthy faith
operate.[6] It does not have to do anything special to be able to
perceive the object of its perception, except to be in its presence.
Faith experiences directly, and accepts what it experiences
without reflection. Just as, for all practical purposes, the world
of sight does not exist for a blind man, for the man without

---

[1] *Lettre à Patricius*, pp. 828–30.

[2] Hom. VIII, pp. 222–5. Gribomont sees in this homily, in the distinction
between the life of the righteous and the life of the monk in the wilderness, a direct
link with the ideas present in the *Liber graduum*, 'Messalianisme', p. 426.

[3] Hom. IX, pp. 344–5 ; see also *Letter to the Monks of Senoun*, p. 71.

[4] Love is also the necessary prerequisite to spiritual knowledge, *Tres tract.*, p.
4 ; Hom. IX, p. 348.

[5] *Tres tract.*, pp. 192–3 ; Homilies II, p. 35 ; III, p. 68. 'When our Lord gave us
this blessing of perceiving him, he delivered to us first of all, faith, with which we
might perceive him. . .', Hom. II, p. 36. See also *Lettre à Patricius*, p. 814.

[6] Hom. IV, p. 77. See also *Lettre à Patricius*, pp. 808, 814, 816.

faith nothing exists beyond the natural world which he can take in with his five senses.[1]

To speak briefly, everything that is of the Spirit, and the whole world of spiritual beings, faith sees and faith perceives. If we do not take faith within our soul, we shall understand nothing outside what can be seen . . . The whole world of the Spirit is perceived by faith, and it seems as if that world could not exist if there were no faith. Observe, then, how great is the power of faith, for all the spiritual things that exist would, without it, be as if they did not exist, and not only living works and spiritual countries, but that Being which is, would be, if we did not have faith, as if he did not exist.

In one sense, faith is the opposite of the modes of learning that belong to the world.[2] The 'knowledge of the world' has as its objects all things that we would think of as falling under the category of natural knowledge—medicine, science, technology, astronomy, agriculture. All human knowledge which is based on study and speculation and reflective thinking is outside the realm of faith. Faith is not something that can be either learned or taught. In short, it is like a sense; either one has it or one does not have it. Through faith, one is able to look at the basic realities of the Christian faith and see that they are true.[3] Only by faith does one perceive the hypostasis of the Word in Jesus Christ.[4] Only by faith does baptism become more than water and oil. Without faith, the eucharist is nothing more than bread and wine.[5] Only by faith does one understand that God exists.[6]

---

[1] Hom. II, p. 35.

[2] 'Knowledge investigates by language (bmeltha) natural things, and faith seizes in silence those things that are above nature. . .', Tres tract., p. 105. The contrasted modes of knowing are sometimes called 'the wisdom of Christ' or 'the wisdom of God' and 'the wisdom of the world', Hom. IV, p. 83.

[3] Tres tract., pp. 107, 193; Hom. II, pp. 33–4; Monks of Senoun, pp. 9–10.

[4] Cf. the comparisons drawn from Exodus, particularly the burning bush, and the staff of Moses; see above, pp. 60 ff.

[5] 'Now to the soul that becomes a pure dwelling place for it, faith gives such power that it does not look upon things as they are, but as it wishes to see them. For behold! You bear upon your hands the live coal of the mysteries, which in their nature are common bread, but faith sees in them the body of the Only One', Homily III, p. 56. 'From him who is baptized, faith is required, and then he receives treasures from the waters; but without faith, everything is ordinary. . . Without faith, baptism is [only water] and without faith, the life-giving mysteries are bread and wine', Hom. III, p. 53. See also pp. 61–2.

[6] 'By faith we learn the fact that [the angels] exist, and not only they, but by faith we also accept that the being who exists by himself, their creator, exists', Homilies II, p. 34, III, pp. 66–7; Lettre à Patricius, pp. 820–2.

Also by faith one can read the Bible with its many apparent inconsistencies and accept it without questioning what is meant or how such things can be.[1] Like a sense, faith simply takes in data; it does not speculate or reflect on what it perceives.[2] Faith, in this sense, is passive, where knowledge, in terms of the world, is active.

Philoxenus speculates upon why God himself rejects knowledge as a way to salvation and accepts simplicity (which is always bound closely to faith)[3] instead. Human knowledge is also good, says Philoxenus; it too is one of the great gifts of God to the world.[4] God has put natural knowledge in all things and given us the tools to seek it out. The answers at which he arrives are plain; worldly knowledge is first of all directed toward the world, and not toward the realm of the Spirit.[5] But second, and more important, while our worldly knowledge comes to us purely as a result of our own efforts, faith comes to us only from God himself.[6] 'Simplicity [as it is bound up with faith], is, then, the gift of nature, and it belongs to the Creator, and nothing belonging to us is mixed up in it, that is to say, nothing of our will and nothing of our work.' Faith is not something we arrive at by any exercise of our own mental processes or will, nor something of which we can be proud.

Faith was originally implanted in our human nature to be

---

[1] *Tres tract.*, p. 111. *Lettre à Patricius*, pp. 814–16; Hom. II, pp. 33–4.

[2] 'Sure faith . . . makes sure that God is and does not inquire; it holds his words to be sure, and does not seek to investigate his nature; it listens to his words and does not judge his deeds and actions. For faith makes one believe God in everything he speaks, without demanding testimonies and proofs of the certainty of his word, the certain proof that it is God who speaks being sufficient for him', Hom. II, p. 26; see also *Lettre à Patricius*, p. 808.

[3] 'By simplicity is not to be understood the simplicity of the world, I mean, stupidity, but the singleness of one thought which is simple to hear and does not judge', Hom. IV, p. 74. Philoxenus explains the relationship between faith and simplicity by the metaphor of the eye: 'For the custom of faith which is mingled with simplicity is that it does not receive instruction by much persuasion, but as the sound and healthy eye does not receive the ray which is set to it by contrivances and inventions, but as soon as it is opened it looks with strength upon the light, because its natural vision is healthy, so also the eye of faith, which is set in the pupil of simplicity, as soon as it hears the voice of God, recognizes it, and there rises in it the light of his Word', Hom. IV, p. 77. It is unclear which is prior, faith or simplicity: Faith is said to be 'born of' simplicity, Hom. VI, p. 162; it precedes simplicity, however, in Hom. VII, pp. 193–4. In Hom. IV, p. 108, the combination of the two constitutes the first stage in the life of perfection.

[4] Hom. IV., pp. 106–7.

[5] *Tres tract.*, pp. 104–7. See also Hom. IV, pp. 82–3.   [6] Hom. IV, p. 108.

the means by which we would live the divine life and know God. Unfortunately, through the corruptions of life in civilization among other men, in most cases, it has been lost.[1] Corrupted faith is Error, a term which is almost hypostatized by Philoxenus, as are its two counterparts, Faith and Truth. Error is faith that has been directed toward the world, rather than at the spiritual realms.[2] Its product is Illusion, the false vision of the world. The Truth, which has at last restored to us the correct vision of all things, is Christ himself, who has in his own person defeated Error.[3]

Philoxenus directly links the corruption of Faith with the life of the town or city. John the Baptist, he says alone among men before the death of Christ, was found worthy to receive full spiritual knowledge; this was because he lived his whole life in the wilderness, away from all other men, so that his natural faculties of perception were not corrupted by any sort of participation in worldly life.[4] Any child, reared completely away from all men, would benefit in the same way.[5] His natural faculties for the perception of divine things would be preserved in the same state of purity that Adam had before the fall. For this reason, Jesus was able to pass on to John the Baptist the full and complete revelation of divine things which even his apostles did not receive until after Jesus' death, and the coming of the Holy Spirit.[6]

'Faith' is also sometimes the name Philoxenus gives to the

---

[1] Faith, however, has not been corrupted and lost in all men, and 'wherever natural faith is preserved in its original state, that man, with whom this faith is preserved is a sheep of the shepherds'. John the Baptist and Matthew, who got up and followed Jesus, leaving everything, both exhibited uncorrupted natural faith, Hom. IV, pp. 77–8; 85–6.

[2] Hom. II, pp. 36–7.

[3] *Tres tract.*, p. 48.

[4] In the *Thirteen Homilies* Philoxenus says of John the Baptist, 'that he should be born without the union of his parents was not fitting, for this belonged to Jesus God alone, but because he was about to receive visions and revelations which were above the old nature, he received the Holy Spirit while he was in the womb after he had been conceived by the union of his parents'. John lived in the natural innocency of Adam before the fall, and he was the only man to whom the full spiritual revelation of Christ was given 'before the dissolution of the curse, and the abrogation of sin'. While Philoxenus says that John was born of carnal union, it was only because it was not fitting for any man other than Christ to be born without it, Hom. IX, p. 302.

[5] Cf. Hom. IV, pp. 85–9.

[6] Hom. IX, p. 302.

object of the spiritual sense, as well as to the sense itself.[1] Conceived of in these terms, the spiritual reality present in the ordinary bread and wine of the Eucharist is called 'faith' : in this use of the word, 'faith' is closely related to one of the primary meanings of the word *theoria*.[2] The general theory of knowledge that lies behind the statement that faith is 'in' the thing to be perceived, includes the notion that what we see in our mind corresponds with a perception that is actually 'in' the thing we know which is external to the mind.

The particular items of the creed are also called 'the faith'. Whether we accept the faith as it is summed up in the credal statements of the church depends, however, not upon our own rational choice, but on whether God has found us worthy to receive them as true.[3] Even our ability to see the truth of the claims of the Christian faith is given by God. This must have been a particularly infuriating argument for Philoxenus' opponents : they disagreed with him because God had not found them worthy to receive the truth of his position ![4]

Faith, like God himself, is uncreated.[5] This is a very strong statement. Faith is, itself, the creative power of God at work in the world, through which the new creation is brought about. In a long poem, modelled on the passage in Proverbs, Philoxenus describes how, while it was through Wisdom that the first creation was brought about, God uses faith as his companion and blue print in the second creation.[6] Faith is the force through which all miracles are performed, the power by which anything is done that falls outside the realm of nature.[7] Holy men make use of it to work wonders; through it, they speak in the name of God himself.[8] Through faith, they call down fire from heaven, raise the dead, or talk to the dead as though they were alive.[9] Faith makes the impossible a reality.[10]

To the sight of the body the kingdom of heaven is far away, yet

[1] Hom. III, p. 54 : ' . . . faith is more deeply seated than knowledge. . . For with respect to created things, knowledge is external, but faith is within the thing itself.'
[2] See below, pp. 106 ff.
[3] 'If one is not worthy to have faith, one will not be attracted to believe', *Monks of Senoun*, p. 90.
[4] See also 'Letter to the Monks of Beth Gaugal', p. 153.
[5] Hom. II, p. 41.   [6] Hom. III, pp. 52–3.
[7] Hom. II, pp. 37 ff.   [8] Hom. II, pp. 45–6.
[9] Homilies II, pp. 45–6 ; III, pp. 57–8 ; *Monks of Senoun*, p. 2.
[10] Hom. II, pp. 39–42.

the eye of faith looks at it; these mansions in the house of the Father which are remote in terms of the body, faith has already lived in. That spiritual light shines in its country gloriously, and faith has already walked in it, and looked at it. The clothing of our glory is in heaven, but faith has already put it on . . . Our race and family and parents are in that country, and faith speaks with them, and is in conversation with them always . . . The powers of life and the ranks of light are in the country of life, and faith glories in them . . . Wherever the self-existent nature of God is, who is remote and far away from everything, he is near to faith . . . Faith is the tongue of God and faith is the command of the Creator. Faith commands, and like God, it is obeyed in everything; it calls and all creation responds. The power of God is the power of faith . . . Faith is the mistress of created things, and as a mistress who gives orders to her maids and is obeyed by them, in the same way, faith commands all creation, and it obeys her.

In christological terms, one might almost be tempted to think that the Incarnation itself is performed by the power of faith. Certainly, the union of divinity and humanity in the hypostasis of the Word is a miracle, and falls entirely outside the natural order. As such, it is quite outside the realm of knowledge, and is accessible only to faith, the sense by which we perceive the non-natural activities of God. Further, says Philoxenus, for all practical purposes, where there is no faith there is no incarnate Word; instead, there is only the man Jesus.[1] In the same way, all the divine realities which exist simultaneously in the realm of nature and in the realm of the Spirit depend, for their practical existence, upon the faith of the human being to whom they are of concern.[2] Because faith is not at all a human power within the control of the individual believer, but is the 'uncreated' power of God himself, Philoxenus' concept of faith cannot be accused of subjectivism. An individual does not 'actualize' the Incarnation for himself. It is God who makes the union of divinity and humanity real within the heart of his elect, so that the Word becomes visible to men.

The Holy Spirit

If faith is the first prerequisite to our knowledge of God, the second is the union of the Holy Spirit with the individual believer.

---

[1] See Hom. II, pp. 35 ff.   [2] Hom. III, pp. 54–6; 61–2, etc.

The Holy Spirit is united to each individual believer at baptism.[1] From this time on, the Holy Spirit remains with each baptized man as a permanent part of him, as the 'soul of his soul'.[2] Through 'putting on the Holy Spirit' a man is re-born and begins to become the New Man. Gradually, as he grows from the state of spiritual babyhood (since the New Man is born as a baby spiritually, just as the Old Man born into the natural world is born a baby) he recognizes the New Man he has become and is able to reap the benefits of his new life in the 'spiritual countries'.[3] The ultimate benefits are perfect love, perfect freedom, and union with God through the Spirit.[4] In all this, the Holy Spirit is conceived of as a kind of higher mind or 'spirit' united to the soul, which acts as an actual part of the man himself, as an internal source of illumination and spiritual guide.[5] The Holy Spirit is not the same as con-science, yet it is the presence of the Holy Spirit that brings about repentance,[6] and it is the internal operation of the Holy Spirit that then also provides for forgiveness following re-pentance.[7] The union of the soul of a man with the Holy

---

[1] Hom. IX, p. 299. See also *Lettre à Patricius*, p. 860.

[2] 'Memra de Philoxène de Mabboug sur l'inhabitation du Saint-Esprit', ed. A. Tanghe, *Le Muséon*, 73 (1960), 50–3. Philoxenus argues for the permanency of the gift of the Spirit partially on these grounds : no one is saved by his works, but only by faith ; even if pagans are baptized and do not immediately mend their conduct, their faith and their confession of right belief has brought them within the fold of salvation. See also cols. 16–17, *De uno e Sancta Trinitate*, where Philoxenus argues that evil deeds do not keep a person from salvation, but rather, that a person's faith provides pardon for his former deeds and is the means of his sal-vation, as was true of the woman who embraced the feet of Jesus and the good thief. Since the gift of the Spirit does not depend on the works of the individual, but rather on the gift of God, the presence of the Holy Spirit in the believer is also not dependent on his works, but rather on God's gift.

[3] Receiving the Holy Spirit through baptism does not mean that a man comes immediately into full union with God. Instead, 'we receive the Holy Spirit by baptism, that it may be to us *the first fruits* of the perfect intercourse which is about to come to us in the mysteries of the Spirit', Hom. IX, p. 299. See also Hom. II, p. 29, *Lettre à Patricius*, p. 834. This new birth and growth do not take place within the world, but follow the leaving the world, Hom. IX, pp. 262–4. Sometimes Philoxenus speaks of two baptisms, one by water and the Spirit, and the other by the going out of the world, *Lettre à Patricius*, pp. 840–2, etc. See also Gribomont, 'Les Homélies ascétiques de Philoxène et l'écho du Messalianisme', *l'Orient syrien* 2, p. 249.

[4] The perfect become spiritual beings while they live on earth, serving God above the law, and being free as God is, Hom. IX, pp. 350–2.

[5] See e.g. Hom. XII, pp. 546–7.

[6] 'Memra sur l'inhabitation du Saint-Esprit', pp. 49–50.   [7] Ibid.

Spirit also provides the opportunity to bring about the 'spirit-
ualization' of the body, which we remember meant the sub-
jugation of the body (conceived of as a wilful power of its own)
and the domination of the body by the soul.[1] Through union
of soul and Holy Spirit, the 'lust of the soul,' i.e. its drive
toward spiritual things and God, is strengthened to such a
degree that it can prevail over the 'lust of the body' toward the
world.[2] In the battle between soul and body, the Holy Spirit
provides supernatural help to the soul.[3] Without the Holy
Spirit, the soul cannot move into its proper realm or participate in the life of the angels, as it ought.

Where faith is conceived of as a sixth sense, roughly analogous to vision, the Holy Spirit as present in the individual
believer is compared to the light in the eye which makes vision
possible.[4] According to one ancient scientific theory explaining
sight, what makes vision possible within the natural realm is a
combination of the presence of light that is actually inherent
in the healthy eye itself with external light in the presence of
some natural, visible object. When the eye is open and healthy,
when there are objects to see, and when the external light of the

---

[1] Homilies XI, pp. 358, 407–8; XI, pp. 463–7, etc.

[2] This 'lust of the soul' is usually the same as the 'lust of the spirit', as in Hom.
XIII, 570–1 : 'The two lusts are placed one against the other, the lust of the body
against the lust of the spirit. . . The vessel of the one is the body, and that of the
other, the nature of the soul ; to the one clings confusion, to the other, order. . .
The lust of the body . . . makes a man weak and dazed . . . but the lust of the
spirit puts might and vigour into the soul. . . The lust of the body is a teacher of
folly . . . but the lust of the spirit not only makes men possess the mental knowledge of the world, but it also dips the understanding in the living motion of the
spirit and clothes a man in readiness and preparation for everything which is
good.' See also p. 577, and Hom. XII, pp. 505–6, etc. The 'lust of the soul' is
sometimes distinguished from the 'lust of the spirit', as in Hom. XII, p. 526.

[3] Hom. XII, '. . . as when a strong man takes hold of the hand of a child, he
takes away his weakness by the association of his own strength, so also the Holy
Spirit takes hold of the thoughts of the soul which is suspended like the hand of the
child, that it may be exalted to spiritual things, and that by its union with the
Spirit it may acquire lightness beyond its nature', p. 546.

[4] 'Natural light is in the pupil of the eye even when it is closed, but it does not
see by its means because the eyelid is stretched over it. But when it is opened, it
sees by the light that was in it when it is united to the external light. Thus also, the
Spirit lives in our soul as light in the pupil, and if carelessness spreads over it, like
the eyelid over the pupil of the eye, although it is in our soul, we do not see by its
means. But if we strip away the inattention from the surface of our mind, and we
direct the purity of our will toward the spiritual light in us, immediately light
meets light as the light of the sun, the natural light in the eye, and by joining the
two, vision receives light', 'Memra sur le Saint-Esprit', p. 51.

sun or a lamp meets the light that is actually in the eye itself, then vision takes place. The basic idea of the necessity of light both in the eye itself and external to the eye is that there must be a likeness between internal and external reality for there to be any internal experiences of the external reality: 'like is known by like', as they expressed it.[1] This basic idea underlies the whole Eastern understanding of the way we know various aspects of God: we only know God as forgiving if we are first forgiving; we do not experience God's love until we have created a counterpart in ourselves by loving.[2] The Holy Spirit as it dwells within the individual believer acts as the internal link belonging to the person himself, linking him with the external reality which is not only the whole of the spiritual realm but also God himself. Unless God himself were present within the soul of a man, even though he were totally surrounded by God and the spiritual realm, he would be unable to experience it or to know God. Without the Holy Spirit, a man is in the position of a blind man who, though he is in the presence of visible objects and sunlight and even has eyes, still cannot see because what must be present in the eye to make it function properly is simply not present. While our modern theory of optics differs from the ancient theory, we can still understand the analogy. One cannot know God unless somehow God himself is actually present within the knower as the actual means of knowing him.

What, then, is the relationship between the Holy Spirit and the free will of the man to whom the Holy Spirit is joined? Philoxenus explains that the soul which is brought to repentance and forgiveness by the indwelling Holy Spirit is quite free to sin or to close its eyes to the 'remembrance of God'.[3]

---

[1] de Halleux (p. 438) points out that faith also acts in this way.

[2] Hom. VI, pp. 171–3, especially p. 172: 'The man who forgives others is himself able to feel the pardon of God, and after this manner also is every good thing of God; until we have become doers of good, we cannot perceive that it is in God. For from the hearing has every man learned that God is good, but from knowledge of the soul alone it is that those who are good perceive his goodness. . .'

[3] The 'remembrance of God' is a frequent phrase in Philoxenus' writings: see Hom. VII, p. 199: the remembrance of God in the mind of the sinner produces fear; the 'remembrance of God' is 'true knowledge', keeping the light of God's judging presence shining into the evil in the soul, Homilies VI, p. 176; XII, pp. 525, 526, etc. For the relationship between the will and the Holy Spirit, see especially 'Memra sur le Saint-Esprit', pp. 49–50.

The Holy Spirit, though not driven out of the soul by any sin except apostasy,[1] does not make its presence felt without the consent of the soul.[2] Philoxenus visualizes an internal struggle between the Holy Spirit and Satan, both of whom stand aside while the soul itself decides to incline in one direction or the other; then, from the time that the soul makes its choice, Satan or the Holy Spirit supports and strengthens it in the direction it has chosen.[3]

On the other hand on a more fundamental level an individual man does not, himself, of his own free will, decide whether or not to be united with the Holy Spirit, even though he is free to be baptized or not to be baptized. Baptism itself is of no use and is totally ineffective unless it is received by *faith*. But faith is entirely outside human control; it is the pure gift of God, given to some, and presumably not to others. God himself gives the gift of the Spirit to whatever man he decides is worthy of it, in terms of his own judgment of worthiness. No man is given the Spirit for his good works[4]—Philoxenus is deeply convinced that all men are sinners—and the Spirit is in the same way not taken away from a man because he sins.[5]

Whether a man is really free in Philoxenus' system cannot be answered simply. In ancient terms 'freedom' was not so much 'freedom to sin': nobody thought that this was freedom. On the contrary, not to be free meant to be so bound up with one's own inner passions and mental illnesses that one was not free to pursue what one knew to be the Good. Freedom in these terms, then, did not so much spring from the will of a man as from the gift of God of his Spirit, who then worked with the individual man synergistically to remove and destroy all the passions, demons, ill-directed loves, and so forth, which bind a man to the world and prevent him from being able to direct his spiritual energy as he himself chooses to direct it. It is only

---

[1] 'Memra sur le Saint-Esprit', pp. 46–8; 51.
[2] Ibid., pp. 49–50.   [3] Ibid.
[4] Though he *is* given the Spirit in baptism, if he has faith.
[5] Philoxenus insists that all men remain sinners, even after baptism. Only the presence of the Holy Spirit enables a man to pray at the Eucharist. The Holy Spirit and baptism are so closely related in Philoxenus' thought, that he can insist that if the Holy Spirit were to leave a man when he sins, his baptism would also leave him, 'Memra sur le Saint-Esprit', pp. 46–7.

after this kind of freedom is acquired by the soul that a man is able to know and love God fully.

When Philoxenus is talking about putting on the Spirit, he is talking about putting on the Spirit of *Christ*: the gift of the Holy Spirit is the direct gift of Christ to his people; only by taking up of the Spirit are we united to Christ and achieve our salvation. Philoxenus makes this equation of the Holy Spirit and the spirit of Christ[1] to such an extent that he often makes such a statement as this :[2]

> I was baptized, therefore, in the name of Him who died for me, and I confess that he in whose name I was baptized died for me, and I believe that I have put on in baptism him in whose name and in whose death I was baptized, according to the words of Paul. For I have put on spiritually in the waters of baptism the spiritual being who became corporeal, and I confess that the living one who experienced death in the flesh is he who raises the dead and gives life ...

When Philoxenus explains the verse, 'the Word became flesh and dwelt in us', to him, the 'in us' means 'the Word dwelt in us by means of the Holy Spirit'.[3] Thus, the spiritual knowledge that we receive through the Spirit Philoxenus can call 'the knowledge of Christ'.[4]

The Law

The first two prerequisites of our knowledge of God are faith and the indwelling of the Holy Spirit. The third is our obedience to the law, the commandments of God.

Although both faith and the presence of the Holy Spirit in our hearts are quite out of human control—only God can bestow them—we are not simply passive recipients of divine knowledge. Though we do not receive either faith or the Holy Spirit originally as the result of our own goodness or sinlessness, we do make progress in the Christian life and our knowledge of God through the direct results of our own labours.[5] The law of God, the Old Testament law, and the commandments of Christ in the New Testament, were given to men for the purpose of healing the broken and distorted mental faculties

---

[1] See e.g. *Tres tract.*, pp. 168–9. See also Hom. IX, p. 299 ; *Monks of Senoun*, pp. 3, 4.

[2] 'Letter to Zeno', p. 172. See also *Lettre à Patricius*, p. 830.

[3] *Tres tract.*, pp. 168–9. See *Monks of Senoun*, pp. 3, 4.

[4] See especially Hom. IX, p. 289.   [5] See e.g. Hom. VII, pp. 210–11.

through which men are meant to experience God.[1] Though God decides ultimately on what state of knowledge a man may stand in, the man himself must prepare himself by obedience to the commandments.

Philoxenus does not always distinguish clearly between the law governing the life of men in the world and the new law given by Christ, governing the monastic life. Generally, however, it appears that for him, the law that governs life in the world is natural law.[2] He himself links the law and life in the natural realm: in fact, he uses it as one of his arguments to demonstrate that Jesus was fully human.[3] Since Jesus came under the law,[4] he had to belong to the realm of nature in his human

---

[1] *Lettre à Patricius*, pp. 806 8. The commandments of Christ are called 'His healthful commandments', Hom. IX, p. 275. Gribomont ('Les Homélies de Philoxène de Mabboug et l'écho du Messalianisme', *L'Orient syrien* (1957), 427) emphasizes rightly that the phrase which Budge translates as 'the righteousness of the law' and which Lemoine interprets in the same way in his French translation of the *Thirteen Homilies* (*Philoxène de Mabboug : Homélies, Sources chrétiennes*, vol. 44, p. 156) does not carry the connotation of the Old Testament law in its oppressive aspect: instead, the phrase suggests 'the evangelical righteousness promulgated for those who do not become monks'. While Philoxenus often distinguishes the law and the realm of nature on the one hand, from the realm of freedom and the Spirit on the other, there is a natural continuity between the Old Testament law and the new commandments of Christ. Philoxenus does, of course, make some strong statements about the necessity of being freed from the law, and the two different orders of existence—that under the law, in the world, and that above the law, outside the world. See e.g. Hom. IX, where the old law is 'laid under nature, because it is impossible that the law be above nature', p. 342 ; Hom. VIII, p. 251. For a typical statement relating all men to the law and the commandments of Christ, see e.g. Hom. VIII : 'The will of Christ ordained the law, that is, he required that all men should journey along the path of the angels . . . but because not every man was able to do this . . . he gave diverse commandments to every man that he might live thereby. . . To the path of the world, the life of righteousness is united, and to the path that is outside the world is attached perfection . . .', pp. 223–4. The life of perfection is also under law, 'the new commandment of love, which Christ gave', *Tres tract.*, pp. 3, 4.

[2] 'The words "what is hateful to yourself, do not do to your neighbour" were written in nature, and were inscribed by signs and by the act of creation of God upon the conscience of every man, that the law of every man might be within himself . . .', Hom. XIII, p. 607.

[3] *Tres tract.*, pp. 182–4.

[4] Hom. VIII, pp. 222–4. Philoxenus speaks ambiguously about Jesus' relationship to the law before baptism. On occasions, he says, before baptism Jesus was 'in bondage to the law' and 'subject to the law as a servant', while after baptism he was 'in freedom', Hom. IX, p. 258. At other times, the law under which Jesus laboured in the world is presented as a new revelation of Jesus, just as the commandments of the life in the wilderness are. Here, 'the law' means 'all the commandments of righteousness and loving kindness', Hom. IX, p. 341.

aspect, for all things belonging to the natural realm fall within the province of the law. The law is not the ritual law of Moses; it is the ten commandments, the law as governing decent and proper behaviour among all men. Joseph knew the law, says Philoxenus, when he was tempted by Potiphar's wife, even though Moses was not yet born.[1] The law as such is inherent in creation itself.

The law of Moses and the Evangelical law combined are not only to regulate our human conduct, but also for the purpose of healing all our injured mental faculties, which have been injured primarily by our involvement in the life of the world. Civilization has destroyed the original purity and simplicity of our nature and made us unable to relate to God on a level beyond the natural level. We have been given the law as a medicine for our illnesses;[2] without following its rigorous discipline we have no hope for recovery. If we follow the law from fear[3] through to its highest stages in the monastic life, we can hope for the complete recovery of our original faculties, and attain to perfect love, and hence, perfect knowledge.[4]

The 'natural' position a man must take with respect to God

[1] This law Philoxenus calls 'the philosophy of the doctrine of Christ . . .', *pîlosophûthâ dhamshîhâ*, Hom. XIII, p. 605.

[2] The Old Testament law did not serve the purpose of healing completely as the new commandments of Christ do, for the new commandments depend, for their efficacy on the previous renewal of our nature through the Incarnation or death of Christ, *Lettre à Patricius*, p. 806.

[3] See e.g. Hom. VII, pp. 198–9. Moses taught the people to fear God so that they might go on to love him. Philoxenus distinguishes between the two rules of life, but he also divides each way of life into three stages. Here there is only *one* stage ruled by fear: 'Jesus laid down in these commandments the restrictions for conduct of life: first, a man must depart from evil and restrain himself from the service of all abominable things; and second, he must do the things that are laid down under the fear of the law; and third, the service of good things which is above the fear of the law; and fourth, he must set out on the path of the discipleship of Christ, which is the perfect going forth from the world; fifth, he must bear labours and sufferings, with which we may make the old man sick; and sixth, we must bear the cross upon our shoulders, and we shall arrive at the fullness of the perfection of Christ. Now in these, two rules of life have been distinguished for us. . . Now the three degrees of righteousness are wrought in the world, and those who perform them are just and righteous; and are neither spiritual beings nor perfect; two degrees are set above the fear of the law, but the third is above both the power and the fear of the law, because it is fulfilled within the heart and inner mind, where the law can neither look nor see', Hom. IX, pp. 334–5.

[4] *Lettre à Patricius*, pp. 806–8: We are restored to purity, and freedom from the passions, from which we go on to love and knowledge. Cf. pp. 838–40; 792–4.

is that of fear.[1] As members of the natural world, all men owe
to God both obedience to the law and fear : they recognize his
majesty and power ; at the same time, they see their own un-
worthiness and sinfulness, and his inevitable judgement loom-
ing over them. The first step toward knowledge of God, then,
is to be in fear of him. This step, once one has the prerequisite
of faith,[2] at least, is within the control of our own will,[3] because
it is in the realm of nature. Fear is the natural attitude of a man
in the presence of God.

Nevertheless, men who live within the world do not need to
remain in a state of fear in the presence of God. When Philoxenus is talking purely about progress within the life of righteousness,[4] he explains that while men start out in fear, they
may progress, first, to a state best described in terms of the
hired labourer. Just as the lowest state of obedience is that of
fear, and one who fears may be thought of as a slave to the law,
in the second stage, one obeys not out of fear, but out of hope
of reward, i.e. heaven. Naturally enough, one who is in this
stage of progress is not yet free of the law.

Sometimes Philoxenus talks as though the highest stage of
obedience to the law within the world is that of love.[5] In this
stage one obeys God neither out of fear of him, nor from hope
of payment. One obeys primarily because one does not wish to
cause pain to God, as one does when one transgresses the commandments. Because one obeys the law out of love of God,
because one sincerely desires what God and the law desire, one
in this stage is 'free' of the law.[6] One has completely inter-
nalized the law : one clothes the naked, feeds the hungry, cares

---

[1] Hom. VII, pp. 210–11 : 'The capacity of loving God does not belong to our
mind, but the capacity with which we were created is to fear God...'

[2] Even so, however, fear also comes about somehow spontaneously : 'The true
fear of God is produced from true faith... And as [a man's] faith does not exist
by means of plans and devices, so also his fear does not consist of skill and knowledge, for as soon as a man believes that God is, he begins to receive the doctrine
of his commandments...', Hom. VI, p. 162.

[3] 'As the crops of the farmers of the world are in the hands of God, while the
ploughing and sowing belong to our own will, even so are the labours and service
of fear placed in our will ; but that we should arrive at the capacity for love, and
gather in the produce from it belongs to the will of God', Hom. VII, p. 210.

[4] Hom. VI, p. 187.

[5] We remember that there are two stages in the life of righteousness placed
above the fear of the law, Hom. IX, p. 334.

[6] Hom. VIII, pp. 245–6.

for the sick, and so forth, not because one ought, but because this is what one most wants to do. The law puts no restraint upon a man in this state.

But Philoxenus does not always talk as though love of God is possible within the life of righteousness, i.e. in the life in the world.[1] He talks just as often about love only as the highest point of progress in the monastic life. The life of righteousness, while it is all that many men can attain to, is nevertheless intended to be the first stage in the life of perfection, i.e. outside the world.[2] The whole of the life within the world, he says, is governed by the law and belongs to the realm of nature rather than to the realm of spiritual beings.[3] But the love of God is something entirely supernatural: no one loves God without his grace. To be in the world is always to be governed by one's passions, and by material things to a certain extent. Fear is the natural position which all men take with respect to God, and even those who have toiled for years in obedience to the monastic law of Christ, laid down in the New Testament, must cultivate an attitude of fear towards God. Whether one loves God depends upon whether one has made oneself worthy to love God. But no man loves God unless God himself puts his love in the man's heart after years of toil for him. Love is the gift of God, just as faith and the Holy Spirit are.[4] But the gift of love differs from these other two by the fact that it is preceded always by preparation on the part of the recipient. The only exception to the rule of the necessity for obedience to the commandments preceding the gift of the highest spiritual gifts was that of the apostles, who received them during the life of Christ.[5]

---

[1] It is unattainable in the world because it follows 'purity of soul' from which is born 'knowledge, the mirror of everything, and from which the understanding rises step by step to divine conversation', Hom. IX, pp. 348–9. The *Lettre à Patricius* also appears to place love right out of the reach of any man outside the monastic life; one must not even aspire to love, according to the letter, unless one's intellect is first made worthy of it by a long discipline in obedience to the commandments. Even then, love and *theoria* are linked in such a way that just as one does not forcibly seek revelations from God, one does not aspire to love him, pp. 832–4. See also *Tres tract.*, pp. 3–4.

[2] Hom. VIII, pp. 222–4, etc.   [3] See *Tres tract.*, p. 184.

[4] 'That we should arrive at the capacity for love, and gather in the produce from it belongs to the will of God', Hom. VII, pp. 210–11.

[5] See e.g. Hom. XI, pp. 484–8. The apostle Paul was given his spiritual revelation by Christ through grace, rather than as a result of his obedience; nevertheless, after his revelation, he spent the rest of his life trying to attain to impassibility and

Nevertheless, although they received the gifts of perfection in advance, they then had to render obedience to the law.[1]

In the life of righteousness, freedom from the law and love go together in this way : the law was given for the purpose of healing the wounded elements in our nature : perfect obedience brings about eventual perfect healing. As one is, therefore, healed, one has no more need of the law. For example, the monastic law regulating what, and how much, one eats serves the purpose of freeing oneself from the unreasonable demands of the body for food. Once one automatically eats only what one needs, the law serves no further purpose.[2] This monk is now free from the law, because he is free of greed. He may eat anything, even meat, with perfect indifference to what he eats. He is in the state of what the Greeks called *apatheia*. He may even move freely among women and sinners.[3] Furthermore, he no longer belongs to the life of nature, which is governed by law. He now belongs properly to the spiritual regions of the angels and the Holy Spirit, which, not being natural, are not governed by law.[4] At this highest stage, he is, of course, not governed by the basic requirements of Jesus' command to feed the hungry and clothe the naked, for he himself, living in absolute poverty, has nothing with which he may do good of this sort.[5]

This perfect freedom and perfect love precede perfect knowledge. It is only at this highest level of freedom and love that a man, entering the presence of God, may perfectly know him.

The Content and Character of Divine Knowledge

Knowledge of God must be contrasted with knowledge of the *world*.[6] The latter term refers to natural knowledge. We

thus love and *theoria* by means of obedience to the commandments. *Lettre à Patricius*, pp. 844–6.

[1] Hom. XI, pp. 484–8. The apostles alone received the Holy Spirit without first fulfilling the law, but after receiving it, they still performed acts of asceticism in order to set an example for us.

[2] Hom. XI, pp. 448–9.   [3] Hom. XI, pp. 482–3.

[4] His whole battle within the life of perfection has been to rise above the realm of nature ; see e.g. Hom. XI, pp. 430–1. 'The gift of the Spirit came to our support, in order that what nature was not able to do of itself it might complete by grace', Hom. XI, p. 425. See also especially *Lettre à Patricius*, p. 808.

[5] '. . . with what shall he clothe the naked and receive strangers, seeing that he himself is both a stranger and naked ?', Hom. VIII, p. 248.

[6] Hom. IV, p. 106, or 'knowledge of worldly affairs', *Tres tract.*, p. 104 ; the 'wisdom of the world', Hom. IV, p. 83.

learn of the world around us through our five senses, through our own reason, through language, by personal experience, which is the most trustworthy and desirable method of learning, and from hearsay, i.e. from teachers.[1] The legitimate subject matter of rational inquiry is the whole of the natural world—what we normally think of as the province of science. All questions having to do with how things are made, and from what, belong to the knowledge of the world. All questions of interest to ancient medicine, even the question of when it is that the soul is joined to the body; the whole field of astronomy, the determining of the position of the heavenly bodies and the prediction of the seasons; the fields of botany and zoology, all belong to it. It also includes the knowledge of all skills and crafts.[2] The world of natural knowledge is the world in which God has no 'natural' place.[3] Hence, the knowledge of the world is a knowledge that excludes God. In its proper place, knowledge of this sort is perfectly good; it was originally given by God himself to the human race, and it is a blessing in the areas it covers. God simply 'prefers' the knowledge that comes through faith, because, on the one hand, the higher knowledge has as its object God himself; on the other hand, 'natural knowledge' comes through human efforts, whereas knowledge of God is always given directly by God himself.[4]

Excluded from natural knowledge are all those things that belong instead to the realm of faith, or spiritual knowledge, for

[1] Through our five senses, Hom. II, pp. 36–7; through reason, see *Lettre à Patricius*, p. 810; through language, *Tres tract.*, p. 105; from teachers or hearsay, Homilies IV, p. 107; XI, pp. 470–1.

[2] See especially *Tres tract.*, pp. 104–6, in which Philoxenus appears to list every conceivable subject open to rational inquiry.

[3] Direct experience of God belongs to the realm of the Spirit or to the realm of miracle, and is quite outside of the natural realm. Philoxenus also believed that God is present within created things, and apprehensible by *theoria* (see pp. 106 ff., below).

[4] 'The wisdom of the world is the gift of God, and why then has he rejected it and chosen simplicity? It is well known that the reason is because our own labour is in it, and because it is collected from those who possess it, whose vision is directed to the world and not to God... Simplicity, then, is the gift of nature, and it belongs to the Creator, and nothing belonging to us is mingled with it, that is to say, nothing of our will and nothing of our work', Hom. IV, pp. 107–8. The primary functions of reason (together with language) to Philoxenus are (1) the praise of God and (2) the discovery of the inadequacy of the human mind in the face of the vastness not only of God himself, but also of all the things there are to know in the world. See e.g. *Tres tract.*, p. 73; Hom. II, p. 27.

example, all the miracles of the Bible,[1] all the articles of the creed,[2] speculation about the Incarnation or the Trinity,[3] on apparent inconsistencies in the Bible,[4] on the angels and the future life,[5] and in short, anything that lies outside the realm of nature, which, as we have said, is what we think of as the world which science investigates. There is nothing at all the matter with the 'knowledge of the world' until those who possess it, such as, according to Philoxenus, the Nestorians, try to apply its methods to problems in the realm that lies outside its legitimate territory.

We cannot 'know' the divine essence, Philoxenus says : God as he is in himself is outside the reach of human capabilities.[6] We cannot know any limitations on the divine essence because there are none. What we can 'know' are the divine activities that we experience and are able to name—mercy, love, judgement, and so forth.[7] But what we know of God is a reflection of what there is already existing in us. We do not know God as forgiving, to repeat an earlier example, until we are first forgiving ourselves, and therefore understand forgiveness.[8] This does not mean that God himself is not really all these things we say about him ; Philoxenus is emphatic that, even before we existed, God was still all these things.[9] It does mean that our conceptualization of God—that is, how we talk and think about him—is a product of the human mind, in so far as our

[1] *Tres tract.*, p. 118.   [2] *Tres tract.*, p. 107 ; Hom. II, p. 34.

[3] *Tres tract.*, pp. 113 ff. ; 173 ; 108.

[4] Or difficulties. *Tres tract.*, pp. 110–12 ; Hom. II, p. 34.

[5] *Tres tract.*, pp. 109 ff.

[6] *Tres tract.*, pp. 4, 5. We only know of it that he exists, pp. 5, 22 ; Hom. II, p. 34. Only God himself knows himself, *Tres tract.*, p. 6 ; not even the angels know him, p. 22. God, in fact, is the only being who is 'an exact knower' of all things that exist, p. 73.

[7] His names really spring from his *will* (though they 'hang from' his nature), because it is the seat of his activities, from which his names come : 'He has no names without actions ; his nature, however, is without actions. Names do not reach his nature, but with his actions his names began. Above action is the nature without names, and the essence without titles. But by deeds, on this side, the names come in, because the deeds are seen', *Tres tract.*, p. 8. Philoxenus talks about the difference between the way God exists in himself and the way in which we experience him : '. . . with respect to himself, he is one, but when he goes out to us, he became many ; with respect to himself, he is not divided ; with respect to us, he is divided by our names. . . . With respect to himself, he is without passion ; by Providence he receives the title of passions. With respect to himself, he has no image ; in visions to us, he is seen in images. . .', *Tres tract.*, p. 9.

[8] Hom. VI, p. 172.   [9] *Tres tract.*, p. 17.

thought is bound to language.[1] The realm of the divine names represents in Philoxenus' theology a kind of mixture of human rational thought and faith, for we do not conceptualize and 'name' God until we first perceive him through faith. Furthermore, while the divine nature is inaccessible to human rational thought, in at least one place, Philoxenus says that even the essence of God may be approached by faith.[2] The reason why God can be approached by faith, even in his most secret places, is undoubtedly to be explained by the fact that faith itself is uncreated and belongs to God.[3]

Philoxenus does not talk so much about the divine names, as about the 'spiritual countries' or *theoria*.[4] The 'spiritual countries' are the territory of the angels and the rest of the heavenly host, as well as being the realm of divine knowledge.[5] Philoxenus thinks of the angels as spiritual beings who inhabit the spiritual countries; they are made out of very thin material, rather than the heavy material we are made of.[6] They are composite, he says in some places, though in other places he implies that they are non-composite.[7] He ascribes to them all sorts of sense impressions, though because their bodies are not

[1] Ibid., p. 79. Nevertheless, 'the spiritual pens which define his names by their words learn from him what to call him. . .', *Tres tract.*, p. 12.

[2] 'Wherever the self-existent nature of God is, who is remote and far away from everything, he is near to faith . . .', Hom. II, p. 40.

[3] Hom. II, p. 41.

[4] In a revealing statement, Philoxenus says that the 'spiritual knowledge of Christ' is the same as what Paul calls 'the kingdom of heaven'. All spiritual knowledge is 'the knowledge of Christ', i.e. knowledge about Christ, and also, the knowledge that comes through Christ; see de Halleux, p. 442. *Lettre à Patricius*, p. 838, 'The true *theoria* of composite and non-composite natures, and that of the Holy Trinity itself . . . is only the manifestation of Christ, which he has shown to men. . .'. 'The true kingdom is the knowledge that does not err and does not doubt, but sees everything in its proper place distinctly, as well as things that are above nature, according to the capacity given to created beings . . .', Hom. XI, p. 470; see also especially Hom. IX, pp. 287–91.

[5] The 'spiritual countries' are also called the 'world of the Spirit', Hom. IX, p. 344; 'countries of the Spirit', Hom. V, p. 123; 'the knowledge of the Spirit' is put in parallel with 'the old world', Hom. IX, p. 295; 'the country of spiritual beings', Hom. V, pp. 124–5, etc.

[6] e.g. *Tres tract.*, p. 20.

[7] Simplicity, or unity, or being non-composite, or being 'in quiet' is a characteristic of spiritual beings, both God (Hom. IV, pp. 81–2; *Tres tract.*, p. 9, etc.) and men. It means, first, being without parts, having no characteristics that would make one able to distinguish between parts within the being. Men are not simple in this way, obviously. God is, and perhaps non-human spiritual beings are. Being non-composite, however, is also a psychological concept, referring to the

like ours, they receive the impressions differently.[1] They taste all over, see all over, hear all over, etc. Their work is the divine service of God. They carry out his orders, and offer him continual worship. These 'spiritual countries' are the proper homeland of human beings, and in fact, Jesus' 'coming into the world took place that he might deliver to the children of men the life and rule of spiritual beings. . .'.[2] In these spiritual countries all the promises of God will eventually be filled; here is the heavenly Jerusalem,[3] though we do not know how; here are the heavenly mansions and the thrones upon which we shall sit and share honour with Jesus and the apostles at the end of time.[4] Speculation on how these things can be, however, is not permitted to us :[5]

Do not meditate in yourself how this kingdom can be, and do not try to search out these spiritual countries in your imagination; do not take upon yourself the customary habit of the thoughts of the body when you hear about incorporeal countries, and do not fashion imaginary forms out of your heart . . . You were not called to search out the kingdom, neither its preparation nor its construction, but only to be an heir and a guest, that you might enjoy yourself out of the overflowing abundance of its spiritual delights.

As we have repeatedly seen when discussing the means of knowing or experiencing divine things, here, too, Philoxenus stresses that we were not 'called to search out the kingdom' in terms of rational or active thought, but 'only to be an heir and guest'.

We participate in the spiritual realm by means of *theoria*.[6] Like the term 'faith', *theoria* has at least two overlapping

ability of spiritual beings, including human spiritual beings, to focus the mind upon one thing alone and perceive and understand it without first going through a process of analysis. To be 'in quiet', or 'non-composite' is to be able to focus the mind inwardly so that it is not directed by the multiple images of the world of the senses or by the analytic world of science; instead, the mind is directed toward God : this is 'pure prayer'. See e.g. *Lettre à Patricius*, pp. 810, 812.

Philoxenus finds the contradiction in the Bible itself; since it is in the Bible, however, we accept it by faith, Hom. II, pp. 33–4.

[1] Ibid.

[2] Homilies VIII, p. 236; VII, pp. 192–3. In Hom. VI, p. 124, our realm is the *image* of the 'spiritual countries'.

[3] *Tres tract.*, p. 110.   [4] Hom. IX, pp. 326–7.   [5] Hom. II, p. 31.

[6] Philoxenus, for all practical purposes, does not use the word *theoria* in the *Thirteen Homilies*. He talks instead of 'spiritual knowledge', 'spiritual wisdom', 'the knowledge of Christ', or even the 'kingdom of heaven', 'the countries of the

meanings. First, *theoria* is in spiritual matters a kind of faculty, by means of which we perceive the hidden and the incomprehensible :[1] 'As for all those things that are incomprehensible to human knowledge, we receive them by faith, and we receive the knowledge about them which comes after the purification of the mind, by *theoria*. . .' In this passage, by faith we perceive that incomprehensible things exist; by their contemplation, we receive knowledge about them.

Second, the term *theoria*, like 'faith', can also refer to the *object* of perception, rather than to the faculty for receiving the perception. In this case, the *theoria* of a thing is its hidden reality or meaning, conceived of as being 'in' the thing.[2] This hidden reality, either in a natural or a spiritual thing, is not accessible to natural knowledge; it is, in fact, accessible only to a mind in a proper state of purification and preparation to receive it. (*Theoria* of natural things is not the same as natural knowledge of them.) Philoxenus speaks in these circumstances

Spirit', etc. It seems clear that he is using all these terms to describe aspects of the reality that *theoria* also describes, for the ascent to the highest levels of knowledge, and our constant participation in the realm of the Spirit or the realm of *theoria* is described similarly, both in the works where the word *theoria* is used, and where it is not used. Faith provides the first and most important starting-point; the need for purification by means of perfect obedience to the commandments is equally important in his major works; the need for love, arrived at only after obedience; the necessity of the Holy Spirit; the necessity for love as the immediate stage preceding knowledge; the emphasis on the 'spiritual' nature of revelation; the notion that the realm of the spirit or *theoria* is one in which the perfect may live continually, not just occasionally, as the righteous men of old—all these themes run through Philoxenus' works. The *Lettre à Patricius* however, expresses these ideas in more Evagrian terminology, perhaps because the recipient is thinking in Evagrian language. Neither the *Thirteen Homilies* nor the *Tres tract.* mention by name the different levels of *theoria*. For an account of the Evagrian elements in Philoxenus' terminology and thought, see I. Hausherr, 'Contemplation et sainteté: une remarquable mise au point par Philoxène de Mabboug', in *Revue d'ascétique et de mystique* (1933), 171–95. See also Guillaumont's *Les 'Kephalaia gnostica' d'Evagre le Pontique*, pp. 207–13. Guillaumont suggests very plausibly that Philoxenus is the translator and editor of one of our two recensions of Evagrius' *Gnostic Centuries*.

[1] *Lettre à Patricius*, p. 820. The difference between faith in this sense and *theoria* is this: faith is compared with vision; it takes in what it sees like a sense, and it 'believes' what it sees without questioning, although it does not always understand. *Theoria*, on the other hand, generally carries a connotation of *understanding*—e.g. one reads the Bible and believes what one reads, by faith. Understanding comes later after the healing of the soul by the purification of the intellect: this understanding is *theoria* or spiritual wisdom. See e.g. *Lettre à Patricius*, pp. 814–16. See also de Halleux, pp. 438–40.

[2] *Lettre à Patricius*, pp. 832–4.

of the *theoria* 'showing itself' to a man, rather than a man seeing it.[1] To try to *force* a revelation of *theoria* at a particular level of reality always ends in disaster and illusion. One must be in a state of preparation for it. Like faith, *theoria* is outside the realm of human will. When we talk about *theoria*, we are talking about knowledge and experience of things that come through a kind of passive receptivity, in which one experiences directly, rather than through any active inquiry.[2]

There are several different levels of *theoria*.[3] Set up in one way, Philoxenus lists three levels: *theoria* of the natural world, *theoria* of the spiritual world, and the *theoria* of the incomprehensible workings of God, including God's providence and future judgement. In another place, the three are, again, natural *theoria*, *theoria* of the spiritual realm, and the *theoria* of the Trinity. He also mentions the *theoria* that the mind has of itself, and the *theoria* of the Bible. Philoxenus does not appear to have a rigid picture of the structure of the levels of *theoria* through which one travels to the highest knowledge of God;[4] on the other hand, he regularly insists that one can only progress in the spiritual realm according to one's state of preparation and purification.[5] This implies movement up through an orderly structure.

[1] Ibid. See also pp. 774, 776, where Philoxenus explains the way one receives *theoria* from the natural world; the illustration holds true, however, for all levels of *theoria* or spiritual knowledge. Gaining the ability to see the *theoria* in a thing is like a child learning to read: at first, he learns only the letters; the *meaning* contained in the words belongs to another order of knowledge. The teacher's job is gradually to bring about the child's ability to see the meaning: 'when the child learns and grows in the means of the study of the symbols, he not only sees the schema of the symbols and their composition, he also receives the *theoria* of the knowledge that is in them'.

[2] See de Halleux, pp. 439–40.

[3] See I. Hausherr, 'Contemplation et sainteté', pp. 187–8.

[4] *Theoria* of all kinds comes to men through the Incarnation, see *Lettre à Patricius*, p. 838. The different levels are given in two different lists in the *Lettre à Patricius*: 'composite natures and non-composite natures, and that of the Holy Trinity, and that of his different dispensations', p. 838. In the other list he says, 'the contemplations of natures are three, two of created natures, rational and irrational, and spiritual and bodily, and one of the Holy Trinity. And outside this there exists another order of *theoria*, all that is incomprehensible has an intelligible contemplation, I mean, creation, the providence of God, and the judgement of all things, and the holy commandments which it is ordained for us to keep. Again, the mind has a *theoria* of itself, and all the words set down in Scripture which are not commandments, but are mysteries, as the holy and divine mysteries celebrated by us all have a spiritual and intellectual *theoria*', p. 820.

[5] *Lettre à Patricius*, p. 842.

The *theoria* of the natural realm, the lowest level, is the understanding of 'why all things are'; this *theoria* is more deeply seated than scientific knowledge, which only deals with *how* things exist, and what they are made of.[1]

The *theoria* of the spiritual realm is the understanding of the non-composite natures of the angels,[2] and perhaps all the mysteries of the church,[3] that is to say, the sacraments.

The *theoria* of the incomprehensible activities of God includes all the work of God in connection with his universe, as it falls outside the natural realm, including the workings of Providence.[4] It is not clear whether this contemplation involves an understanding of *why* God acts as he does, or how. On the one hand, it may possibly refer to the holy man's ability to see into the future. On the other hand, it may refer to the experience of seeing and being aware of God acting in all things, creating and healing, ordering and sustaining his new creation which is above nature.

Theoria of the self refers to the individual's ability to reflect upon himself, as he looks into his own heart and seeks to discover his own motives.[5]

Theoria of the scripture is the immediate understanding of it by faith and simplicity. It is the direct knowledge of the commandments of God which comes from reading the Bible in a consciously reflective and passive state without conscious *active* reflection upon what one reads.[6] Philoxenus does not use the term *theoria* to refer to the product of the allegorical method; in fact, he appears to be mistrustful of the allegorical method when the individual believer sits down to read the Bible.[7] The

[1] This *theoria* of composite natures is arrived at after the defeat of the passions; it is contained in everything in the world, 'for everything created by God was created by spiritual wisdom . . . and this was for the sake of teaching the intellect, which is not able to arrive at spiritual wisdom simply, when it does not have perceptible raw material', ibid., p. 774. This is also called the *theoria* of composite natures, p. 834.

[2] Ibid., p. 820. See Hom. II, pp. 32 ff.

[3] Philoxenus does not explicitly say where the *theoria* of the sacrament falls. It may well go in the next category.

[4] See fn. 4, p. 108 above.

[5] This is speculative. Philoxenus does not explain what he means by this; we are assuming with Hausherr that it is an Evagrian idea, 'Contemplation et sainteté', p. 174.

[6] *Lettre à Patricius*, pp. 812, 866.

[7] One must accept what one reads in the Bible, without questioning, ibid., p. 814.

theoria of the biblical law is our direct apprehension of what we are immediately required by God to do.[1] Philoxenus contrasts this way of reading the biblical commandments with the analytical approach in which one applies human reason to adjudge the appropriateness and consistency of the prescriptions. Conscious thought, as analysis, only sets up a barrier between the man and the Word of God in the text.[2] This does not mean that Philoxenus reads his Bible literally, however. Though he forbids the monks to whom he writes to apply analysis and conscious study to the text, Philoxenus was an ancient man influenced by the techniques of allegorical exegesis, just as Theodore of Mopsuestia was. He found Christ all over the Bible, even in the staff of Moses.

In every case Philoxenus stresses our immediate and direct experience of the thing that falls under *theoria*.[3] At every level of experience he sets out as axiomatic that what we experience directly ourselves is more valuable than what we can be taught by human language.[4] This principle tends to give Philoxenus' over-all theology an air verging on the anti-intellectual. He warns the monks against reading, on the grounds[5] that it unsettles the mind and scatters its powers, except in the case of a mind already directed toward the world. Reading even in the Bible is unsettling; one only reads to be able to go on to pure prayer.[6] In the same way, while a teacher or spiritual guide is assumed to be necessary, and one must learn the dogmas of the church, the role of the teacher has only a secondary importance.

The highest level of *theoria* is that of the Holy Trinity.[7] In the *Letter to Patricius*, Philoxenus says that *love* is the 'first *theoria* of the Trinity'.[8] He does not explain what he means by this, but it is surely safe to link the passages on the *theoria* of the Trinity with those in which he speaks of union or mixture with the

---

[1] Ibid., p. 866.   [2] Ibid., p. 814.   [3] See de Halleux, pp. 439–40.

[4] 'He whose life is established by means of the motions of flesh and blood is unable to become heir to this knowledge [which is the spiritual knowledge of Christ], and if it happens that he receive it by the tradition of words, he hears the words of others, and it is not the knowledge which itself has revealed itself in his soul, for this knowledge is beyond words, and beyond appellations and names . . .', Hom. XI, pp. 470–1.

[5] *Lettre à Patricius*, pp. 810–12.   [6] Ibid.

[7] Ibid., pp. 838, 820.   [8] Ibid., p. 828.

Trinity through our union with the Holy Spirit.[1] Whatever this *theoria* is, it is not describable in human language, for a characteristic of all spiritual *theoria*, i.e. *theoria* at its highest levels, is that it is indescribable by human language.[2]

This brings us to our final point. Philoxenus' *theoria* of the spiritual regions and of God himself is essentially mystical. God, though he used to speak directly to men, and perhaps even appear to them, no longer speaks in an audible voice or appears in any bodily form,[3] unless, he says, God in *theoria* sometimes appears to the perfect.[4] But even here, Philoxenus is extremely mistrustful of any experience resembling visions which may be described in language.[5] The Gnostic systems are to be mistrusted because they describe in words what is indescribable. He tells the story of Satan who appeared disguised first as an angel of light and then as Christ himself to one of the holy men. The holy man was rightfully mistrustful and refused to look, saying only that even if it *were* Jesus Christ himself, he did not seek to see him 'outside his place'.[6] One does not directly seek any vision of God. If one is especially blessed, God himself may bestow some revelation of himself, but one does not try to wring it out of him. All knowledge of God is the free gift of God alone.

Conclusion

Severus started with a Platonic epistemology in which there are different levels of being, but in which a single reality can extend through more than one level of being. His attempted solution to the christological problem is cast in terms of this epistemology.

Philoxenus starts with an epistemological distinction between

---

[1] Hom. XII, p. 524. In the same homily, however, Philoxenus also describes what appears to be the ultimate union of the soul and God as the 'mixture' of the soul in the ultimate and perfect beauty of Christ, pp. 504-7.

[2] *Lettre à Patricius*, pp. 848-50 ; Hom. IX, pp. 351, 352.

[3] Though God formerly spoke in bodily form to men, even to sinners, as he did to Adam, Cain, and Noah. After this early period, however, he spoke only to holy men, prophets, and the righteous, *Lettre à Patricius*, pp. 862-4.

[4] Ibid. Today he does not need to speak to men in a bodily fashion because he has bestowed upon men the gift of the Spirit, pp. 862, 864.

[5] Ibid., pp. 800, 852.

[6] Ibid., p. 800. See de Halleux, pp. 439-40.

natural knowledge and something that is also a kind of knowledge, but following different rules, a kind of supernatural
knowledge, called *theoria*, mediated through an epistemological
faculty called 'faith'. His christology builds on this epistemological distinction.

PART III

JACOB OF SARUG

WE have already found significant differences in the doctrines of knowledge of Severus and Philoxenus, and hence in their christologies. Our third figure, Jacob of Sarug, is quite different from either of the others. His theory of knowledge has distinct gnosticizing tendencies which produce a very different picture of Christ. Where Philoxenus to a certain extent, and Severus to a large extent, can be characterized as belonging to a school of thought deeply affected by Christian Platonism, Jacob's thought is far more mythological or symbolic, far closer to the thought world in which gnosticism flourished than to the world of Greek philosophy and theology.

The Mythological System

We begin our study of Jacob with a summary of his basic account of the reasons for, and the way in which, the Word entered the world to save mankind.

Mankind, in the person of the 'great Adam'[1] had originally been created by God the Father in the image of his Son as he was to appear on earth, that is, in the image of Jesus.[2] Adam and Eve had been set in Paradise to be the gardeners; this is the natural and proper territory of the human race.[3]

---

[1] Hom. 125 (iv.578), *Homiliae selectae Mar-Jacobi Sarugensis*, ed. P. Bedjan, Paris, 1905.

[2] 'Before the created things, the Father sealed the image of his Son,
And formed him and showed him how he would shine among earthly beings.
The Father looked at the image of his son and formed Adam . . .' (Hom. 125 (iv.591)).
See also Letter 11, *Jacobi Sarugensis: epistulae quotquot supersunt*, ed. G. Olinder, Louvain, 1937, CSCO, vol. 110, Scriptores Syri, T. 57, p. 42.

[3] As the good thief explains to the cherub who guards the way into Paradise, Hom. 177 (v.686):
'To you the chariot belongs, and to us the High One entrusted Paradise . . .
Return to your chariot that we may be returned to Eden . . .'
This Homily is one of the best sources for Jacob's gnosticizing mythology, as it deals with aspects of his system apart from those directly relating to Christ. In it,

Unfortunately, however, in 'the first contest' with the Great Dragon,[1] Adam was defeated, and a 'wall of enmity'[2] was established between God and the human race, 'the upper beings and the lower beings'.[3] Adam was driven out of the garden and set to live on earth, separated from Eden, not only by an enormous mountain of fire,[4] and a cherub with a sword, but also by a great and dangerous sea of fire which could not be crossed over.[5] At the same time, some of the cherubim and/or the Watchers came to live in Eden, usurping the place of Adam.[6]

From this time, earth was to be for Adam and his descendants both a natural home and a place of great danger, for in it, they would forget their true country.[7] At death, Adam and those coming after him entered 'the Dark City'[8] and fell entirely into the control of 'the keepers of the night',[9] and 'Adam the Great

Jacob describes the trip of the good thief from the cross to the gate of Eden, including his instruction and preparation by Christ on the cross, his crossing of the sea of fire, and his conversation with the cherub who does not wish to admit him to Eden.

[1] Jacob calls Satan an astonishing number of different names. To list a few: 'the Great Dragon' or 'the Dragon', Letters 11, p. 44, 19, p. 119; 'the Dragon who ate the dust of Adam', Hom. 40 (ii.196); 'the great serpent', ibid.; 'the Serpent', Letters 19, p. 103, 29, p. 233, Hom. 53, part 6 (ii.564); 'the Demon', Homilies 53, part 7 (ii.595), 94 (iii.641); 'the Wicked Ruler', Letter 12, p. 47, 'the Seizer of the Dark World', ibid.; 'the Master of the Contest', ibid.; 'the Tyrant', ibid.; 'Satan', Letter 12, p. 51, etc.; 'the Slanderer', Hom. 53, part 3 (ii.489); 'the Archon' or 'Ruler who guards the air', Homilies 56 (ii.642), 53, part 3 (ii.492); 'Beelzebub', Hom. 49 (ii.351); 'the Kidnapper', Letter 13, p. 54; 'the Rebel Archon', Letter 29, p. 104; 'the Cockatrice', Letter 19, p. 233; 'the Killer', Letter 29, p. 233.

[2] Letter 3, p. 17; 19, pp. 103, 119, etc.

[3] The 'upper beings' appear to include the angels as well as God. Cf. Homilies 94 (iii.644); 125 (iv.577), etc.

[4] Sometimes also called a 'wall' of flame, Hom. 177 (v.671, 674).

[5] Homilies 177 (v.671, 673); 53, part 4 (ii.507).

[6] Cf. Hom. 177 (v.686).

[7] Letter 9, p. 40. Speaking of the world, Jacob writes, 'See! it is sweet to us, beloved to us, beautiful to us, true to us, while it deceives us. See! it excites us, overthrowing us who would go out of it, and we are bound by love of it'.

[8] Sheol also has many names which, as in the case of Satan, reveal something about its character. To list a few, 'the Dark City', Letter 13, p. 53; 'the City of the Dead', Letter 30, p. 235, 'the city of heroes', Letter 16, p. 81; 'the Dark World', Letter 19, p. 108; 23, p. 202.

[9] 'The Keepers of the Night', Hom. 53, part 6 (ii.564). These demons in charge of hell are also called by a variety of names. The names of the demons and the various names for Sheol suggest that there was some link between the city of the dead, guarded by the 'keepers of the night' and the city and its hostile watchmen in the Song of Songs, in Jacob's thought.

Image'[1] lay corrupting in hell, separated from the 'Hidden Father'[2] by a seemingly insurmountable barrier.

Meanwhile, the human race grew up, progressively falling into the control of the 'Evil Archon', 'the Ruler of the Air'. Through him, idolatry sprang up, darkening human understanding, and bringing about more and more alienation between God and men. Error held sway. Finally, God sent the Truth to combat error, first in the Law on Sinai, and then through the prophets.[3] From the time of Moses to the time of Christ, the history of humanity is the history of the elemental struggle between Truth and Error, Light and Darkness.[4] During this period, the world was under the control of Satan— sealed with his seal.[5]

At last, God the Father, the Great King, in his mercy decided that he could no longer allow his image to remain corrupting in Sheol in the power of the Great Dragon.[6] He made a decision, and sent his son, 'the Son of the Kingdom',[7] to creation, 'the city of the Father'.[8] The Son was sent by an undiscoverable and untreadable path, and he entered the world through 'the gate without opening'[9] and came to dwell in the womb of the virgin 'in the schema of a man'[10] so that Mary became a 'sealed letter full of secrets'.[11] Within the womb,

---

[1] Hom. 53, part 7 (ii.596).   [2] Hom. 125 (iv.578).

[3] Letter 19, pp. 105, 106.   [4] Ibid.

[5] Letter 12, p. 52, 'He suffered on their behalf in order that the alien seal be removed from them, and the seal of their true Lord fall upon them'. See also Letter 19, p. 104, referring to a seal of freedom, which God originally placed on the world. The Word in the Incarnation 'received the seal of the house of Abraham', Hom. 53, part 1 (ii.455).

[6] 'The image of his Father which in the midst of the depth had fallen and perished,
    He sought to carry from the destruction in which it had grown old' Hom. 94 (iii.642).
   See also Homilies 53, part 7 (ii.594); 40 (ii.195).

[7] 'The Son of the Kingdom came down in the road of the King, his Father . . .', Hom. 53, part 1 (ii.455). The place from which the Son is sent is frequently called 'the House of the Father', ibid., p. 457; Hom. 53, part 7, p. 589; Letter 12, p. 48.

[8] 'The Only One entered creation, the City of his Father', Hom. 53, part 6 (ii.564).

[9] 'He came to the world by an untreadable path, by a road without clearing, by a crossing without a bridge, by a gate without opening', Letter 13, p. 53.

[10] Hom. 53, part 1 (ii.457), or 'the schema of the servants', Hom. 94 (ii.591).

[11] Homilies 39 (ii.181); 94 (iii.591); Letter 36, p. 262. This notion of the secret letter sent from heaven to men appears in the Syrian Christian gnostic tradition, in Ode 23 of the Odes of Solomon and in 'The Hymn of the Soul'.

the Word put on his humanity, called 'the image of the servant',[1] to be first a disguise so that the archons and keepers of
the Dark City should not recognize him ;[2] second, he put it on
as 'equipment' for his journey into Hell ;[3] and third, to make
himself visible to *men* as the 'Hidden One' who was later to
'come to revelation'.[4]

From his birth, the Word carefully maintained his disguise.
By almost none[5] was he recognized, for 'to sight he was a man,
though by nature he was God'.[6] While a few of the simple
recognized him by faith,[7] the rulers and archons did not. In
the wilderness, Satan held a contest with him to learn his
identity, but he did not learn it, because, while Christ was able,
'he was not willing' to turn stones into bread.[8] Thus Satan
assumed he was only a man.

During his ministry, to those able to see and understand,
that is, to the simple, Jesus demonstrated his divinity by the
miracles he performed, and by his teaching, mankind was
attracted to the Father.[9]

Finally, at the crucifixion, Jesus for the last time fooled the
earthly authorities into assuming that they were crucifying
a mere man.[10] Not until his death was it at last revealed to
the Evil Archon and the large bulk of humanity that they
had crucified the Word, 'the Lord of Glory' who holds in
being all created things.[11] At this time, it was 'the dumb

[1] Letter 16, p. 77, etc.   [2] Letter 13, p. 55, Hom. 94 (iii.591).
[3] Letter 13, p. 54; 33, p. 249.
[4] Letter 3, p. 18. Christ is frequently called 'the Hidden One who has come to revelation'.
[5] Only the good thief openly acknowledged him and did not remain silent at the crucifixion, Hom. 177 (v.677).   [6] Letter 13, p. 53.
[7] The 'wise', those who reason about his identity and the manner of his entry into the world, will never recognize him: only those who exercise 'faith', i.e. the 'simple', recognize him. Letter 13, pp. 49–51; Sermon 39 (ii.175); Homilies 40 (ii.190–1); 94 (iii.622–6); 125 (iv.567–8).
[8] Letter 12, p. 47.
[9] Ibid.: 'He began to act and teach, that by his acting, it would be known whose Son he is, and by his teaching, humanity would be attracted to the house of his Father.'
[10] Herod wished to question Jesus because he had heard of his miracles, but Jesus refused to answer, because if Herod knew who he was, he would not have allowed the crucifixion to take place. Hom. 53, part 5 (ii.529).
[11] Jacob vividly describes the way in which creation hangs in the void, suspended only by the power of God in the same way that a rock thrown by a human hand is suspended only by the power of the one who throws it, while there is nothing above it, and nothing below it, Hom. 125 (iv.552–3).

natures'[1] who revealed his identity by the seeming threat of their extinction—the sun by darkening, the earth by quaking, and so forth.

At death, Christ had dived into hell like a brave swimmer to retrieve 'the pearl, precious to the waters',[2] the Image of the Father. This he did by allowing Death to swallow him, Death assuming that he was wholesome food, rather than the Lord of Life.[3] But Christ acted as poison within Death, and Death choked on him and died.[4] Christ then, after remaining three days in Sheol, released the Great Adam and then all the prisoners, and returned Adam to Paradise.[5] The work of Christ being over, he returned once again to the country of his Father.

The human race is now left in a new condition. The great wall of enmity separating the upper and lower beings from each other has been broken down; God and men are no longer angry with each other.[6] The 'Great Dragon who ate the dust

---

[1] 'Dumb natures were witnesses and preachers to him,
    And from them, the earth learned who he was in the
        time of his death . . .' (Hom. 53, part 7 (ii.591)).
The theme of the 'dumb natures' is extremely common. Letters 2, p. 14; 12, p. 49; 16, p. 77, etc.

[2] The pearl imagery reminds us of the 'pearl of great price', and of the pearl in the Syriac 'Hymn of the Soul'. Jacob uses it to stand, not only for the image of God perishing in Sheol, Homilies 53, part 8 (ii.599), 94 (iii.642), Letter 19, p. 110, but also for the Word made flesh, Letter 16, pp. 75–7, and the faith, Letter 16, p. 74.

[3] Hom. 94 (iii.615).

[4] See e.g. Hom. 94 (iii.615):
    'He was embodied, and he set himself before death;
    All his life was hidden in him, while he was dead.
    And when death had swallowed up the dead one who was
        full of life . . .
    As ordinary food, he ate him, when he ate him,
    And life bubbled up from him and choked him when
        he swallowed him.
    When he ate him, he thought that he was a man,
    And when he swallowed him, he knew he tasted the fact
        that he was God.'
See also Letter 21, p. 141.

[5] The release of the prisoners: Hom. 94 (iii.616); Letter 41, p. 295; 23, p. 178, etc. The release of Adam: Homilies 94 (iii.641, 645); 53, part 7 (ii.596), 40 (ii.194–5), etc.

[6] It is not simply God who is angry with men: men are also angry with God and in need of reconciliation. See e.g. Hom. 41 (ii.205) for a typical statement: 'He became the mediator, and he gave satisfaction to the sides who were angry . . .'; Homilies 94 (iii.644); 125 (iv.578); 53, part 5 (ii.530), etc.

of Adam'[1] has been killed, and men are now able to return to
Eden, rather than to Sheol at death. They are, furthermore,
now equipped for the journey across the sea of fire which
separates this world from that : they have been given the proper
garments, a key to the gate, and a 'passport of life'.[2] The faintly
hostile angels have been driven out of Eden[3] and sent back to
their throne-chariot,[4] and order—peace[5]—has been established. The world is no longer 'sealed with the alien seal' of
Satan, but with the seal of the Son. Finally, Christ has left a
path by means of which men are able to ascend to the Father,[6]
and in the mind of the perfect, the Word may now dwell as he
dwelt in the womb of Mary.[7]

[1] Hom. 40 (ii.196).
[2] Jesus addresses the good thief on the cross:
> 'I will clothe you in a robe of light in the high bridal bed.
> A key of light take for yourself, and go to the garden of
>   good things . . .
> Ride upon the fire and go down in the way of the flame;
> Tread on the gulf of fire and do not be terrified . . .
> And if the ranks of fire meet you, you will not be
>   terrified' (Hom. 177 (v.669)).

The garment, the key, and the passport are all assumed by baptism:
> 'The thief washed in the baptism mixed with blood,
> And he put on from it, the outer garment of light, and
>   going, went out.
> He carried for himself the key to the lock of fire, the
>   Word of the Son,
> And in his right hand, the passport which he had written
>   with the blood of life.
> By baptism, the power of the Son was assumed,
> That when he would pass over the sea of fire, he would
>   not be singed' (Ibid., p. 670).

The lock and key are mentioned again on pp. 674, 676, 680, 685, the garments
of baptism woven 'out of his living blood', p. 680.

[3] The 'watchers' do not wish to let the good thief into Eden, in spite of his special
equipment for a safe entry: the cherub even tries to trick him into descending to
hell to help Jesus. There is also a glimpse of the dangers involved in the entry into
'Paradise' in early Jewish tradition, in the legends surrounding the entry into Paradise of Akibha, Ben Azai, Ben Zoma, and Aher; see e.g. G. Scholem, *Jewish Gnosticism, Merkabah Mysticism, and Talmudic Tradition*, Chapter III, pp. 14 ff.

[4] Hom. 177 (v.686, 687). See also Hom. 125 (iv.602), etc.

[5] This notion of 'peace', *shaynâ*, settling on creation in some cosmic sense, is very
common in Jacob. See e.g. Homilies 41 (ii.205–6); 94 (iii.620,644); 125 (iv.577,578),
etc.

[6] Letter 7, p. 34: 'He prepared the path of life for human beings, that they
might go to his glorious Father.'

[7] 'Open the gate of your mind (*hawnâ*) to the miracle, that he may dwell in you
when you are perfect as he dwelt in the womb of the virgin when she was sealed
up', Letter 3, p. 20.

The Absolute Oneness of Christ

At the root of Jacob's christology is the uncompromising insistence on the absolute oneness of Jesus, which he sometimes expressed in traditional monophysite language. Jesus is[1]

> one Son, one number, one hypostasis, one nature,
> one God who was enfleshed from the holy virgin,
> one of the Trinity who was seen in the flesh . . .

In Jesus there is one nature and hypostasis, without division.[2] Jesus is not a union of a complete man and God;[3] he is God who without change has become man.[4] In him there is only one will[5]—the will of God—and one operation[6]—the operation of the Word made flesh. In him there are no separate proprieties,[7] belonging to the humanity and the divinity; all things belong to the Word. In him, there are no 'names' or 'parts', 'ranks' or 'numbers'.[8]

---

[1] Letter 3, p. 19.

[2] '[I anathematize those] who, after the union, divide (*mphalgîn*) and name and count in the one Christ natures and their proprieties, and their individualities, and their operations', Letter 16, p. 70. For the prohibition against 'dividing' see also Letters, 16, pp. 65, 72; 33, pp. 247, 248; 14, pp. 60, 61; 6, p. 31. The root in all these cases is *plg*.

[3] As Jacob says the Nestorians believe, Letters 14, p. 61; 21, pp. 137, 139; 19, p. 118.

[4] This theme of the divine 'coming into being without change' to de Halleux characterizes Philoxenus' theology. See *Philoxène*, pp. 319 ff. For this idea in Jacob, see e.g. Letter 6, p. 32: 'One is the true son in whom are neither hypostases nor numbers arranged. . . Not that the Word destroyed his nature, nor was he changed from the properness of his being . . . But while remaining in that first condition which he naturally possessed, he descended to the extremity hypostatically and willingly, while he did not destroy that first state, for he was God and became a man, but he remained in what he was, [namely], God'; Letters 13, p. 56; 36, p. 264.

[5] Cf. Hom. 53, part 3 (ii.502). Jacob does not even paint Jesus as having two 'wills' as Philoxenus and Severus do, as though Jesus contained within him two warring drives, that of the Word, and that of the human element which strives toward self-preservation and life in the world.

[6] Letter 16, p. 71. The Nestorians know 'in Immanuel two hypostases, one the receiver of passions, and one the worker of powerful things; the high things were given to the one, and the lowly things to the other'. See also Letters 21, pp. 139, 140; 12, p. 50, etc.

[7] In Letter 14, p. 61, he condemns those who 'arrange natures after the union, and speak about natures and their proprieties and individualities'; Letters 16, pp. 65, 70; 19, p. 115.

[8] It was important to Severus that there are no 'names': a self-subsistent

Jesus is one nature and one hypostasis. Jacob uses the word 'nature' to refer to a concrete being, an entity which can be counted.[1] The sun, the earth, and the various natural elements which, by their upheaval, announced the identity of Christ at the time of the crucifixion, are customarily called 'the natures'.[2] This use of the word 'nature' is by far the most frequent one in Jacob's writings. In a christological context, Jacob also customarily calls the divine element in Christ, which did not die at the crucifixion, his 'nature.'[3] As we shall see, Jacob usually thought in terms of the Word as the real 'being' or identity in Christ, to which one would assign the term 'nature', while the humanity had a kind of secondary existence to which the term would not be assigned.

When Jacob uses the word 'hypostasis' in a technical sense, it appears to be a synonym for 'nature'.[4]

One nature and hypostasis, then, means 'one being', 'one actual identity'. Jacob explicitly rejects the 'two nature' christology of those whom he considers to be Nestorians because two natures has to mean two basic 'beings' in Christ, the man

hypostasis was characterized by the fact that it could be counted as an entity (i.e. it had a number) and that it had a name of its own, such as 'Jesus' or 'the man' or 'the Incarnate Word'. That there are no ranks means that the Word cannot be divided into a lowly and a glorious part. There are no names: Letters 16, p. 65; 14, p. 61. There are no parts: Letters 6, p. 31; 33, p. 247; no ranks or degrees: Letters 19, p. 118; 21, pp. 139, 140; 33, p. 247; no numbers: Letters 16, p. 65; 14, p. 61; 6, pp. 31, 32; 19, p. 118; 21, pp, 139, 140.

While Jacob emphasizes that in Christ there is to be complete unity, without number, distinction, or rank, he does occasionally talk as though he is using either Chalcedonian language or at least the language of Severus of Antioch. In letter 21 he seems to suggest that there may be two natures in Christ, but they must not be separate. Nestorius' error was that he and his followers counted 'ranks and numbers and numbers of natures. . . And they teach that the propriety of the natures are preserved and their distinction known. . . [But] there are no ranks or numbers or distinctions of natures' (p. 139, Letter 21). Here there is no explicit rejection of two natures, only the 'distinction of natures'. Nevertheless, Jacob goes on to use the above mentioned phrase: 'He died in truth for the sake of human beings, *while the life of his nature was preserved*'. He basically thinks in terms of the one divine nature of Christ.

[1] See J. Lebon, *La Christologie du monophysisme syrien*, p. 461, who says that monophysites in general had a tendency to use 'nature' in this concrete sense.

[2] Letters 2, p. 14; 12, p. 49; 13, p. 54.

[3] Letter 13, p. 56. Christ is 'one of the Trinity who was enfleshed . . . the pitier of the dead, who became one of the dead, while the life of his nature was preserved in him'; Letters 21, p. 141; 36, p. 264.

[4] See T. Jansma, 'The Credo of Jacob of Serugh', p. 26. The whole article contains an excellent summary of the Alexandrine elements in Jacob's thought.

Jesus and the Word,[1] and along with these two basic beings, two 'numbers' and two 'ranks', not to mention two operations. To confess two natures means to assign the 'small things' to the man and the great things to God. To confess two natures means to hold to such a view of the union that one must say that the Word assumed the man who is worshipped with him, as a king assumes the purple which is worshipped with him.[2]

Within this context, Jacob affirms the doctrine of the hypostatic union—that the body of the Word came to him through his second birth,[3] the birth from the virgin. It was his body, belonging to him as any man's body belongs to him,[4] and it did not belong to him as the purple belongs to the king.[5] The Word did not *assume* a man; he *became* a man.[6]

While the Word made flesh is one, and not two, Jacob insists that he is complete in his humanity and in his divinity:[7]

> He is the one who is from the Father and from us.
> . . . He is God with his Father, and the same one,
> with us, the son of man.

Jesus' real human body belonged to him as his own. He was really born, in a miraculous fashion from a virgin, and really suffered physical pain on the cross and died.[8] He bought food and ate when he was hungry and slept when it was appropriate to sleep.[9] Jacob will even cautiously admit that Jesus prayed,

---

[1] See e.g. Letters 14, p. 61; 27, pp. 137, 139; 33, p. 249. The Nestorians worship a quaternity: Letter 31, pp. 238–41.

[2] Letter 19, pp. 123–7.

[3] The theme of the two births is also frequent in Jacob's writings: Letters 2, p. 13; 3, p. 18; 6, pp. 32, 33; 13, p. 53; 14, p. 60: 29, p. 233, etc.

[4] Cf. Letter 19, p. 118. The humanity and divinity both belonged to his hypostasis: 'His body is not known outside him in number, and his divinity is not foreign to his embodiment . . . because hypostatically, he took the image of the servant, and not as a possession.'

[5] Letter 19, pp. 123–7.

[6] 'The humanity of our Lord did not come into being, but it was our Lord who became a man', Letter 6, p. 31.

[7] Letter 3, p. 19. For other similar statements, see Homilies 53, part 3 (ii.496); 49 (ii.348); 94 (iii.619). For the statement that he is complete both in his humanity and in his divinity, Letters 13, p. 56; 17, p. 86, etc.

[8] But this pain did not belong to him, in so far as his nature was unembodied: it belongs to him only as part of the economy, Letter 33, p. 249. And he was able to die, only because he was willing: Homilies 49 (ii.354); 40 (ii.190); 94 (iii.597); 53, part 4 (ii.505), etc.

[9] Homilies 40 (ii.187); 94 (iii.624).

though he points out that he had no need of it, since as God he is the one who receives prayers.[1]

On the other hand, Jacob only rarely makes any sort of reference to the human mind or soul of Jesus, and does not even have a vestigial notion of a kind of second will in Jesus which represents a non-divine drive toward the world, such as we find in Severus' and Philoxenus' thought. While Jesus suffers physical pain, it does not appear that he ever suffered mental anguish. It is not surprising to discover that Jesus is absolutely omniscient.[2]

While Jacob frequently affirms that Jesus shared all things with us, with the exception of sin,[3] he says, at least once, that Jesus shared everything except sin and *'corruption'*.[4] If the text can be trusted at this point, then, we can say that Jacob was probably a monophysite of the aphthartodocetist persuasion.

Jacob is an unambiguous monophysite within the context of the christological controversy: in his letters[5] he unambiguously emphasizes the complete unity of Christ and the one nature and hypostasis of the 'one God who was made flesh from the holy virgin'. However, of the three monophysites we have studied in detail in this work, he is the only one who is almost totally un-interested in the human element in Jesus.

Schema

One of the keys to the understanding of Jacob's christology is to be found in his use of the concept of schema. Jesus is God by nature, but in the image and schema of a man. In a typical statement Jacob says of the Word,[6]

---

[1] Hom. 53, part 3 (ii.496–8, 500–2).

[2] Hom. 53, part 2 (ii.470, 471). Jacob is concerned that Jesus should have chosen as his apostle a man who would ultimately betray him. He explains that it is analo-gous to the fact that God knew before he created them that both Adam and 'the ruler who guards the air' who was also 'a chosen apostle' should turn away from him, Hom. 53, part 3 (ii.489–92).

[3] Hom. 94 (iii.619); Letter 19, p. 118, etc.

[4] 'Christ is one, who is like his Father in everything, except for the embodiment and passions, and he is like us, in everything except for sin and corruption (*ḥbhālā*)', Letter 19, p. 118.

[5] Jacob rarely uses the language of the christological controversy in his homilies, perhaps because he had mixed audiences of Chalcedonians and monophysites, or just as likely, because it did not appear to him to be suitable material in sermons.

[6] Hom. 94 (iii.591). 'In the schema of servants', *b'ēskîm 'abhdê*. For other similar statements, see Hom. 53, part 1 (ii.457); Letter 21, p. 139.

He took the image of the servant from the womb of the
    blessed one,
And in the schema of servants he visited the servants
    and freed them.
He dwelt in the daughter of a man, and became the son
    of man by these things . . .

Primarily, in Jacob's language, a schema is a mode or manner
of existence. The word 'schema' can be applied to the way in
which a monk lives[1]—life in the city, life in a monastery, and
the life of the solitary are three different schemata. It can also
be applied to the states in which Mary found herself after the
birth of Jesus—the states of being a virgin and being a mother.[2]
The heavenly beings each praise God according to their
schemata,[3] that is, in their own way which is fitting for them,
the seraphim as seraphim, the cherubim as cherubim, and so
forth. The prisoners in hell, freed by Jesus, appeared before him
in their various schemata.[4]

A person or thing can change schemata. Jacob consoles a
monk suffering under the attack of demons by reminding him to
hope that[5] 'from humbleness, he will be snatched up to the
height in another schema'. Presumably, this new schema would
be one in which he would not be under the attacks of the
demons.

In a specifically christological context, Jacob also gives two
examples of a person or 'thing' existing simultaneously in two
different schemata. A thought (Jacob calls it a 'word') can
exist in two schemata at the same time: in one schema, in the
mind of the writer of a letter, and in a second, in the form of
writing on the page.[6] In the first schema, the word is intangible

---

[1] Letters 39, pp. 287, 289; 40, pp. 292, 293.

[2] Letter 36, p. 262. See also Hom. 39 (ii.183), where the word 'degree', *dargâ*,
replaces 'schema' in an almost identical passage.

[3]   'The seraphim of fire . . . beat their wings in
                their sanctifyings;
        The cherubim of powers who bless him in their descent,
        Companies and ranks who shout for him in their hosannas,
        Multitudes of powers and hosts in their schemata,
        Distant created beings whom he created . . .'
                                    (Hom. 53, part 4 (ii.512)).

See also Hom. 125 (iv.545, 563).

[4] Hom. 53, part 7 (ii.595, 596).   [5] Letter 38, p. 276.

[6] Cf. Hom. 38 (ii.163-4); Letter 4, pp. 21-3, where the idea is expressed without
the use of the word 'schema'; Letter 36, pp. 262-3.

and unlimited; in the second, it is both tangible and limited.[1]
No one has access to the thought in the *mind* of another person,
so long as it is in his mind; on the other hand, one has immediate
access to the same thought if it is written down. Jacob uses
Mary, after the birth of Jesus, to illustrate another way in which
it is possible to exist simultaneously in two schemata. After
giving birth, Mary remained a virgin and 'was known to be a
virgin in truth and a mother in truth, without being counted
as two, while she stood in two schemata, because she was a
virgin and a mother, and Mary is one, and she is a mother, and
she is a virgin'.[2]

Especially by these last two examples, Jacob illustrates that
the concepts 'nature' and 'schema' are quite different. Indeed,
he argues in one place that if one accepts the Nestorian version
of the two natures in Christ, '[God] will not be born of a
woman and be like us, and empty himself and take the image
of the servant or fight in a schema like a man'.[3] In another
place although Jacob does not use the word 'schema' itself, he
expresses his awareness of the difference between the real
identity of Jesus, and his apparent identity. The Word was
able to trick 'the keepers of the dark city' and disguise himself from them because 'he was a man to sight, but God by
nature'.[4]

While Jacob uses the word 'nature' in the context of christology to express the concrete being and stable identity of a
person or thing, a schema, at least in the case of a human being,
is something that can be chosen or rejected or changed. One
is born with one's nature: one is born a single human being, and
retains one's basic identity throughout life. Mary was Mary
when she was a baby, and she was still Mary after she bore
Jesus.[5] But while one is born into a certain schema, the schema
is not part of one's nature, for the schema must change—sometimes by choice, sometimes not. Babies grow up to become
marriageable young women, marriageable young women may

---

[1] Letter 4, p. 22.
[2] Letter 36, p. 262; see also Hom. 39 (ii.183).   [3] Letter 21, p. 139.
[4] Letter 13, p. 53, *badh'nāshā bhaḥzāthā 'alāhā dhēn bakhyānā*. They did not know
him, because 'he showed himself to them as a man, while he is God'.
[5] See e.g. Letter 36, p. 262. Cf. the monk who asks to have his schema changed,
Letter 38, p. 276; the various forms of monastic life are also called schemata,
Letters 39, pp. 287, 289; 40, pp. 292, 293.

choose to remain in the schema of virgins, or they may change
their schema, marry, and bear children.

Jacob wishes us to understand that while Jesus is *one* nature
and hypostasis, he exists on earth in two schemata: he exists
in the mode of being of both God and man. While the Word is
God, he has come into being in the schema of a man.[1] Jacob
insists that Jesus is a complete man in so far as he has a body,
just as any man does; it is his own, not a possession belonging to
him as the purple belongs to the king.[2] He suffered physical
pain and hunger; he grew weary and slept.[3] He experienced
both birth and death, and all these things belonged to him, not
because he was a man by nature, but because he was in the
schema of a man.[4]

The word 'schema' was a dangerous one within the context
of the christological controversy. Nestorius talks about it.[5]
Severus also uses it to explain the way in which angels appear to
men: they appear in various schemata according to the circumstances in which they appear; they do not appear as they really
are.[6] Jacob sometimes uses 'schema' in this sense himself. He
explains in one homily that at the time of the transfiguration,
Elijah and Moses appeared with Jesus 'in truth' and not 'in
schema'.[7] In a christological context once Jacob uses the expression 'in schema' himself, to contrast the way in which those
who deny the reality of the bodyhood of Christ regard his
humanity with those who affirm it.[8]

Thus we see that Jacob uses the word schema in two different
ways: the first, in contrast with 'nature', and the second, in
contrast with 'in reality'.

In the context of the analogy of the letter, we find that Jacob
used the concept of the two schemata to reduce the humanity

[1] Letter 21, p. 139; Homilies 53, part 1 (ii.457); 94 (iii.591).

[2] Letter 19, pp. 123–7.

[3] Homilies 40 (ii.189); 94 (iii.624), etc.   [4] Cf. Letter 33, p. 249.

[5] See e.g. Bedjan edition, *Le Livre d'Héraclide*, pp. 117, 244 ff.

[6] Hom. LXXII (P.O. xii.76, 77).

[7] The disciples 'saw in truth and not in schema, and not in an image . . . He did
not ask a schema of the prophets and our Lord brought them', Hom. 49 (ii.360).
See also p. 361. Philoxenus refers to a false vision of Elijah's chariot and fiery
horses as being only a schema, rather than a reality. *Lettre à Patricius*, p. 854; cf. pp.
834–6.

[8] Letter 14, p. 61: 'The church condemns those . . . who say he was not embodied
from the virgin . . . but he was seen in *phantasia*, in image, and in schema.' One
manuscript leaves out 'in schema'.

of Jesus to little more than that of a symbol, in the same way
that all written words are only symbols and vehicles for thought.
Mary is described as 'a letter full of secrets',[1] and the bearer of
the message, the bodyhood of Jesus, is the writing within the
letter, and the real message is the Hidden Word himself:[2] 'He
came to be embodied from the seed of the house of David and
Abraham, and in the revelation of his bodyhood, as in the
mark of writing, he is visible and audible and embraced and
touched.' Thus 'anyone who saw him and read him knew that
he was God'.[3]

However, when Jacob uses this image of the letter he is
working in a decidedly gnosticizing context. The idea of a
secret letter, sealed and sent from heaven to those who are to be
saved, is one found frequently in gnostic literature. Nevertheless,
given the gnosticizing framework of Jacob's thought, the fact
that Jesus' humanity is only a kind of external trapping, a sign
pointing to his real identity, does not mean that Jesus is less
'human' than other men. To a real gnostic, the humanity of
all men has a kind of unreality compared with their true identity as dwellers in another realm, who have been misplaced and
now must dwell on earth. Even human intellect has little to do
with the true identity of human beings.

The Image of the Servant

The phrase 'the schema of a man' often appears in Jacob's
writings in conjunction with the phrase 'the image of the
servant'. To understand what he means by this last motif, we
have to look at the idea of the 'image' in Jacob's basic mythological framework.

In the beginning, when God created Adam, he created him,
not just to be his own image, in the image of the 'Great Mind',[4]
but in the image of the human Jesus who was to come to earth.[5]

---

[1] Homilies 39 (ii.181); 94 (iii.591); Letter 36, p. 262.   [2] Letter 4, p. 23.
[3] Hom. 39 (ii.174). To Philoxenus, the schema of a word is the written word,
composed of letters, rather than the meaning of the word. *Lettre à Patricius*, p. 774.
[4] Hom. 125 (iv.557).
[5] 'Before the created things, the Father sealed the image of his Son,
   And formed him and showed how he would shine among the earthly beings.
   The Father looked at the image of his Son and formed Adam. . . .
   Because of this, he said, "Let us make man in our image,"
   In this image of the child of Mary, the only begotten' (Hom. 125 (iv.591)).

While this human Jesus did not exist in actuality at the time of the creation of man, he already had a kind of potential existence.[1] Mankind was created originally, then, as a kind of double image—as an image of the Son, who is the image of the Father, but also as the image of the Son made man. What Ezekiel saw on the throne-chariot, says Jacob, was itself also a kind of double image; it was the image of the servant, but also the image of God the Father.[2]

The humanity of Christ, then, is in a primordial relationship to the human race.[3] Adam is in a very special sense the image of God. Again and again Jacob describes the necessity of Christ's mission to Sheol, not just to rescue Adam, but to save 'the Great Adam'[4] or 'the Great Image',[5] the Image of the Father.[6] The title of Christ as 'the second Adam'[7] has special significance in Jacob's system, which is almost bewildering with its series of images of God and man, reflected and re-reflected from the beginning of creation until the coming of the Word in the Image of the Servant.

Thus Christ is 'the heavenly being, the second Adam who

---

[1] Hom. 125 (iv.575); only the image of the body of Christ was seen on the chariot; the vision was of things to come.

[2] In this important homily Jacob is arguing with a Jew over who was actually the one seen upon the chariot. Apparently the Jew is arguing that it is God the Father. Jacob says, 'Ezekiel saw the hidden Father on the chariot as a man, but the form was of his only one', Hom. 125 (iv.588). But the Son who is the image of the Father appears as the image of the servant, who is, of course, made in the image of the Son.

[3] Hom. 94 (iii.590):

'The image of the Son, the only one, he gave to Adam,
While he was its creator, he took it from him when he
    visited him . . .
While he was its creator, he was related to him who gave
    him the image . . .
To his own he came; in his image he dwelt in the daughter of Adam,
Who was formed in his image, and because of this, he was
    related to him.'

[4] Hom. 125 (iv.578).

[5] Hom. 53, part 7 (ii.596).

[6] 'The image of God was perishing in Sheol, and the Son descended
To seek and find the image of his Father which was perishing' (Hom. 53, part 7 (ii.594)).
Homilies 94 (iii.642); 40 (ii.195).

[7] Hom. 53, part 7 (ii.589). In one place Jacob says that the Word was embodied in Adam: Hom. 53, part 6 (ii.555): 'he was in him, and put on his body, and came into being from him'.

came down from the house of the Father'[1] to annul all the curses that fell upon Adam after the Fall,[2] to pay off Adam's debt,[3] and to rescue him from the clutches of Sheol.[4]

Although in Jacob's thought, the humanity of Jesus is only a sort of ambiguous half-humanity, at the same time the humanity of all men who are the descendants of the Great Adam appears to have no more than a tenuous semi-reality itself, being merely a reflection of an image of God.

The Secret Jesus

Within Jacob's mythological framework, at the time of the coming of Christ, Adam and all mankind were suffering under the rule of the enemy or enemies of God. As a result of Satan's first defeat of Adam, mankind came to languish under the worship of idols[5]—Error—and was subject to the destruction of death. The fact that at the time of the birth of Christ, the world was 'sealed with an alien seal', that is, was almost entirely under Satan's control,[6] meant that the Word must enter creation, not openly, as its Lord, but *secretly*, in order once more to engage Satan in battle on behalf of the human race, the Image of God. This secret existence of the Word in creation provides another important key to our understanding of Jacob's christology.

As we have already suggested, on a very basic level, Jacob regarded the humanity of Jesus as a disguise,[7] much in the way that the clothing of the Egyptians is assumed as a disguise by the child who leaves his heavenly home to go out in search of

---

[1] Hom. 53, part 7 (ii.589). Jacob makes heavy use of the themes of the parallel events in the life of Adam and Christ. Golgotha is linked with Eden frequently; e.g. it is called 'the Eden of God', Letter 17, p. 83.

[2] He annulled the curses by enduring everything Adam endured following the fall, but he endured them in a 'healthy' manner; while Adam's sweat was 'unhealthy', Christ's was not, because he was without sin. Hom. 53, part 3 (ii.503–4).

[3] Letter 41, p. 296.

[4] This theme appears innumerable times, Letter 30, p. 235; Homilies 53, part 6 (ii.555); 40 (ii.195); 94 (iii.641), etc.

[5] See above, p. 115; Letter 19, pp. 103–4.   [6] Letter 12, p. 53.

[7] 'The Only One entered the city of his Father, creation,
      That he might inspect the merchants and provide in it all goods.
      The keepers of the night despised him. . . .
      But because he bore the image of the servant they did not know him. . . ' (Hom. 53, part 6 (ii.564, 565)).
   See also Letters 12, pp. 49, 50; 13, p. 53, etc.

the pearl in the gnostic 'Hymn of the Pearl'. While the humanity in both cases is *real*, at the same time, it is intended to hide the true identity of its bearer. In the 'Hymn of the Pearl', of course, the humanity is so real that its bearer forgets his true identity, in a fashion typical of gnostic mythology. In Jacob's system, while the humanity is intended to be equally real, there is never any suggestion that Jesus might forget his true identity: he is Lord of creation. Jesus' disguise never broke down. He successfully deceived the 'rulers of the dark world':[1]

he astounded them; he made them err . . . He hid his riches in his poverty, his divinity in his humanity, his hiddenness in the revelation of his coming, and he was in our world as one of the sons of the world, and the rulers did not know him, and the Seizers of the dark world did not discover him.

This humanity with which the hidden one 'equipped himself usefully from the womb of the virgin'[2] in order to go out 'after the track of the Kidnapper'[3] is often called 'the Image of the Servant', the expression frequently in parallelism with 'the schema of a man'. For the purpose of the disguise, the chief characteristics of the Image are lowliness, humility, poverty, apparent powerlessness, and the ability to suffer in the flesh and die.[4] Likewise the temptation of Christ in the wilderness Jacob interprets as a contest between Satan, who is trying to discover his identity, and Jesus, who successfully conceals it by his refusal to perform the miracles. Because of Jesus' apparent inability to turn stones into bread, Satan is left in doubt.[5] Again and again Jacob insists that it was Jesus' seeming lowliness and weakness that fooled his demonic enemies:[6]

When they saw powers in him, they said, 'he is not a human being'. He showed them weakness; they said, 'he is not God'. And because of this, the Rulers of the World did not know him, for if they had known him, they would not have crucified the Lord of glory.

Jacob is always careful to remind us that this weakness and lowliness of Jesus is only apparent; one of his favourite themes is the recounting of the dangers to which the enemies of

[1] Letter 13, p. 55. [2] Letters 13, p. 54; 33, p. 249.
[3] Letter 13, p. 54. [4] Letters 2, p. 14; 12, p. 49.
[5] See above, p. 116; Letter 12, pp. 49–50. [6] Letter 2, p. 14.

Jesus exposed themselves in daring to lift a hand against the divine Fire who was able to burn them to cinders with one spark.[1]

All this disguise serves one purpose: to allow for the secret entry of the Son into Sheol, so that he may recover the Image of his Father.[2] Not only during his lifetime on earth was the true identity of Jesus hidden, but also during his entry into hell. In order to trick Death,[3]

> he received the clothing of the dead and the colour of the dead
>   when he entered [Sheol] . . .
> He was like the inhabitants of the place when he entered . . .

The Word being disguised, Death swallowed the Lord of Life, expecting him to be 'wholesome food'.[4] Instead, Death himself choked to death on him, and the prisoners in Sheol were released.

Jesus, disguised in his humanity, is the great Secret, the Hidden One of God. On the one hand, the disguise and the Secret serve the purpose of deceiving all those beings, both demonic and human, who are aligned against him. But the concept of the Secret is also a positive one. Even apart from his existence in the world as Jesus, the Word is called the Secret of the Father.[5] He is the one great Secret which lies behind and gives meaning to all the secrets of prophecy.[6]

---

[1] Hom. 53, part 4 (ii.507). When Judas approached Jesus to kiss him, and Jesus said,

> '". . . I am the one", the demons fell,
> For before all his power, the world was unable to stand.
> The sea of his fire was kindled to consume them.
> But his fire cooled in his mercies, so that he preserved them'.

See also ibid., p. 511; Homilies 53, part 5 (ii.525; 532); 53, part 6 (ii.554), etc.

[2] Homilies 53, part 7 (ii.594, 596); 94 (iii.642); 40 (ii.195).

[3] Hom. 53, part 7 (ii.594).   [4] Hom. 94 (iii.615); Letter 21, p. 144.

[5] Hom. 125 (iv.574). Christ secretly created and commands all the servants of his Father, Hom. 53, part 4 (ii.512). He is also 'the hidden altar who is served secretly', the one who secretly brought down the riches of his Father to earth, Hom. 125 (iv.607).

[6] 'The Son of God is the breath of prophecy . . .

> Just as the body cannot stand without the soul,
> Neither can prophecy [stand] without the secrets of the Son of God. . . .
> What riches does the sun have except its light?
> And what secret does the Father have unless it is his Son?
> By his hands, secrets go out to revelation from the house of his Father,
> For he is the secret of all secrets of prophecy . . .' (Hom. 125 (iv.574)).

Christ is, then, above all, 'the hidden one, come to revelation'[1] in Jesus.

While a few recognized Jesus' true identity during his lifetime (the disciples are often called 'the sons of his secret'),[2] it was not until the crucifixion that it was openly revealed who he really was, and all the world had access to knowledge about him.[3]

The secret identity of Jesus which was revealed was not simply that Jesus was the Word. The *gnosis* about Jesus included a knowledge of 'who he was, and the son of whom, and for whom he came, and what he asked him to do'.[4] Often another element is added: praising John the Evangelist, Jacob congratulates him for revealing to every man

> who [his] Lord is, and what is his country,
>   indeed, the Son of whom,
> And for whom he came into being.[5]

Variants of this formula appear reasonably frequently. In all, there are five elements in it, not all of which are used each time: (1) 'who he is',[6] (2) 'the Son of whom',[7] (3) 'for whom he came',[8] (4) 'what his country is',[9] and (5) 'what he was asked to do'.[10] Occasionally Jacob expands on one or more of these points, as he does in the fifth part of his long work on the crucifixion. Jesus is asked by Pilate what his country is, but is unable to tell him, because if he did, the secret would be given away and the crucifixion could not have taken place. The answer that Jacob makes for Jesus reveals some more of the gnostic flavour of his thought:[11]

> The country of your Father is your country; you do not go
>   astray with us.
> Your Father in heaven is the one whom you serve among
>   earthly beings;
> Your country is hidden; why are you oppressed in the
>   countries?

---

[1] Letters 2, p. 13; 3, p. 18; 13, p. 56; 17, p. 86; 33, p. 248; Hom. 39 (ii.184), etc.
[2] Homilies 49 (ii.352); 53, part 1 (ii.455); 53, part 2 (ii.482).
[3] Hom. 40 (ii.189); Letters 2, p. 14; 12, p. 48; 19, p. 110, etc.
[4] Letter 13, p. 53.   [5] Hom. 38 (ii.161).
[6] Letter 13, p. 53; Hom. 49 (ii.350); Letters 2, p. 14; 12, p. 49.
[7] Hom. 38 (ii.161); Letters 13, p. 52; 2, p. 14; 12, p. 49.
[8] Letter 13, p. 53; Hom. 38 (ii.161); Letter 12, p. 49.
[9] Homilies 38 (ii.161); 53, part 5 (ii.527).
[10] Letter 13, p. 53.   [11] Hom. 53, part 5 (ii.527, 528).

Above the archons, the upper beings are to you a country. . . .
Hidden worlds and those revealed in their circuits;
The shining country of the ardent crowds of the house of
    Gabriel. . . .
The company full of a thousand thousands of heavenly beings. . . .
These are your countries, Son of God. . . .
You wished, my Lord, and you came from the high buildings
    of your Father. . . .
Heaven is your country; why are you oppressed in the
    countries?

Mixture

In Jacob's conception of the union between humanity and
divinity in Christ, we find that, as in Philoxenus' writings, one
of the most frequently used terms is 'to mix'. He uses this
term most significantly within the context of the hypostatic
union, to describe the way in which the Word Incarnate
brought about a reconciliation between the two 'sides' who were
angry with each other, God and mankind, bringing them into
a state of peace. In this section we shall try to determine the
content of the word ḥlṭ within the context of the union. For
the sake of convenience we shall consistently translate it as 'to
mix'. Jacob uses it in at least four different ways in a non-
christological context.

First, he says, to discover the meaning of a biblical text, one
'mixes' or 'joins' (nqp) various texts by setting them side by
side to discover their meaning.[1] 'Mix', in this context, carries
no connotation of what we think of as a mixture of liquids, but
appears to mean only 'place together', 'set next to each other'.

Second, Jacob says, God originally created Adam by 'mixing'
dust and water. Here the term ḥlṭ applies to the type of mixture
in which the two things joined are not only brought together:
their union produces a third entity, different from the original
ingredients, namely, a man.[2]

Third, writing a letter to the monks dwelling on Mount

---

[1] Letter 24, p. 206. ḥlṭ and nqp are set in parallel to each other. Similarly in
Letter 38, p. 281, Jacob says that the holy man is not to mix (ḥlṭ) the moon with
the sun, or thought of possession with thoughts of God.
[2] 'When God made his image stand upon the dust and made him the likeness
    from formed clay . . .
    A grain of dust and a drop of water the creator mixed together . . .' (Letter 23,
p. 193).

Sinai, Jacob congratulates them on the way in which, in them, the two sacred mountains, Sinai and Golgotha, representing the law and the gospel, are 'mixed'.[1] In this case, the 'mixture' takes place through the intermediation of the monks who act as a kind of common ground between the law and the gospel, metaphorically speaking. Their own being provides the link between the law and the gospel,[2] bringing about what we might think of as 'mixture by mediation'.

Fourth, Jacob describes the way in which Judas left Jesus to betray him:

'He fled from the Light to go and mix with the darkness', and he 'mixed his essence with the hateful night of all darkness'.[3] In this sense, 'mixture' appears to represent a kind of gnostic idea in which the individual elements or adherents of darkness go to their source to participate in it.

He also uses the word 'to mix' in at least four different ways to describe Christ's relationship to men in different contexts where the hypostatic union is not explicitly being talked about.

First, Jacob says that the Word 'mixed' among Jews and Galileans, while in the flesh.[4] This 'mixture' suggests no more than the English expression 'to mix in a crowd'.

In the second type of mixture between Christ and a person, or thing, some change takes place in the person or thing mixed with Christ, yet not the kind of change we had in the case of mixture of dust and water to form Adam. Instead, the person or thing comes to be endowed with new, and better, characteristics. For example, Jacob describes the way in which Jesus is 'mixed' in love with Peter, after he sees how much Peter loves him.[5] This 'mixture' serves the purpose of giving to Peter extraordinary psychological strength to withstand the agony of the crucifixion. Another example of a similar type of union: Jacob instructs a monk who is fighting the demons to pray to Christ, reminding himself to remember that 'on my behalf he

---

[1] Letter 7, p. 36.   [2] Ibid.

[3] Hom. 53, part 3 (ii.493). Hom. 53, part 2 (ii.472): the disciples ask Jesus, 'Who has gone out of the sphere of the light of our Lord, to go and mix with the darkness in a great movement?'.

[4] Hom. 53, part 5 (ii.528). See also Hom. 40 (ii.186), and perhaps Hom. 53, part 3 (ii.496).

[5] Hom. 53, part 6 (ii.569).

descended to the contest; my fall was mixed in his resurrection'.[1] In this 'mixture' the weakness and helplessness of the monk is transformed into the strength of Christ, and the fall reversed.

The term 'to mix' is also used by Jacob to describe the union between Christ and the church.[2] He insists that the two of them, Christ the rich bridegroom, and the Church, the poor bride, are made *one*.[3] We are unable to determine, however, exactly the way in which they are conceived of as being one, though Jacob is using the analogy of marriage. It is unclear whether the church comes to belong to Jesus as an extension of his own body, or whether they are to be 'one' in the way in which any husband and wife are one. At the same time this use of the term 'to mix' also involves a change in the condition of the thing, the Church, which is mixed with Christ: in this case, the poor bride goes to become the wife of a rich husband.

In another place, we have what may possibly be an example of union with Christ conceived of in gnostic terms, analogous to the union between Judas and the darkness. Jesus is trying to wash Peter's feet; after Peter is made to understand the importance of the washing, he insists that Jesus wash all of him: nothing is to be 'alien' to 'mixture with him'.[4] In this case, one suspects that Jacob conceives of the mixture as a kind of gnostic rejoining of Peter to the Word in Christ.

We are now ready to look at the way in which Jacob uses *ḥlṭ* to describe the 'hypostatic union' itself, the way in which the Word was joined to the individual human element in Christ; he also uses it to describe the new relationship which comes to exist between the whole of the human race and God the Father as a result of the hypostatic union. Christ brought about this new relationship, reconciling the two 'sides' who were angry

---

[1] Letter 38, p. 273.

[2] Letter 23, p. 174. Jacob also uses *ḥlṭ* and *mzg*, another 'mix' word, to describe the relationship between Christ and the bread and wine of the eucharist: 'Behold, his body is mixed with the bread and his blood is mingled with the wine', Letter 38, p. 273.

[3] Christ came to 'take the church and mix it with his body and make it from him, and the two of them would be one . . . the groom from the virgin and the bride from baptism', Letter 23, p. 174; 'The rich bridegroom is united to the poor bride and the two of them become one', Letter 2, p. 15.

[4] Hom. 53, part 1 (ii.464).

with each other, and making peace between them, by acting
as the mediator between them, thereby 'mixing' them in each
other and making them one.[1]

A complication is caused by the fact that Jacob conceives
of human nature as a concrete collective, much in the way
many fourth-century thinkers did.[2] He thought of the union
between the Word and the humanity of Jesus in such a way that
the Word was united not only to the individual humanity of
Jesus: through Jesus, the Word was joined to the whole of the
human race. Jacob does not, in fact, make a clear distinction
between the 'mixture' of the Word in humanity in general and
the 'mixture' of humanity and divinity in Jesus.[3] The human
race is an organic unity which is far more real than the separation one sees between individual members of the human race.
In exactly the same way, for the *Word* to be joined to humanity
means that the Father himself is brought into close relationship
with the human race, and this relationship is also called
'mixture'.[4]

This 'mixture' between mankind and God the Father depends on the fact that the 'mediator', Christ, who brings it
about, is absolutely 'one',[5] one being who is at the same time
fully man, except for sin, and fully God, except for suffering.[6]
Only a being who belongs to the two 'sides' can stand between

---

[1] Letters 3, p. 17; 19, p. 119; 21, p. 140; 29, p. 233; Homilies 40 (ii.195); 41
(ii.205); 53, part 5 (ii.530); 94 (iii.619, 644); 125 (iv.578). For a typical statement,
see Letter 29, p. 233, 'The love of God was revealed to the world in the cross of his
son, and that cross broke down the wall of enmity which the Serpent built between
Adam and God, and he released the decree of that death which was given to Adam
for the transgression of the commandment. And he made peace between the upper
beings and the lower ones and he mixed the sides in each other that the first
enmity should be forgotten . . .'

[2] Jansma, in 'The Credo of Jacob of Serugh', suggests that Jacob was a man
'who was born too late', and wanted no part in the christological controversies of
his own time; according to Jansma, Jacob's position is really pre-Chalcedonian,
pp. 32, 33.

[3] The Word is said to have been 'the one mediator between the two sides [the
Father and humanity, who] cast down peace, and embraced them in his hypostasis, reconciling them', Hom. 94 (iii.620), but see Letter 19, p. 119, 'he took a body
without sin into his hypostasis . . .'. See also e.g. the following ambiguous and
typical passages: Letter 21, pp. 139–40, Hom. 40 (ii.186–7).

[4] He came 'for his Father that he should be a Father for us . . . and he mixed us
with respect to genus with his begetter', Letter 19, p. 120.

[5] Letter 16, pp. 80–1, etc.

[6] Hom. 94 (iii.619); Letter 2, p. 13.

them, inclining in favouritism toward neither side.[1] Jacob
rejects the Nestorian version of the union because to the
Nestorians Christ is not one but two, and is therefore himself in
need of a mediator between God and mankind.[2]

Exactly how the 'mixture' of humanity and divinity comes
about through the hypostatic union is unclear. Only two conclusions seem worthwhile drawing. First, Jacob himself does not
seem to have been aware that he was using 'mixture' in
different senses in different contexts, or if he was aware of their
different meanings, they perhaps all seemed similar to him or not
incompatible. Most probably, when he used 'mixture' the word
carried with it all or many of its various connotations most of
the times he used it. In the Syrian tradition 'mixture' was not
a technical word, but one rich with a variety of meanings. The
hearers of Jacob's homilies would almost certainly not question
his use of the word. The other conclusion that we can surely
draw is that none of the specific uses of the word 'mixture'
found in Jacob's writings could be taken as the basis of a
workable doctrine of the hypostatic union: either Jacob was
thinking in basically unacceptable terms, or he simply did not
have anything very specific in mind when he used the word
'to mix' in the context of the union. In fact, Jacob's thought
seems to provide us with a good example of why Chalcedon
rejected the language of 'mixture' to describe the relationship
between the humanity and the divinity in Christ. The language
of 'mixture' was part of the Syrian tradition inherited from
Ephraim, but Jacob sometimes seemed to use it in a gnostic
sense—though of this we cannot be certain. It is even possible
that he used it in the sense of the way two liquids were mixed
together to describe the union: there is simply no way of
knowing what he had in mind.

The Chariot of Ezekiel

One of the most striking and significant of the images which
Jacob uses to describe the incarnate Word is that of the fire,
the flame, or the coal.

[1] He made for us 'a true reconciliation, because he did not incline, in the middle
position, to one of the sides which he took . . . But he was from the two sides, one
intermediate Son who in the union of his hypostasis made one in great peace those
who were angry at each other', Letter 19, p. 120.
[2] Letters 21, pp. 139–40; 6, p. 32.

Christ himself is frequently called 'the fire': Jesus is called 'the living fire which came down from heaven'.[1] He is also called 'the flame': John approached Jesus at the last supper; he 'embraced the fire and began to question the flame'.[2] Again, the parts of Jesus' body are referred to as belonging to this divine 'fire'. At the last supper, speaking of the fact that Jesus lay down to eat, Jacob says,

> The breast of the fire, also the limbs of the flame,
> And the living spirit lay down in a miracle by the table.[3]

Jesus is sometimes called the coal: at the judgement of Jesus before the crucifixion, speaking of Judas' betrayal, Jacob says,[4]

> The briar approached and kissed the burning coal
> and it did not burn up.

In his heavenly, non-human existence, the Word is described as the source of a great fire which flows from him.[5] At the same time, he is said to be surrounded by flame.[6] The cherubim and seraphim make up his armies, 'companies of flame'.[7] A sea of fire is even said to divide the realm of spiritual beings from our human realm.[8]

If we ask what this fire, and its biblical origin, is, we find that a large part of it takes its inspiration from Ezekiel's vision of the throne-chariot. The language of the coal would appear to be inspired by the vision in Isaiah, chapter 6. But we also know that speculation on the fiery aspects of the throne-chariot comprised at least a part of Jewish gnostic interpretation of the throne-chariot (so-called *merkabhah* mysticism).[9] In the light of the fact that Jacob, in his homily devoted to the throne-chariot, specifically argues with an unnamed Jew on the interpretation

---

[1] Hom. 53, part 1 (ii.457). See also Letter 31, p. 238, Homilies 53, part 2 (ii.476), 94 (iii.602); 177 (v.664).

[2] Hom. 53, part 2 (ii.476). See also Homilies 53, part 4 (ii.511); 94 (iii.602, 633), etc.

[3] Hom. 53, part 2 (ii.476).

[4] Homilies 53, part 4 (ii.511); 94 (iii.602), etc.   [5] Hom. 94 (iii.583).

[6] Homilies 53, part 1 (ii.464); part 8 (ii.607), the Son is 'the Strong One whom the flame surrounds'.

[7] Homilies 125 (iv.543); 53, part 4 (ii.512); part 8 (ii.602); 177, p. 662.

[8] Homilies 177 (v.669).

[9] G. Scholem, *Jewish Gnosticism, Merkabah Mysticism, and Talmudic Tradition*, pp. 31 ff.

of the vision,[1] and therefore appears to be in direct contact
with Jewish thought on this point, it seems probable that some
of his fire imagery was shared by his Jewish colleagues. The
possibility of Persian influence is, of course, also there.

The language of the fire or the flame serves three purposes.
First, it points to the total 'otherness' of the divinity of God,
even in the world, in the sense that divinity is dangerous to
approach, especially for the sinner. Second, it points to the
unapproachability of God through the ordinary channels of
human knowledge. Third, it stands for the vitality and life-
giving character of God, in so far as he reveals himself.

The first use of the flame imagery is obvious: again and again
Jacob paints a picture of the Word in the world, disguised as
a man, but in reality the divine Fire who is able to flash out
and destroy the whole world without a moment's notice.[2]
Jacob stresses that the presence of the Word in the world was
not only a source of blessing to the world, but also a potential
source of great danger. Only God's mercy held back the con-
suming fire of his judgement.[3]

The second use of the flame imagery is to emphasize the
absolute unapproachability of God:[4]

> A fearful fire flows from you . . .
> You are very far from the one who worships and
>   believes in you.
> You are very fearful to the one who is eager to track
>   you down.

The fire holds back the one who would approach God for the
purpose of 'investigation':[5]

> Who is able to tell of his way amongst the coals,
> To investigate the fire or walk on the flame?

The third idea represented by the fire imagery is that of the

---

[1] See e.g. Hom. 125 (iv.588).

[2] Homilies 53, part 2 (ii.476); part 4 (ii.507, 511); part 5 (ii.525, 532); part 6
(ii.554).

[3] See e.g. Hom. 53, part 4 (ii.507). On the day when Judas betrayed Jesus, 'The
sea of his fire was kindled to consume [the crowd who came to seize him], but his
fire cooled in his mercies, so that he preserved them'. In one particularly interesting
place, Jacob suggests that if, after Judas had betrayed Jesus, he had been able to
weep tears of repentance, the tears would have quenched the fire of judgement,
Hom. 53, part 6 (ii.568).

[4] Hom. 94 (iii.583).   [5] Ibid., p. 602.

revelation of the Word, occasionally to men, and commonly and regularly to 'the watchers'[1] (the latter being the intermediate class of heavenly beings, including the cherubim and seraphim, whose natural dwelling-place, created especially for them, is the throne-chariot). When the fire language is used in this sense, it is often paralleled with language referring to the Word as the light or the sun.[2]

The chariot itself was created to be the natural territory of the seraphim and the cherubim.[3] This is not only the place where the cherubim and the seraphim belong; it is also the source of life for them, and it represents the place and manner in which God is revealed to them, according to what they are capable of receiving.[4]

Just as, after the crucifixion, the cherubim are warned away from Eden, because it is not their natural territory, men are warned away from aspiring to a revelation of God in the throne-chariot.[5] In this respect, Jacob utterly rejects Jewish *merkabhah* mysticism. At the same time, he appears to reject any notion of contemplation (he does not ever, to my knowledge, use the word *theoria*) involving the mystical ascent of the mind to God. While God reveals himself to the angels on the chariot, he reveals himself in a comparable manner to men on the altar of the eucharist:

> In all the heights amongst his crowds he shows himself,
> In whatever images he knows that they are able to see him.
> To the upper beings, in a great thing which is
>   unspeakable . . .
> And to intermediate beings, another crowd, he yoked the
>   chariot.
> And he made the Secret descend; he arranged by it that
>   his account should come to the world.

---

[1] Hom. 125 (iv.602).

[2] Homilies 53, part 3 (ii.493); part 2 (ii.473), where Christ is called 'Fire and Light'.

[3] Homilies 125 (iv.602); 177 (v.686).   [4] Hom. 125 (iv.599).

[5]   'See! He is revealed and stands among the earthly messengers . . .
        All the secrets and types and beauties of the heavenly beings—
        See! they are in him; no man should desire far off things.
        See! In the service of the holy altar in the time of the Mysteries,
        The powers in their hallowings are arranged and stand.'
He goes on to say that the coals of the chariot appear on the altar in the eucharist, available to the sight of the whole world, Hom. 125 (iv.607).

And in the midst of the world, he established the altar
    for bodily creatures,
And he became a body from whom they should eat, their
    dwelling place.[1]

Do not seek him above, oh sinner, when you look for him;
He has come to you; in your place look at him who—
    see—is with us,
To the altar as far as you who see him who dwells upon
    the table.
And from the pieces of bread of his body, all creation is
    satisfied.
You now desire to see him in the place of the angels . . .
Blessed be his place, the altar, his place amongst earthly
    beings.
To this draw near, oh cancerous man, and he will heal
    your soul.[2]

Faith and Knowledge

In the final analysis, we are cut off entirely from rational
knowledge of God in Christ because Christ belongs entirely to
the realm of the supernatural.[3] Unlike Severus, especially,
but also unlike Philoxenus, Jacob does not seem to be willing
to assign to reason any area in which it may properly function
in order to gain knowledge of God. He says categorically that
reason belongs to the realm of the visible.[4] Those who apply its
methods to trying to make sense of the presence of God in
Christ are 'the wise', those who engage in 'controversy'.[5]
'Controversy', the attempt to solve the theological problems
raised by Greek philosophy, is the work of Satan; he uses it to
disturb the praise that mankind owes to God.[6] 'The wise' are
the disciples of Satan, just as the demons are.[7]

Only faith or love can approach and know God,[8] and this

---

[1] Hom. 125 (iv.602).   [2] Ibid., p. 606.   [3] See e.g. Letter 3, p. 20.
[4] 'The wisdom of the world is in visible nature alone', Hom. 94 (iii.587).
[5] For reference to the 'wise' and 'controversy', see Letters 2, p. 13; 13, pp. 55–6;
Hom. 49 (ii.349), etc.
[6] Letter 19, p. 103.
[7] See e.g. Letter 13, where 'devils', 'archons', and 'scribes' are lumped together.
[8] 'To love he is near and revealed, and he stands like the day;
But from the controversy of the knowers he is really far away. . . .
Oh wise men, [you cannot interpret him]. . . .
Oh proud scribe, know yourself and see yourself.
And not in pride will you speak the account of Immanuel.

is given only to 'the simple':[1] these 'simple' are ignorant men,[2] as we see in the case of Jesus' original disciples. Only these are able to exercise faith, and thus able to praise[3] God and wonder at his miracles in Christ without raising questions, or trying to 'investigate him' or 'track him down'.[4]

Conclusion

Thus we see that Jacob holds to a christology which is unsatisfactory in many areas. Furthermore, while he actually uses the language of the monophysite side of the christological controversy, the monophysitism to which he holds is incomplete if judged by the standards of both Severus and Philoxenus. Jesus, in his system, does not seem fully human, in spite of his affirmation to the contrary. His theory of knowledge about God appears to be over-mythological in a gnosticizing fashion, and to reject natural knowledge completely as a route to any kind of knowledge about the things of God. Further, Jacob does not have an adequate version of the union between God and man in Christ, relying as he does on an unclear notion of the mixture between the two. His theory of the human schema of the Word seems to make the humanity merely modal. All in all, Jacob's position is one which, upon reflection, appears to me to have been rightfully worthy of rejection by both Chalcedonians and such monophysite theologians as Severus and Philoxenus.

In the simplicity of faith, in perfection, in humility speak the account when it is spoken' (Hom. 40 (ii.191)).
See also Hom. 49 (ii.349); 'the light of the soul is faith', and it alone is able to approach difficult questions of Biblical interpretation, Letter 24, p. 203, etc.
[1] Hom. 94 (iii.622–6).   [2] Ibid.
[3] The ability to praise God is the gift of God. Homilies 40 (ii.185); 94 (iii.582); 38 (ii.158, 160); 125 (iv.567–8), etc.
[4] Letters 2, p. 11; 26, p. 223. Christ 'came to enlighten the world, not to be investigated by the world; he came to save the captives, not to be tracked down by the saved; he came to make the unclean clean, not that their mouths make propositions about him . . .'.

CONCLUSION

SEVERUS' vision of the hypostatic union of divinity and humanity in Christ serves one major purpose: it allows us to talk about the absolute unity and single identity of Christ as the Incarnate word at the same time that it accounts for the presence of all human things in Jesus, including a human will. This view of the union, coupled with Severus' Christian Platonic view of reality as three hierarchically arranged levels of being, means that Severus is able to explain how it is that a single identity may exist simultaneously in two (or more) levels while retaining its actual unity of being. As we have said, in the case of men, the body is the iconic representation of the psyche in the sensible level. Both body and psyche function in their own levels, each in the way appropriate to that level, yet the two elements are bound in their hypostatic union into one identity, neither element existing without the other. In the same way, the humanity of Christ, including the human will, is an iconic representation of the divinity, and while the two exist together in one identity, as one being, the humanity forms a perfect image of the divinity, on the created level in which it functions. It is this humanity that offers us our vision of God, and acts as our model in our own 'new creation': We are divinized in the image of Christ.

When we go on to characterize the key to Philoxenus' christology, we find, first, that there is no 'natural' humanity in Christ, and no 'natural' participation of mankind in God. Philoxenus' christology and epistemology are rooted in his sharp distinction between the natural and the supernatural. Reality is not a series of three hierarchical levels, each a lesser image of the one above it, as it is in Severus' thought. Instead, reality consists of two realms which can, and do, exist simultaneously in the same place at the same time, but which are totally unlike each other—the realm of the natural, and the realm of the supernatural. The whole Christian reality belongs to the supernatural realm, including the Incarnation, our perception of it through faith, our knowledge of God even at the level of natural *theoria*, and the whole of our life as baptized

Christians. At the same time, we as men, and Christ as God, continue to remain inexorably in the realms of our own natures. The one essential weakness in Philoxenus' system seems to be this: Christ is fully human, yet we know that he is, only because Philoxenus tells us that he must be: there is nothing in Philoxenus' system which makes full humanity necessary for Jesus. On the other hand, Philoxenus is as acutely aware of our radical dependence on grace and faith as Luther: men are always in the hands of God, dependent upon him in the natural world for good crops, health, and shelter, but outside the needs of the body, men are dependent upon him in a special way, directly, so to speak, and not indirectly, through the smooth functioning of the laws of nature. The division between the natural and the supernatural realm allows him to locate all our face-to-face experiences of God in the realm of the supernatural. As we said, here we meet him in Christ, in the sacraments, in prayer, and in contemplation. In this supernatural realm, God and men meet on terms of freedom which cannot exist in the natural realm.

The fundamental reality of Christ in Jacob's thought is the hidden and secret presence of the Word disguised in Jesus, and revealed to believers. For Jacob, the saving knowledge of God is our knowledge of Jesus's identity: 'who he is and the son of whom, and for whom he came, and what he asked him to do'. Jacob insists as firmly as Severus and Philoxenus that Jesus was complete man, as well as complete God; in Jacob's thought, Jesus truly suffered and died on the cross, and he was truly resurrected from the dead, just as we shall also be at the last judgement. Nevertheless, Jacob's thought is characterized by a sense of the proper alienness and transitoriness of the life of *all* men, as well as of the life of Jesus, in this temporal world which snares us and destroys us by our love of it. If Jesus' humanity sometimes seems to be an illusion in Jacob's system, fallen humanity is also illusory. It is Eden, which the good thief reaches only by crossing the sea of fire, that is our 'natural' home.

BIBLIOGRAPHY

TEXTS AND TRANSLATIONS

The Acts of Thomas, translation, introduction, and commentary by A. Klijn (Leiden, 1962).

AHOUDEMMEH, 'Sur l'homme', ed. and transl. by F. Nau, *Patrologia Orientalis*, III (Turnhout, 1971), 97–115.

ATHANASIUS I, Monophysite Patriarch, *The Conflict of Severus*, ed. and transl. from the Ethiopic by E. J. Goodspeed, *Patrologia Orientalis*, IV (Turnhout, 1971), 575–717.

BARDAISAN, *The Book of the Laws of Countries : Dialogue on Fate of Bardaisan of Edessa*, ed. and transl. by H. J. W. Drijvers (Assen, 1965).

CONYBEARE, F. C. (ed. and transl.), '*Anecdota Monophysitarum*', transl. from the Armenian, *American Journal of Theology*, 9 (1905), 719–40.

DIONYSIUS THE AREOPAGITE, *The Divine Names and the Mystical Theology*, transl. by C. E. Rolt (London, 1920).

——, *La Hiérarchie céleste*, transl. by G. Heil, with an introduction by R. Roques (*Sources chrétiennes*, Vol. 58 (Paris, 1958).

——, *Mystical Theology and the Celestial Hierarchies*, transl. by the editors of The Shrine of Wisdom, 2nd ed. (Fintry, Brook. Nr. Godalming, Surrey, 1965).

DRAGUET, R., 'Pièces de polémique antijulianiste,' *Le Muséon*, 44 (1931), 255–317.

EBIED, R. Y., and WICKHAM, L. R., 'A Collection of Unpublished Syriac Letters of Timothy Aelurus', *Journal of Theological Studies*, 21 (1970), 321–69.

EPHRAIM, *Commentaire de l'Évangile concordant ou Diatessaron*, Introduction, translation, and notes by L. Leloir (*Sources chrétiennes*, 121) (Paris, 1966).

——, *Hymnes sur le Paradis*, transl. by R. Lavenant; introduction and notes by F. Graffin (*Sources chrétiennes*, 137) (Paris, 1968).

——, *A Letter of Ephrem to the Mountaineers*, ed. and transl. by A. Vööbus, Contributions of the Baltic University, XXV (Pinneberg, 1947).

——, *Saint Ephraim's Prose Refutations of Mani, Marcion, and Bardaisan*, ed. and transl. by C. W. Mitchell, Text and Translation Society, 2 vols. (London, 1912–21).

EVAGRIUS PONTICUS, 'Seconde partie du traité qui passe sous le nom de "La grande lettre d'Évagre le Pontique à Melanie l'ancienne" ' Ed. and transl. by G. Vitestam, *Scripta Minora*, 3 (Lund, 1964).

——, 'Les Six centuries des "Kephalaia gnostica" d'Évagre le Pontique', transl. and ed. by A. Guillaumont, *Patrologia Orientalis*, XXVIII (Paris, 1958), 5–264.

FROTHINGHAM, A. L., *Stephen Bar Sudaili, The Syrian Mystic, and the Book of Hierotheos* (Leyde, 1886).

GARITTE, G., 'Fragments coptes d'une lettre de Sévère d'Antioche à Sotérichos de Césarée', *Le Muséon*, 65 (1952), 185–98.

GRAFFIN, F., 'La Catéchèse de Sévère d'Antioche', *L'Orient syrien*, 5 (1960), 47–54.

HATCH, W. H. P., 'A Fragment of a Lost Work on Dioscurus', *Harvard Theological Review*, 19 (1926), 377–81.

HAUSHERR, I., 'L'Imitation de Jésus-Christ dans la spiritualité byzantine', in *Études de Spiritualité Orientale* (Rome, 1969).

——, 'Le Traité de l'oraison d'Évagre le Pontique,' *Revue d'ascétique et de mystique*, 15 (1934), 34–93; 113–70.

JACOB OF SARUG, 'Deux homélies inédites de Jacques de Saroug', ed. and transl. by P. Mouterde, *Mélanges de l'Université Saint Joseph*, 26 (1944–6), 1–37.

——, 'La Deuxième Homélie de Jacques de Sarug sur la foi du Concile de Chalcédoine', transl. by P. Krüger, *L'Orient syrien*, 2 (1957), 125–36.

——, *Epistulae quotquot supersunt*, ed. by G. Olinder, *Corpus Scriptorum Christianorum Orientalium*, vol. 110; Scriptores Syri II, 57 (Louvain, 1937).

——, 'Extraits de l'homélie sur l'amour de l'argent' and 'Extraits de l'homélie sur la décollation de Saint Jean-Baptiste', transl. by J. Babakhan, in 'Vulgarisation des homélies métriques de Jacques de Saroug, évêque de Batnan en Mésopotamie (451–521)', *Revue de l'orient chrétien*, 2nd ser. 9 (1914), 61–8, 143–54.

——, 'Homélie sur la descente du Très-Haut sur le Mont Sinai, et sur le symbole de l'Église', transl. by J. Babakhan, in 'Essai du vulgarisation des homélies métriques de Jacques de Saroug, évêque de Batnan en Mésopotamie (451–521)', *Revue de l'orient chrétien*, 2nd ser., 7 (1912), 410–26; 8 (1913), 42–52.

——, 'Homélie sur la fin du monde et sur le mariage', transl. by J. Babakhan, in 'Vulgarisation des homélies métriques de Jacques de Saroug, évêque de Batnan en Mésopotamie (451–521)', *Revue de l'orient chrétien*, 2nd ser., 8 (1913), 358–74.

——, 'Homélie de Jacques de Saroug sur la mort d'Aaron', transl. by M. Wurmbrand, *L'Orient syrien*, 6 (1961), 255–78.

——, 'Homélie sur Saint Thomas, l'apôtre de l'Hinde', transl. by J. Babakhan in 'Vulgarisation des homélies métriques de Jacques de Saroug', *Revue de l'orient chrétien*, 2nd ser., 8 (1913), 147–67; 252–69.

——, *Homiliae selectae Mar-Jacobi Sarugensis*, ed. by P. Bedjan, 5 vols. (Paris, (1905–10).

——, 'Jacob of Serugh's Homilies on the Spectacles of the Theatre', ed. and transl. by C. Moss, *Le Muséon*, 48 (1935), 87–112.

——, 'Lettres de Jacques de Saroug aux moines du Couvent de Mar Bassus, et à Paul d'Edesse', ed. and transl. by P. Martin, *Zeitschrift der deutschen morgenländischen Gesellschaft* 30 (1876), 217–75.

——, 'Mimro de Jacques de Saroug sur les deux oiseaux', transl. by F. Graffin, *L'Orient syrien*, 6 (1961), 51–66.

——, 'Mimro de Jacques de Saroug sur la synagogue et l'eglise', transl. by M. Albert, *L'Orient syrien*, 7 (1962), 143–62.

——, 'Mimro de Jacques de Sarug sur la vision de Jacob à Bethel', transl. by F. Graffin, *L'Orient syrien*, 5 (1960), 225–46.

JOHN OF BETH APHTHONIA, *Vie de Sévère*, ed. and transl. by M.-A. Kugener, *Patrologia Orientalis*, Vol. 2 (Paris, 1907), 207–64.

JOHN OF EPHESUS, *Lives of the Eastern Saints*, ed. and transl. by E. W. Brooks, *Patrologia Orientalis*, 17–19, (Paris, 1923–6), vol. 17, 1–307; T. 18, 513–698; T. 19, 153–285.

JOHN RUFUS, *Plérophories*, ed. and transl. by F. Nau, *Patrologia Orientalis*, VIII (Paris, 1911), 5–208.

JOHN THE SOLITARY, *Dialogues sur l'âme et les passions des hommes*, transl. by I. Hausherr, *Orientalia Christiana Analecta*, 120 (Rome, 1939).

Liber Graduum, ed. and transl. by M. Kmosko, *Patrologia Syriaca*, 3 (Paris, 1926).

MACARIUS THE EGYPTIAN, *Fifty Spiritual Homilies of St. Macarius the Egyptian*, transl. by A. J. Mason (London, 1921).

MARSH, F. S., *The Book Which Is Called the Book of the Holy Hierotheos*, Text and Translation Society, 10 (London and Oxford, 1927).

NAU, F., 'Notice inédite sur Philoxéne, évêque de Maboug (485–519)', *Revue de l'orient chrétien*, 8 (1903), 630–3.

——, (ed. and transl.), 'Textes monophysites', *Patrologia Orientalis*, XIII (Paris, 1916), 162–269.

NESTORIUS, *The Bazaar of Heracleides*, transl. by G. R. Driver and L. Hodgson (Oxford, 1925).

——, *Le Livre d'Héraclide de Damas*, ed. by P. Bedjan (Paris, 1910).

——, *Le Livre d'Héraclide de Damas*, transl. by F. Nau (Paris, 1910).

The Odes and Psalms of Solomon, ed. and transl. by J. Rendel Harris, in 2 parts (Cambridge, 1909).

The Odes of Solomon, transl. by J. A. Robinson, Texts and Studies, Vol. VIII (Cambridge, 1912).

PHILOXENUS OF MABBUG, *The Discourses of Philoxenus, Bishop of Mabbogh*, ed. and transl. by E. A. W. Budge, 2 vols. (London, 1894).

——, *Homélies*, introduction, translation, and notes by E. Lemoine, *Sources chrétiennes*, 44 (Paris, 1956).

——, 'A Letter of Philoxenus of Mabbug Sent to a Friend', transl. by G. Olinder, *Göteborgs Högskolas Arsskrift*, 56 (Göteborg, 1950).

——, 'A Letter of Philoxenus of Mabbug Sent to a Novice', transl. by G. Olinder, *Göteborgs Högskolas Arsskrift*, 47, 21 (Göteborg, 1941).

——, 'La lettre à Patricius de Philoxène de Mabboug', ed. and transl. by R. Lavenant, *Patrologia Orientalis*, XXX (Paris, 1963), 725–883.

——, 'La Lettre de Philoxène de Mabboug à "Abou-Niphir"', ed. and transl. by J. Tixeront, *Revue de L'orient chrétien*, 8 (1903), 623–30.

——, 'La Lettre de Philoxène de Mabboug à un supérieur de monastère sur la vie monastique', transl. by F. Graffin, *L'Orient syrian*, 6 (1961), 317–52, 455–86; 7 (1962), 77–102.

——, 'Une lettre inédite de Philoxène de Mabboug à un avocat, devenu moine, tenté par Satan', transl. by F. Graffin, *L'Orient syrien*, 5 (1960), 183–96.

——, 'Lettre inédite de Philoxène de Mabboug à l'un de ses disciples', transl. by M. Albert, *L'Orient syrien*, 6 (1961), 243–54.

PHILOXENUS OF MABBUG, 'Une lettre inédite de Philoxène de Mabboug à un Juif converti engagé dans la vie parfaite', transl. by M. Albert, *L'Orient syrien*, 6 (1961), 41–50.

——, *Lettre aux moines de Senoun*, ed. and transl. by A. de Halleux, *Corpus Scriptorum Christianorum Orientalium* 231–2. Scriptores Syri 98–9 (Louvain, 1963).

——, 'Memra de Philoxène de Mabboug sur l'inhabitation du Saint-Esprit', ed. and transl. by A. Tanghe, *Le Muséon*, 73 (1960), 39–71.

——, 'Nouveaux textes inédits de Philoxène de Mabbog. I : Lettre aux moines de Palestine ; Lettre liminaire au synodicon d'Éphèse', ed. and transl. by A. de Halleux, *Le Muséon*, 75 (1962), 31–62.

——, 'Nouveaux textes inédits de Philoxène de Mabbog. II : Lettre aux moines orthodoxes d'Orient" ed. and transl. by A. de Halleux, *Le Muséon*, 76 (1963), 5–26.

——, *Philoxeni Mabbugensis tractatus tres de Trinitate et incarnatione*, ed. and transl. by A. Vaschalde, *Corpus Scriptorum Christianorum Orientalium*, 9 10. Scriptores Syri, 9, 10 (rep. Louvain, 1955, 1961).

——, *Sancti Philoxeni episcopi Mabbugensis dissertationes decem de uno e sancta Trinitate incorporato et passo*, I and II only, ed. and transl. by M. Brière, *Patrologia Orientalia*, 15 (Paris, 1927), 439–542.

——, 'Textes inédits de Philoxène de Mabboug', ed. and transl. by J. Lebon, *Le Muséon*, 43 (1930), 17–84 ; 149–220.

——, *Three Letters of Philoxenus, Bishop of Mabbôgh*, ed. and transl. by A. Vaschalde, Catholic University of America, Dissertation for the Degree of Doctor of Philosophy (Rome, 1902).

PROCLUS, *The Elements of Theology*, translation, introduction, and commentary by E. R. Dodds, 2nd ed. (Oxford, 1963).

SEVERUS OF ANTIOCH, 'A Collection of Letters from Numerous Syriac Manuscripts', ed. and transl. by E. W. Brooks, *Patrologia Orientalis*, 12, 14 (Paris, 1919–20), 163–342; 1–310.

——, *Eiusdem ac Sergii Grammatici : Epistulae Mutuae*, ed. and transl. by J. Lebon, *Corpus Scriptorum Christianorum Orientalium*, 119–20, Scriptores Syri, 4, 7 (Louvain, 1949).

——, *Les Homiliae Cathedrales de Sévère d'Antioche* in the Syriac translation of Jacob of Edessa, ed. and transl. in *Patrologia Orientalia* (Turnhout, Belgium, and Paris, 1922–72). Homilies XXXII-LI : M. Brière, F. Graffin, and C. Lash (P.O. xxxv. 288–379, xxxvi. 8–137, 396–528) ; Homilies LII-LVII : R. Duval (P.O. iv. 1–94) ; Homilies LVIII-LXXVI : M. Brière (P.O. viii. 209–396, xii. 1–163) ; Homilies LXXVII (Greek and Syriac texts) : M.-A. Kugener and E. Triffaux (P.O. xvi. 761–863) ; Homilies LXXVIII-XCVIII : M. Brière (P.O. xx. 273–434, XXII. 1–176, XXV. 1–174) ; Homilies XCIX-CIII : I. Guidi (P.O. xxii. 207–312) ; Homilies CIV-CXXV : M. Brière (P.O. xxv. 625–815, xxvi. 265–450, xxix. 74–262).

——, *The Hymns of Severus and Others in the Syriac Version of Paul of Edessa, as Revised by James of Edessa*, ed. and transl. by E. W. Brooks, *Patrologia Orientalis*, 6, 7 (Paris, 1911), 1–179 ; 593–802.

SEVERUS OF ANTIOCH, *Liber contra impium Grammaticum*, ed. and transl. by
J. Lebon, *Corpus Scriptorum Christianorum Orientalium*, 93, 94; 101, 102;
111, 112, Scriptores Syri, 45, 46; 50, 51; 58, 59 (Paris and Louvain,
1929-38).
——, *Orationes ad Nephalium*, ed. and transl. by J. Lebon, *Corpus Scriptorum
Christianorum Orientalium*, 119, 120, Scriptores Syri, 4, 7 (Louvain, 1949).
——, *Le Philalèthe*, ed. and transl. by R. Hespel, *Corpus Scriptorum Christianorum
Orientalium*, 133, 134, Scriptores Syri 68, 69 (Louvain, 1952).
——, *La Polémique antijulianiste*, ed. and transl. by R. Hespel, *Corpus Scrip-
torum Christianorum Orientalium*, 244, 245, Scriptores Syri, 104, 105
(Louvain, 1964).
——, 'La Première Homélie cathedrale de Sévère d'Antioche', transl. by
E. Porcher, *Revue de l'orient chrétien*, 19 (1914), 69-78; 135-142.
——, *The Sixth Book of the Select Letters of Severus, Patriarch of Antioch, in the
Syriac Version of Athanasius of Nisibis*, ed. and transl. by E. W. Brooks,
4 vols. (London, 1902-4).
THEODORE OF MOPSUESTIA, *The Commentary of Theodore of Mopsuestia on the
Lord's Prayer and on the Sacraments of Baptism and the Eucharist*, Wood-
brooke Studies, vol. VI (Cambridge, 1933).
——, *The Commentary of Theodore of Mopsuestia on the Nicene Creed*, ed. and
transl. by A. Mingana, Woodbrooke Studies, Vol. V (Cambridge, 1932).
——, *Les Homélies catéchétiques de Théodore de Mopsueste*, transl. and introd.
by R. Tonneau and R. Devreesse, *Studi e Testi* 145 (Vatican, 1949).
THEODORET, *The Ecclesiastical History, Dialogues, and Letters of Theodoret*,
transl. by B. Jackson, Nicene and Post-Nicene Fathers, 2nd Ser, vol.
III (Grand Rapids, [1892].)
ZACHARIUS RHETOR, *The Syriac Chronicle Known as that of Zachariah of
Mitylene*, transl. by F. J. Hamilton and E. W. Brooks (London, 1899).
——, 'Vie de Sévère', ed. and transl. by M.-A. Kugener, *Patrologia Orien-
talis*, II (Turnhout, 1971), 7-115.

LITERATURE

ABRAMOWSKI, L., Review of *Philoxène de Mabbog. Sa vie, ses écrits, sa théologie*,
by A. de Halleux, *Revue d'histoire ecclésiastique*, 60 (1965), 859-66.
ALTANER, B., and STUIBER, A., *Patrologie* (Frieburg, 1966).
ARNOU, R., 'Unité numérique et unité de nature chez les Pères, après le
Concile de Nicée', *Gregorianum*, 15 (1934), 242-54.
BAETHGEN, F., 'Philoxenus von Mabug über den Glauben', *Zeitschrift für
Kirchengeschichte*, 5 (1882), 122-38.
BALL, C. J., 'Jacobus Sarugensis', in *A Dictionary of Christian Biography* (New
York, repr. 1967), III. 327-8.
BARDY, G., 'Sévère d'Antioche', *Dictionnaire de théologie catholique*, Vol. 14
(1941), coll. 1988-2000.
BARKER, J., *Justinian and the Later Roman Empire* (Madison, Wisconsin, 1966).
BECK, E., 'Philoxenos und Ephraem', *Oriens Christianus* 46 (1962), 61-76.
——, *Die Theologie des heiligen Ephraem in seinen Hymnen über den Glauben*,
Studia Anselmiana, 21 (Vatican, 1949).
BETHUNE-BAKER, J. F., *Nestorius and His Teaching* (London, 1908).

LITERATURE 149

BOTTE, B., 'Le Baptême dans l'Église syrienne', *L'Orient syrien*, 1 (1950), 137–55.

BRIÈRE, M., 'Introduction générale aux homélies de Sévère d'Antioche', *Patriologia Orientalis*, XXIX (Paris, 1960), 7–72.

BROWN, P., *The World of Late Antiquity* (London, 1971).

BURGHARDT, W., *The Image of God in Man According to Cyril of Alexandria* (Woodstock, Maryland, 1957).

BURKITT, F. C., *Saint Ephraim's Quotations from the Gospel*, Texts and Studies, vol. VII, no. 2 (Cambridge, 1901).

BURY, J. B., *History of the Later Roman Empire from the Death of Theodosius I to the Death of Justinian*, 2 vols. (London, 1931).

BUTLER, H. C., *Early Churches in Syria*, ed. by E. B. Smith (Princeton, N. J., 1929).

CASEY, R. P., 'Julian of Halicarnassus', *Harvard Theological Review*, 19 (1926), 206–13.

CHABOT, J. B., *Littérature syriaque* (Paris, 1934).

CHADWICK, H., 'Eucharist and Christology in the Nestorian Controversy', *Journal of Theological Studies*, N.S. 2 (1951), 145–64.

CHARANIS, P., *Church and State in the Later Roman Empire : The Religious Policy of Anastasius the First* 491–518 (Madison, 1939).

CHESNUT, G. F., 'Fate, Fortune, Free Will and Nature in Eusebius of Caesarea', *Church History*, 42 (1973), 165–82.

——, 'The Pattern of the Past: Augustine's Debate with Eusebius and Sallust', in *Our Common History as Christians*, ed. J. Deschner, L. T. Howe, and K. Penzel (New York, 1975).

CHESNUT, R., Review article of *The Rise of the Monophysite Movement*, by W. H. C. Frend, *Anglican Theological Review* (1974), 64–8.

CHITTY, D., *The Desert a City* (Oxford, 1966).

CRUM, W. E., 'Sévère d'Antioche en Égypte', *Revue de L'orient chrétien*, 3 ser., 3 (1922–3), 92–104.

DANIÉLOU, J., *Platonisme et théologie mystique* (Paris, 1944).

DE HALLEUX, A., *Philoxène de Mabbog. Sa Vie, ses écritis, sa théologie* (Louvain, 1963).

DEVREESSE, R., *Essai sur Théodore de Mopsueste*, Studi e Testi, 141 (Vatican, 1948).

——, *Le Patriarcat d'Antioche depuis la paix de l'Église jusqu'à la conquête arabe*, Études palestiniennes et orientales (Paris, 1945).

DE VRIES, W., 'La Conception de l'Église chez les Jacobites', *L'Orient syrien*, 2 (1957), 111–24.

——, 'Die Eschatologie des Severus von Antiochien', *Orientalia Christiana Periodica*, 23 (1957), 354–80.

——, *Sakramententheologie bei den syrischen Monophysiten*, Orientalia Christiana Analecta, No. 125 (Rome, 1940).

DIEPEN, H. M., ' "L'assumptus homo" à Chalcédoine', *Revue thomiste*, 51 (1951), 573–608, and 53 (1953) 254–86.

DOWNEY, G., *A History of Antioch in Syria from Seleucus to the Arab Conquest* (Princeton, 1961).

DRAGUET, R., 'Julien d'Halicarnasse', *Dictionnaire de théologie catholique*, Vol.
8 (1925), col. 1931–40.

——, *Julien d'Halicarnasse et sa controverse avec Sévère d'Antioche sur l'incor-
ruptiblité du corps du Christ*, Univ. Cath. Lovan. Dissert. ad gradum
magistri in Fac. Theol., II, 12 (Louvain, 1924).

EMMET, D., 'Theoria and the Way of Life', *Journal of Theological Studies*, N.S.
17 (1966), 38–52.

ENGBERDING, H., 'Wann wurde Severus zum Patriarchen von Antiochien
geweiht ?', *Oriens Christianus*, 37 (1953), 132–4.

EVERY, G., '*Theosis* in Later Byzantine Theology', *Eastern Churches Review*,
(1969), 243–52.

FREND, W. H. C., *The Rise of the Monophysite Movement* (Cambridge, 1972).

GALTIER, P., 'Théodore de Mopsueste : sa vraie pensée sur l'Incarnation',
Recherches de science religieuse, 45 (1957), 161–86, 338–60.

GREENSLADE, S. L., *Schism in the Early Church* (London, 1964).

GREER, R., 'The Antiochene Christology of Diodore of Tarsus', *Journal of
Theological Studies*, N.S. 17, 2 (1966), 327–41.

——, *Theodore of Mopsuestia : Exegete and Theologian* (London, 1961).

GRIBOMONT, J., 'Les Homélies ascétiques de Philoxène de Mabboug et
l'écho du Messalianisme', *L'Orient syrien*, 2 (1957), 419–32.

——, 'Le Monachisme au IVᵉ siècle en Asie Mineure : de Gangres au
Messalianisme', *Studia Patristica*, vol. II, *Text und Untersuchungen zur
Geschichte der altchristlichen Literatur*, 64 (Berlin, 1957), 400–15.

GRILLMEIER, A., *Christ in Christian Tradition from the Apostolic Age to Chalcedon
(451)*, transl. by J. S. Bowden (New York, 1965).

——, and BACHT, H., *Das Konzil von Chalkedon. Geschichte und Gegenwart*, 3
vols. (Würzburg, 1951–4).

GROSS, J., *La Divinisation du chrétien d'après les Pères grecs* (Paris, 1938).

GUILLAUMONT, A., 'Étienne bar Soudaili', in *Dictionnaire de la spiritualité*,
Vol. 4 (1961), coll. 1481–8.

——, *Les 'Kephalaia gnostica' d'Évagre le Pontique et l'histoire de l'origénisme chez
les grecs et chez les syriens*, Patristica Sorbonensia, 5 (Paris, 1962).

HARB, P., 'L'Attitude de Philoxène à l'égard de la spiritualité "savante"
d'Évagre le Pontique', in *Memorial Mgr. Gabriel Khouri-Sarkis* (Louvain,
1969), 135–55.

——, 'La Conception pneumatologique chez Philoxène de Mabbûg',
Recherches orientales, 5 (1969), 5–15.

HAUSHERR, I., 'Contemplation et sainteté. Une remarquable mise au point
par Philoxène de Mabboug (†523)', *Revue d'ascétique et de mystique*, 14
(1933), 171–95.

——, 'De doctrina spirituali Christianorum Orientalium. Quaestiones et
Scripta', *Orientalia Christiana*, 30 (1933), 149–216.

——, 'L'Erreur fondamentale et la logique du Messalianisme', *Orientalia
Christiana Periodica*, 1 (1935), 328–60).

——, 'Les Grands Courants de la spiritualité orientale', *Orientalia Christiana
Periodica*, 1 (1935), 114–38.

——, 'Un grand auteur spirituel retrouvé : Jean d'Apamée', *Orientalia
Christiana Periodica*, 14 (1948), 3–42.

LITERATURE 151

HAUSHERR I., *Hésychasme et prière*, Orientalia Christiana Analecta, 176 (Rome, 1966).

——. *Philautie. De la tendresse pour soi à la charité selon Saint Maxime le Confesseur*, Orientalia Christiana Analecta, vol. 137 (Rome, 1952).

——, 'Spiritualité syrienne : Philoxène de Mabboug en version francaise', *Orientalia Christiana Periodica*, 23 (1957), 171–85.

HAYES, E. R., *L'École d'Édesse* (Paris, 1930).

HONIGMANN, E., *Évêques et évêchés monophysites d'Asie antérieure au VIᵉ siècle* Corpus Scriptorum Christianorum Orientalium, 127, Subsidia, 2 (Louvain, 1951).

JANSMA, T., 'The Credo of Jacob of Serugh : A Return to Nicea and Constantinople', *Nederlandsch Archief voor Kerkgeschiedenis*, 44 (1960), 18–36.

——, 'Die Christologie Jakobs von Serugh und ihre Abhängigkeit von der alexandrinischen Theologie und der Frömmigkeit Ephraems des Syrers', *Le Muséon*, 78 (1965), 5–46.

——, 'Encore le crédo de Jacques de Saroug', *L'Orient syrien*, 10 (1965), 75–88 ; 193–236 ; 331–70 ; 475–510.

——, 'L'Hexaméron de Jacques de Sarug', *L'Orient syrien*, 4 (1959), 3–42 ; 129–62 ; 253–84.

——, 'Investigations in the early Syrian Fathers on Genesis. An Approach to the Exegesis of the Nestorian Church and Comparison of Nestorian and Jewish Exegesis', *Oud Testamentische Studien*, Deel XII (Leiden, 1958).

JUGIE, M., 'Julien d'Halicarnasse et Sévère d'Antioche', *Échos d'orient*, 28 (1925), 129–62 ; 257–85.

——, 'La Primauté romaine d'après les premiers théologiens monophysites', *Échos d'orient*, 33 (1934), 181–9.

KHOURI-SARKIS, G., 'Note sur les mètres poétiques syriaques', *L'Orient syrien*, 3 (1958), 63–72.

KRÜGER, P., 'Le Caractère monophysite de la troisième lettre de Jacques de Saroug', *L'Orient syrien*, 6 (1961), 301–8.

——, 'Das Problem der Rechtglaübigkeit Jakobs von Serugh und seine Lösung', *Ostkirchliche Studien*, 5 (1956), 158–76 ; 225–42.

——, 'Untersuchungen über die Form der Einheit in Christus nach den Briefen des Jakob von Serugh', *Ostkirchliche Studien*, Würzburg, 8 (1959), 184–201.

——, 'War Jakob von Serugh Katholik oder Monophysit ?', *Ostkirchliche Studien*, 2 (1953), 199–208.

KUGENER, M.-A., 'Allocution prononcée par Sévère après son élévation sur le trône patriarcal d'Antioche', *Oriens Christianus*, 2 (1902), 265–82.

LEBON, J., 'La Christologie du monophysisme syrien', in *Das Konzil von Chalkedon : Geschichte und Gegenwart*, ed. by A. Grillmeier and H. Bacht (Würzburg, 1951), I. 425–580.

——, *Le Monophysisme sévérien. Étude historique littéraire et théologique sur la résistance monophysite au concile de Chalcédoine jusqu'à la constitution de l'Église jacobite*, Univ. Cath. Lovan. Diss., ad gradum doct. in Fac. Theol., II.4 (Louvain, 1909).

——, 'Le Sort du consubstantiel nicéen', *Revue d'histoire ecclésiastique*, 47 (1952), 485–529 ; 48 (1953), 632–82.

LEBON, J., 'La Version philoxénienne de la Bible', *Revue d'histoire ecclésiastique*, 12 (1911), 413–36.

LEMOINE, E., 'Physionomie d'un moine syrien : Philoxène de Mabboug', *L'Orient syrien*, 3 (1958), 91–102.

——, La Spiritualité de Philoxène de Mabboug', *L'Orient syrien*, 2 (1957), 351–66.

LOOFS, F., *Nestorius and His Place in the History of Christian Doctrine* (Cambridge, 1914).

LOSSKY, V., *The Vision of God*, transl. by A. Moorhouse (London, 1963).

MARRIOTT, G. L., 'The Messalians and the Discovery of Their Ascetic Book', *Harvard Theological Review*, 19 (1926), 191–8.

MATHEW, G., *Byzantine Aesthetics* (New York, 1963).

MINGANA, A., 'New Documents on Philoxenus of Hierapolis, and on the Philoxenian Version of the Bible', *The Expositor*, 9th ser. 19 (1920), 149–60.

MOELLER, C., 'Le Chalcédonisme et le néo-chalcédonisme en Orient de à la fin du VIᵉ siècle', in *Das Konzil von Chalkedon : Geschichte und Gegenwart*, ed. by A. Grillmeier and H. Bacht (Würzburg, 1951), I. 637–720.

MOUTERDE, P., 'Le Councile de Chalcédoine d'après les historiens monophysites de langue syriaque', in *Das Konzil von Chalkedon : Geschichte und Gegenwart*, ed. by A. Grillmeier and H. Bacht (Würzburg, 1951), I. 581–602.

NORRIS, R. A., *Manhood and Christ : A Study in the Christology of Theodore of Mopsuestia* (Oxford, 1963).

OLINDER, G., *The Letters of Jacob of Sarug : Comments on an Edition* (Lund, 1939).

ORTIZ DE URBINA, I., *Patrologia Syriaca* (Rome, 1965).

PEETERS, P., 'Jacques de Saroug appartient-il à la secte monophysite ?', *Analecta Bollandiana*, 66 (1948), 134–98.

PORCHER, E., 'Sévère d'Antioche dans la littérature copte', *Revue de l'orient chrétien*, 12 (1907), 119–24.

PRESTIGE, G. L., *St. Basil the Great and Apollinaris of Laodicea*, ed. by H. Chadwick (London, 1956).

QUASTEN, J., *Patrology*, vol. III (Maryland, 1960).

RAVEN, C. E., *Apollinarianism : An Essay on the Christology of the Early Church* (Cambridge, 1923).

REFOULÉ, F., 'La Christologie d'Évagre et l'origénisme', *Orientalia Christiana Periodica*, 27 (1961), 221–66.

ROUSSEAU, D. O., 'La Rencontre de Saint Ephrem et de Saint Basile', *L'Orient syrien*, 2 (1957), 261–84; 3 (1958), 73–90.

SAFFREY, P. H. P., 'Le Chrétien Jean Philopon et la survivance de l'école d'Alexandrie au VIᵉ siècle', *Revue des études grecques*, 67 (1954), 396–410.

SALAVILLE, L., 'Hénotique', *Dictionnaire de théologie catholique*, vol. 6 (1920), coll. 2153–78.

SAMBURSKY, S., *The Physical World of the Greeks*, transl. by M. Dagut (London, 1956).

——, *Physics of the Stoics* (London, 1959).

SCHOLEM, G., *Jewish Gnosticism, Merkabah Mysticism, and Talmudic Tradition*, 2nd ed. (New York, 1965).

SELLERS, R. V., *The Council of Chalcedon : A Historical and Doctrinal Survey* (London, 1961).

——, *Eustathius of Antioch and His Place in the Early History of Christian Doctrine* (Cambridge, 1928).

——, *Two Ancient Christologies* (London, 1954).

SHELDON-WILLIAMS, I. P., 'The Pseudo-Dionysius', *The Cambridge History of Later Greek and Early Medieval Philosophy*, ed. by A. H. Armstrong (Cambridge, 1967), 457–72.

SMITH, W., and WACE, H. (eds.), *Dictionary of Christian Biography*, 4 vols. (London, 1877–87).

SULLIVAN, F., *The Christology of Theodore of Mopsuestia*, Analecta Gregoriana LXXXII (Rome, 1956).

TISSERANT, E., 'Philoxène de Mabboug', *Dictionnaire de théologie catholique*, vol. 12 (1935), coll. 1509–32.

VAN DER MEER, F., and MOHRMANN, C., *Atlas of the Early Christian World*, transl. and ed. by M. Hedlund and H. H. Rowley (London, 1966).

VAN ROEY, A., 'Les Débuts de l'Église jacobite', in *Das Konzil von Chalkedon, Geschichte und Gegenwart*, ed. by A. Grillmeier and H. Bacht (Würzburg, 1953), ii. 339–60.

VASILIEV, A. A., *Justin the First : An Introduction to the Epoch of Justinian the Great*, Dumbarton Oaks Studies, I (Cambridge, Mass., 1950).

VENABLES, E., 'Philoxenus', *A Dictionary of Christian Biography* (New York, repr. 1967), IV. 391–3.

——, 'Severus (27)', *A Dictionary of Christian Biography* (New York, repr. 1967), IV. 637–41.

VILLER, M., 'Aux sources de la spiritualité de Saint Maxime. Les oeuvres d'Évagre le Pontique', *Revue d'ascétique et de mystique*, 11 (1930), 156–84; 239–68; 331–6.

VÖÖBUS, A., *Early Versions of the New Testament : Manuscript Studies*, Papers of the Estonian Theological Society in Exile, 6 (Stockholm, 1954).

——, *Handschriftliche Überlieferung der Mēmrē-dichtung des Ja'qob von Serūg*, Corpus Scriptorum Christianorum Orientalium 344, 345, Subsidia 39, 40, 2 vols. (Louvain, 1973).

——, *A History of Asceticism in the Syrian Orient. A Contribution to the History of Culture in the Near East* (Corpus Scriptorum Christianorum Orientalium 184, 197, Subsidia 14, 17, 2 vols. (Louvain, 1958–60).)

——, *Literary, Critical and Historical Studies in Ephrem the Syrian*, Papers of the Estonian Theological Society in Exile, X (Stockholm, 1958).

——, *Les Messaliens et les réformes de Barçauma de Nisibe dans l'église perse*, Contributions of the Baltic University, vol. 34 (Pinneberg, 1947).

——, 'New Data for the Solution of the Problem Concerning the Philoxenian Version', *Festschrift K. Kundzins* (Eutin, 1953), 169–86.

WARE, K. T., ' "Pray Without Ceasing" : The Ideal of Continual Prayer in Eastern Monasticism', *Eastern Churches Review*, 2 (1969), 253–61.

WIDENGREN, G., *Researches in Syrian Mysticism* (Leiden, 1961).

WOLFSON, H. A., 'Philosophical Implications of Arianism and Apollinarianism', *Dumbarton Oaks Papers*, No. 12 (Cambridge, Mass., 1958), 3–28.
WOODWARD, E. L., *Christianity and Nationalism in Later Roman Empire* (London, 1916).
WRIGHT, W., *A Short History of Syriac Literature* (London, 1894).

INDEX

Note: A reference to a footnote carried over from a previous page is given in the form 'n*', as in '26n*'.